PRESCHOOL

The IDEA MAGAZINE FOR TEACHERS® MAILBOX®

2004–2005
YEARBOOK

The Education Center, Inc.
Greensboro, North Carolina

The Mailbox® 2004–2005 Preschool Yearbook

Managing Editor, *The Mailbox* Magazine: Leanne Stratton

Editorial Team: Becky S. Andrews, Kimberley Bruck, Karen P. Shelton, Diane Badden, Sharon Murphy, Karen A. Brudnak, Sarah Hamblet, Hope Rodgers, Dorothy C. McKinney

Production Team: Lisa K. Pitts, Margaret Freed (COVER ARTIST), Pam Crane, Rebecca Saunders, Jennifer Tipton Cappoen, Chris Curry, Sarah Foreman, Theresa Lewis Goode, Ivy L. Koonce, Clint Moore, Greg D. Rieves, Barry Slate, Donna K. Teal, Zane Williard, Tazmen Carlisle, Irene Harvley-Felder, Amy Kirtley-Hill, Kristy Parton, Cathy Edwards Simrell, Lynette Dickerson, Mark Rainey

ISBN 1-56234-663-6
ISSN 1088-5536

The Education Center, Inc.
P.O. Box 9753
Greensboro, NC 27429-0753

Contents

Departments

Features

BULLETIN BOARDS
AND DISPLAYS

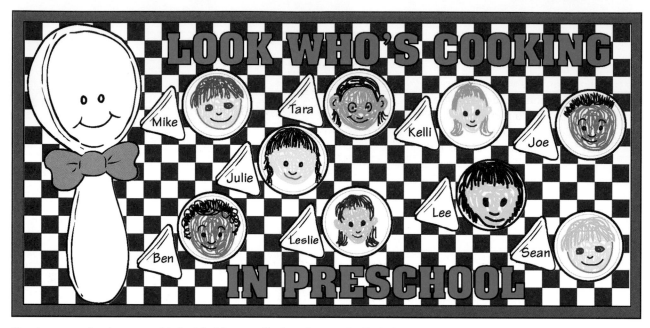

LOOK WHO'S COOKING IN PRESCHOOL

Get the new school year cookin' with this cute display. Cover a bulletin board with an inexpensive, plastic, checked table cover. Have each child draw her face on a paper plate. Mount each face on the background; then add a folded paper napkin with the child's name next to her plate. Add the title shown and a simple spoon character. This delicious display is done!

Laurie Birt, Belinder Elementary, Prairie Village, KS

Crunch into a study of apples with this "tree-mendous" idea! Cut a length of white bulletin board paper; then paint a tree trunk on the lower half. Have your preschoolers add green paint handprints to the top for leaves. Then invite them to crumple red tissue paper into balls. Glue most of these apples to the tree, adding a few at the bottom. Finally, post next to the tree the poem shown, and teach your little ones to recite it.

Sara Andrew—Preschool Handicapped
Jefferson Preschool Center
Charlottesville, VA

Tree trunk at the
bottom;
Leaves at the top.
Apples falling off
the tree—
Plop, plop, plop!

Your preschool pardners will say, "Yee-haw!" when they see this welcoming display! During preschool orientation, take a photo of each of your new students. Mount each photo on a wanted poster. (See page 271 for a pattern. Mask out the poem before photocopying.) Mount the posters over a background of bandana-print fabric. Ta-da! The Wild West—preschool style!

Tina Rumburg—PreK
Gaston Day School
Gastonia, NC

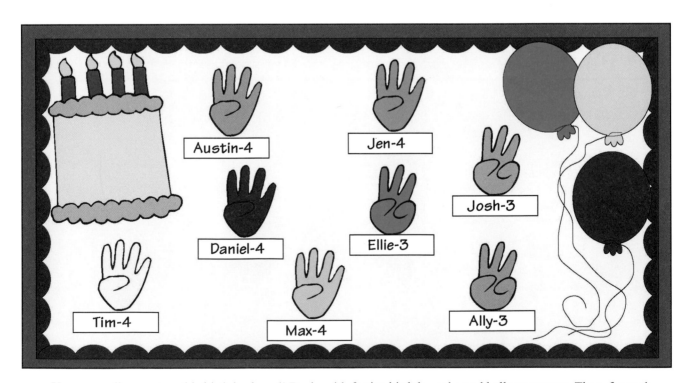

You can really count on this birthday board! Begin with festive birthday cake and balloon cutouts. Then, for each child, die-cut a hand shape and fold the fingers to show the child's age. Mount each hand on the board, along with a strip showing the child's name and age. When a child has a birthday, unfold one of the fingers to show his new age, and update his name strip.

Bev Christiansen—Preschool, Whittier Elementary, Clinton, IA

Fall is in the air and on this display too! Have each child paint a white paper towel with tempera paint in a variety of fall colors. Then have her spritz the towel with water to make the colors blend. After the towels have dried, cut out leaf shapes. Attach a brown bulletin board paper tree trunk to a wall; then add the leaves to create a beautiful fall tree!

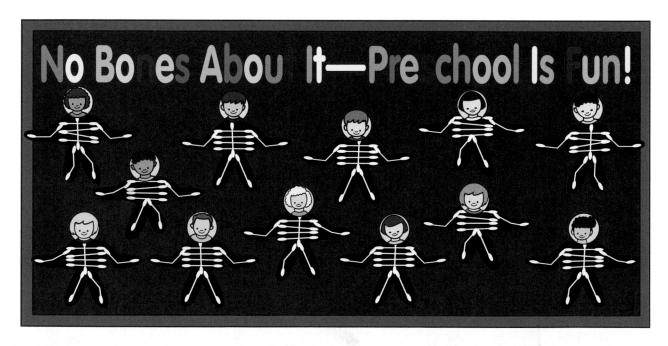

Cute is the best word to describe this clever bulletin board! Have each youngster glue cotton swabs to black construction paper to make a skeleton. Allow the glue to dry. Take a photo of each child to use as the head of his skeleton. Attach the skeletons to a bulletin board with the title shown.

Michele Slaughter and Diane Harrison—PreK, Barton Elementary School, Patchogue, NY

AND DISPLAYS

We're Sweeter Than Pumpkin Pie!

Carlos · Pam · Kent · Clevell · Barry · Becky · Kelly · Ivy · Ann-Marie · Jennifer · Clint · Cayce

A pumpkin patch takes shape when youngsters make this bulletin board. Have each child mix red and yellow paint on an old cookie sheet to make a thin layer of orange. Then help her press a large pumpkin-shaped white construction paper cutout in the paint to make a print. When dry, write each child's name in the center of her pumpkin. Attach the pumpkins to a bulletin board and title the display as shown.

Nancy O'Toole—Preschool, Ready Set Grow, Grand Rapids, MN

Twinkle, twinkle, little star.
How I wonder what you are,
Up above the world so high,
Like a diamond in the sky.

Stars twinkle on this pretty display. Have each child dip a star-shaped cookie cutter in glue and then press it on a sheet of dark blue construction paper to make several prints. Help each child sprinkle gold or silver glitter over the glue. When dry, shake off the excess. Next, attach each child's paper to a wall to create a sky scene. Post the words shown to complete the display.

Jennifer K. Adamson—Toddlers and Preschool, Lifespan School and Daycare, Allentown, PA

BULLETIN BOARDS

Light up your classroom this season with a display of Rudolph's red-nosed friends! First, tape a string of Christmas lights with red bulbs across your board, making sure the plug reaches an outlet. For each reindeer, trace a child's shoe and both hands. Cut out the tracings and attach the hand-shaped antlers to the shoe cutout. Have the child add eyes and a mouth. Then cut a hole for the nose and attach the reindeer over a bulb at its base. Ho, ho, ho—what a glow!

Michael Marks
Harding Elementary
Lebanon, PA

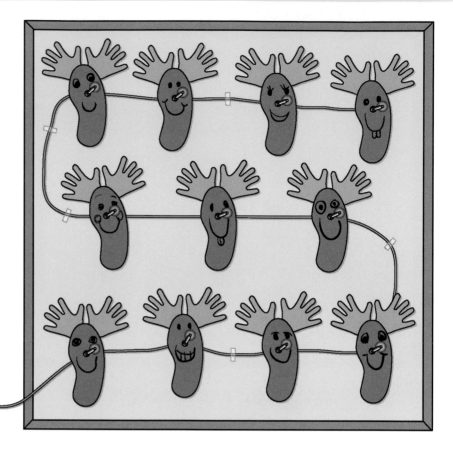

Craft a batch of gingerbread people for this yummy display! Duplicate the pattern on page 17 onto brown construction paper to make a class supply. Have each child decorate a cookie with rickrack, yarn, ribbon, paper reinforcements, craft foam shapes, or paper punches. Display the finished cookies on aluminum baking sheets or large pieces of aluminum foil.

Pam Sartory, City of Palm Beach Gardens Recreation Dept., Palm Beach Gardens, FL

Shhh! These bears are sleeping! Display some of your students' best bear artwork in a snowy cave. Crumple brown craft paper and attach it to a bulletin board to make a cave shape. Add some white cotton batting around and on top of the cave for snow. Then mount student-made bears inside the cave and add a title.

Bonnie Martin, Hopewell Country Day School, Pennington, NJ

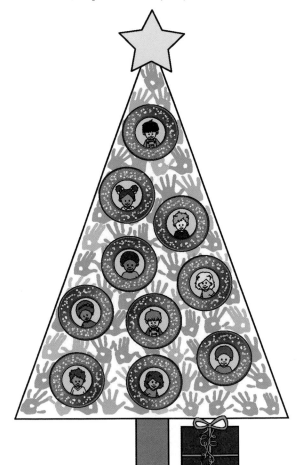

This display is a holiday "tree-t"! Cut a triangle tree shape from a long length of white bulletin board paper. Have students cover the tree in green paint handprints. Have each child make an ornament by painting a small paper plate red and then sprinkling on glitter while the paint is wet. Cut the child's photo into a circle and glue it to the dried plate. Add these ornaments to the tree. Then add finishing touches, such as a star atop the tree and a big present below. Happy holidays!

Theresa Booth
Little Acres Learning Center
Vineland, NJ

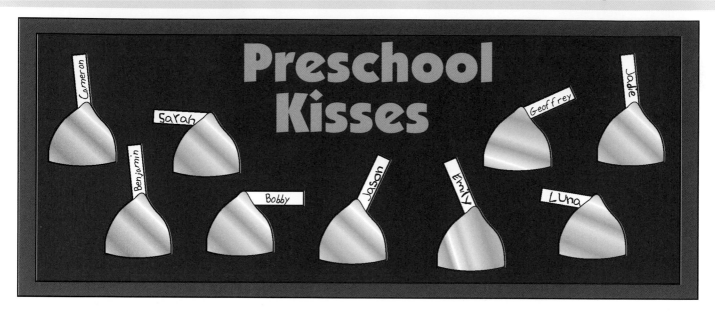

This sweet bulletin board will get youngsters ready for Valentine's Day! Cut out a candy kiss-shaped piece of poster board for each child. Give each youngster a cutout, a length of aluminum foil, a strip of white paper, and a pencil. Then have him write his name on his strip. Instruct him to use the foil to wrap his cutout to cover his kiss. Help each child tape his name strip to his cutout. Attach the kisses to a bulletin board and title the display "Preschool Kisses."

Fran Chupper, Lil Sprouts Preschool, Toms River, NJ

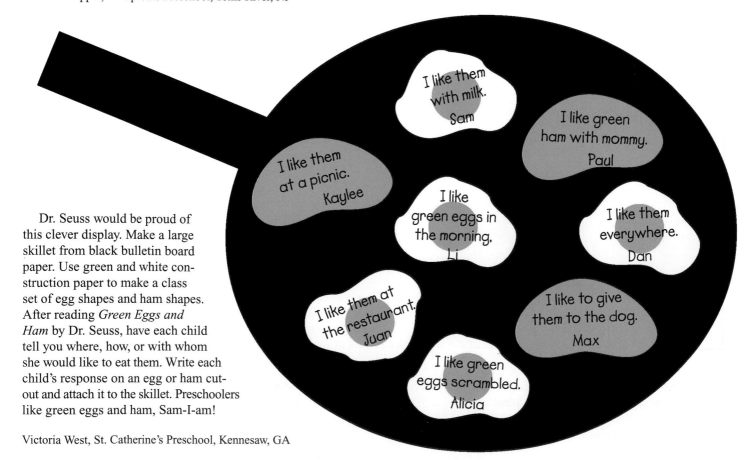

Dr. Seuss would be proud of this clever display. Make a large skillet from black bulletin board paper. Use green and white construction paper to make a class set of egg shapes and ham shapes. After reading *Green Eggs and Ham* by Dr. Seuss, have each child tell you where, how, or with whom she would like to eat them. Write each child's response on an egg or ham cutout and attach it to the skillet. Preschoolers like green eggs and ham, Sam-I-am!

Victoria West, St. Catherine's Preschool, Kennesaw, GA

12

AND DISPLAYS

Jelly beans are nearly jumping out of this festive display! Cut out a large jelly bean shape from pastel construction paper for each child. Drop a small plastic egg in each of several containers of paint. For each child, place a jelly bean shape in a shoebox and then have her spoon two or three different eggs into the box. Use a rubber band to secure the lid on the box. Invite the child to hold the box as she jumps. After the paint dries, display the jelly beans in and around a brown bulletin board paper basket. Pretty!

Barbara Carothers Ulmer
Allisonville Christian Church Preschool
Indianapolis, IN

The luck of the Irish will be in your classroom when this bulletin board is created. Use green tempera paint to paint the palms and fingers of a child's hands. Help him make three sets of handprints, as shown, and then make a print of his finger (for a stem). Display the shamrocks on a bulletin board titled "Happy St. Patrick's Day!"

Barbara Desnoyers, Clark Elementary

Make this display on a rainy day to help your little ones appreciate spring rain! In advance, take a full-length photo of each child. To make one project, cut closely around the child's body in the photo and then glue the cutout to a sheet of construction paper. Have the child fold a cupcake liner in half and glue it above her head in the photo, as shown, to resemble an umbrella. Add a pipe cleaner handle. Then have the child draw green grass and spring flowers on the ground near her feet and clouds and rain above and beside her. Display all the photos on a bulletin board with the title "Rainy Day Treasures."

Cathy Welwood
Learning Experience
Calgary, Alberta, Canada

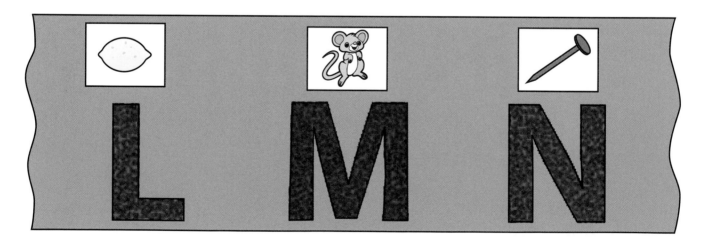

Help your little ones learn letter formation with a display of sandpaper letters. Cut the alphabet from sheets of sandpaper; then display it along a wall at children's eye level where it's easy to touch. Add a picture above each letter to represent the corresponding beginning sound.

Angela Lenker, Montgomery Early Learning Center/Head Start, Pottstown, PA

Enhance a study of nursery rhymes with this cute bulletin board! To begin, make a few copies of the nursery rhyme character patterns below and on page 18. Ask each child to choose one of the characters and snap his photo as he makes a face expressing the character's feelings. Then cut the child's head from the photo and glue it onto one of the patterns. Color the pattern and cut it out. Then mount all the pictures on a bulletin board for a super silly nursery rhyme display!

Maria Cella, Rainbow Academy, Iselin, NJ

Nursery Rhyme Character Patterns
Use with the display on this page.

A Picture-Perfect Class
Thanks for the Memories!

Review the school year with this memorable display! Draw a simple camera, similar to the one shown, and make a copy for each child. Have each child color her camera. Cut out the lens and tape a photo of the child to the back of the camera. Post the cameras on a board and have each child dictate a favorite preschool memory to mount near her camera. Then just add the title!

Heather Campbell, HCDS, Pennington, NJ

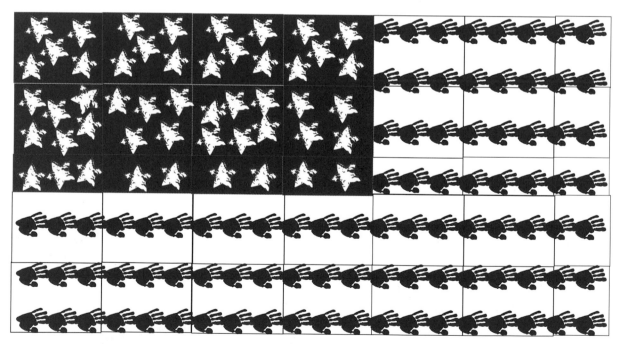

What a glorious Old Glory! For this giant flag, have youngsters paint large pieces of white paper blue. Use these to form the field of blue and then sponge-paint fifty white stars on it. Have youngsters make red handprints on white paper for the flag's stripes. Assemble the flag on a bulletin board for a super salute to the USA!

Debbie Vrana, Jefferson Elementary, Princeton, IL

Nursery Rhyme Pictures
Use with the nursery rhyme display idea on page 15.

BUSY HANDS

BUSY HANDS

Creative Learning Experiences
for Little Hands

BUTTON, SNAP, AND ZIP!

Little hands get some independent dressing practice and strengthen fine-motor skills while buttoning, snapping, and zipping through these ideas.

SORTING LAUNDRY

It's laundry day! So grab three laundry baskets and a collection of clothes with buttons, snaps, and zippers. Label each basket with a label from page 32. Then have a little one work the closures and sort the clothes into the correct basket. Before he leaves the area, have him undo the closures to ready the center for the next visitor. Zzzip!

BABY DOLL DUDS

Youngsters won't be able to resist dressing your classroom dolls in real baby clothes! Ask parents to donate baby clothing and sleepers with snaps, buttons, or zippers. Have each child choose a doll and a piece of clothing to dress it in. Encourage her to line up the snaps or buttons evenly before fastening them. After she dresses the doll, have the child undress and re-dress the doll in clothing with a different type of closure. All buttoned up and beautiful!

MAKING AN IMPRESSION

Play dough makes an impressive medium when it comes to exploring buttons, snaps, and zippers! Gather three old pieces of clothing with different closures. Put them in your play dough center. Pair students; have one of the little ones flatten a ball of play dough and then gently press a clothing closure into it while his partner closes her eyes. After the clothing is removed from the dough, have the partner look at the impression and determine which clothing piece was used. Have her tell why she's come to her conclusion. Then have youngsters switch roles and complete the activity again. A button made those prints. I can see the holes!

A FEEL FOR FASTENERS

Encourage youngsters to use their sense of touch to help them zip, button, and snap when you create a feely box full of fasteners! In each side of a fairly large lidded box (such as a detergent box), cut a hole that is just large enough for a youngster to put her hand inside. Put inside the box an item with a zipper, an item with large buttons, or an item with snaps. Then invite a child to slip her hands into the holes, pick up the clothing item, and try to work the fastener(s). When she thinks she's zipped, buttoned, or snapped, she can take the top off the box to check her success.

Ada Goren
Winston-Salem, NC

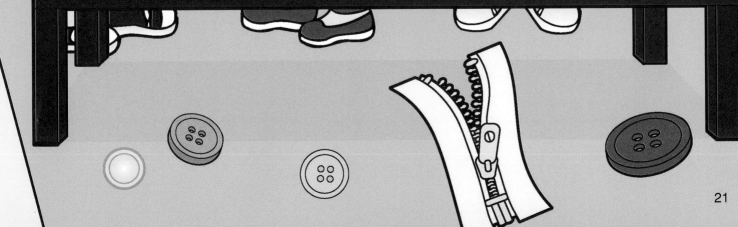

BUSY HANDS

Creative Learning Experiences for Little Hands

PUMPKIN PIZZAZZ!

Harvest plenty of hands-on learning using real—and some not-so-real—pumpkins.

ideas by Suzanne Moore, Irving TX

A PUMPKIN FAMILY

There's a new family in town—the Pumpkins! Place three different-size pumpkins on a table to represent a papa pumpkin, a mama pumpkin, and a baby pumpkin. Also include on the table dry-erase markers, hats, wigs, scarves, ties, sunglasses, and a dry sponge. Invite each child to draw facial features on each pumpkin and then dress them using the props. After sharing his pumpkin family with classmates, have him remove the props and then use the dry sponge to erase each pumpkin face.

BLOCK FACES

A jack-o'-lantern's nose doesn't have to be a triangle. It could be any shape! Cut out large pumpkin shapes from orange poster board and place them in the block center. Encourage children to use different-shaped blocks to transform the pumpkins into jack-o'-lanterns. Easy!

PUMPKIN PRINTS

Here's an art activity that will increase each child's motor skills and create an attractive display at the same time. To prepare, cut mini pumpkins in half so that the half with the stem (handle) can be used to make prints. Clean out any strings and seeds. Stock a center with the pumpkin halves, shallow trays of orange paint, and a class supply of 12" x 18" white construction paper. Have each student hold the stem of a pumpkin, dip the cut side of the pumpkin in paint, and then make prints on personalized paper. After the paint has dried, use the papers to decorate a bulletin board, to make placemats, or as booklet covers!

FEELY PUMPKIN

Need a tactile activity for busy little hands? Look no further! In each of two large plastic jack-o'-lanterns place three or four mini pumpkins, an apple, an orange, and green shredded tissue paper. Invite each student in a pair to take a jack-o'-lantern, close his eyes, reach inside, and try to find the mini pumpkins. Tell the pair how many mini pumpkins there are in each jack-o'-lantern. When each child thinks he's removed all of the pumpkins, have him open his eyes to check. If he's removed an item other than a pumpkin, instruct him to return it to the jack-o'-lantern, close his eyes, and continue his search. No peeking!

PUMPKIN PLAY DOUGH

Stir up your favorite play dough recipe; then work in a little pumpkin pie spice and orange food coloring to make pumpkin-scented play dough. Stock a center with the play dough, rolling pins, pie pans, pumpkin-shaped cookie cutters, and plastic knives. Invite little ones to shape the dough into pumpkins, pumpkin pies, and cookies. Yum!

BUSY HANDS

Creative Learning Experiences for Little Hands

WRAPPING PAPER, BOXES, AND BOWS

Little hands get some independent fine-motor practice with these activities focused around wrapping paper, boxes, and bows.

ideas contributed by Janet Boyce, Cokato, MN

"BOW-TIFUL" WRAPPING PAPER

Invite youngsters to create their own unique wrapping paper with this stamping activity. To make stampers, glue spools to the bottoms of various bows. Also glue spools to small jewelry gift boxes—some to the box tops and some inside the box bottoms as shown. Pour paint in pans to create thin layers. Provide each child with a piece of newsprint or bulletin board paper. Have him write his name on his paper and then choose a stamper, dip it in paint, and make multiple prints on his paper. Encourage him to repeat the activity with a different stamper and another color of paint. After the paper is dry, use it to wrap parents' gifts before sending them home!

PRETTY BOW PATTERNS

Youngsters will be wrapped up in this bow-patterning activity for days! In advance, gather a large supply of bows. Use colored sticky dots to make patterning cards appropriate for your group, similar to those shown. Put the patterning cards and a gift bag full of bows at a center. Invite students to visit the center, choose a patterning card, and then create the pattern using the bows. For an added challenge, have children use the bows to copy and then extend the pattern.

WRAP IT UP

Add some wrapping practice to your block center with this idea! Cut inexpensive wrapping paper into pieces appropriately sized to fit the blocks in your classroom. Place the paper, a supply of blocks, a tape dispenser or Post-it flags (for a reusable alternative) at a table. Invite a group of youngsters to use the supplies to wrap the blocks. For fun, have them pretend it's time to open gifts and unwrap the blocks to ready the center for the next group of students. This idea is all wrapped up!

A ONE-OF-A-KIND CARD

All you need for this activity is wrapping paper, construction paper, glue, and bows. Give each child a folded construction paper card. Have her cut or tear scraps of wrapping paper and then glue the pieces to the front of her card. After the glue has dried, invite her to attach a self-adhesive bow to the front of the card to resemble a wrapped gift. Write a desired sentiment on the inside of the card, and it's ready to accompany a gift!

BAUBLE BOXES

Jewelry boxes make the perfect manipulative to help little hands practice fine-motor skills. Collect a variety of small jewelry boxes. Attach a bow to the top of each lid. Separate the lids from the bottoms, and place them in a large gift bag. To play, have a child sort the box lids and bottoms. Then instruct him to match each lid with its corresponding bottom and then fit them together. When each box is complete, have him take them apart and return them to the gift bag for the next student.

BUSY HANDS

Creative Learning Experiences for Little Hands

STAMPIN' AND STICKIN'

Keep little hands busy with these ideas, which use some of preschoolers' favorite tools—stamps and stickers!

ideas by Angie Kutzer, Garrett Elementary, Mebane, NC

NIFTY NAMEPLATES

This idea helps youngsters learn the spelling of their names while creating nameplates for their tables. To begin, give each child a 4" x 12" tagboard strip and, if needed, his name printed on a small piece of paper. Encourage him to use alphabet stamps and stickers to form his name on the strip. Then invite the child to look through the rest of your supply to find other stamps and stickers of items he likes and use them to decorate the space around his name. After the names are finished, allow each child to share his project before taping it to the table at his seat. (If your children don't have assigned seats, these nameplates also make great flash cards for lining up or transitioning between activities.) That's my name!

WE GO TOGETHER

Use stamps and stickers to introduce youngsters to attributes and sorting. Look through your collection of stamps and stickers to get ideas of commonalities. Decide on an attribute or a group name. Then, for each child, label a divided sheet of paper as shown. Have each youngster choose stamps and stickers and make stamp prints and attach stickers in the appropriate places on her paper. After everyone finishes, give each child a chance to share her paper with the group.

ONE TO ONE

Practicing one-to-one correspondence gets sticky here, but in a good way! Give each child a half sheet of one-inch grid paper. Instruct each child to put one sticker in each square to fill the page. If your stickers are in short supply, have students stamp prints in the squares instead. One to one is lots of fun!

STICKER STORIES

Get ready for lots of language practice when you use this storytelling activity. Have each child use a collection of stickers and stamps to create a story scene of his choice. Provide crayons and markers for him to use to add any extra details. After the scene is complete, ask him to tell about his picture; then add his dictation to the scene. Compile students' pictures into a class book titled "Our Sticker Stories."

LOVE IS IN THE AIR

Mounting these "heart-y" collages together on a bulletin board will surely fill your room with Valentine's Day spirit! Cut out a large heart shape from colorful construction paper for each child. Then encourage her to fill her shape with as many heart-shaped stamps and stickers as possible.

For more enrichment, have each child estimate how many hearts will fit inside the cutout before beginning. Then help her count the hearts in her finished project. Use the hearts to decorate your room and then send them home as Valentine's Day cards for family members. Hip, hip, hooray for hearts!

The bug is climbing up the tree because he wants to munch on a leaf.

Max

BUSY HANDS

Creative Learning Experiences for Little Hands

NIFTY NEWSPAPER USES

Here's a news flash! Newspaper is neat for all kinds of motor skills practice!

ideas by Lucia Kemp Henry, Fallon, NV

NEWSPAPER COLLAGE

Ripping and tearing are required for this artistic newspaper activity! Demonstrate for little ones how to tear a sheet of newspaper into strips. Encourage each child to experiment with tearing strips of different widths. After youngsters have torn a supply of strips, mix equal parts of water and liquid starch. Have each child dip each strip in the mixture and then slide her fingers along the strip to remove the excess liquid. Then instruct her to place the strip on a 12" x 18" sheet of construction paper in any fashion she likes. Encourage her to continue to add strips to her paper to make a unique collage. Invite each student to share her dried collage with the group. Then attach the collages to a bulletin board and title the display "Nifty Newspaper Collages!"

PAPER SCRUNCH

Want students to strengthen their fine-motor skills? Try this idea! To begin, have each child lay a half sheet of a newspaper (12" x 22") on a table. Instruct her to place the palm of her hand on the center of the paper. Then have her use only her fingers to scrunch the paper together until she has gathered it up in her hand, making a ball. Encourage each youngster to try this task with her other hand too. Then challenge little ones to repeat the activity with larger pieces of newspaper. Have students toss the newspaper balls in a box to use with "Painting With Newspaper" on page 29. Scrunch, scrunch!

Painting With Newspaper

Use newspaper balls as stand-ins for sponge printers in this easy painting activity! To prepare, crumple newspaper into balls or use the paper balls from "Paper Scrunch" on page 28. Also cut newspaper into half sheets (12" x 22"). At your painting center, have each child clip a newspaper page to his easel. Then instruct him to grasp a newspaper ball, dip it in paint, and press it repeatedly on his paper to make prints. Invite him to repeat the printing process with a fresh newspaper ball and a different color of paint. After he finishes painting, have each student place his paint-dipped newspaper balls in the trash. Display the paintings along with the title "Crumple, Dip, Print, Print, Print!"

Shredded Paper Sensory Search

Turn your sand table into a great sensory experience. Shred newspaper with a paper shredder to make enough filler for your empty sand table. Then hide consecutive numbers of spring objects in the newspaper, such as one plush bunny toy, two gardening gloves, three plastic flowerpots, four silk flowers, five seed packets, and six plastic chicks. Make a numbered picture key on chart paper and display it next to the table. Encourage each student who visits the center to use her sense of touch to explore the table's contents to find all the items on the chart. Happy spring, and happy searching!

Newspaper Toss

Making these beanbags is a snap! Shred newspaper with a paper shredder to make a large supply. Give each child a resealable plastic bag. Have her fill her bag with shredded newspaper. Before sealing each child's bag with clear packing tape, drop in three or four jingle bells. Have youngsters decorate their bags with stickers if desired. Place a hoop on the floor and have students toss their bags in the hoop from varying distances. Ready, set, toss!

BUSY HANDS

Creative Learning Experiences for Little Hands

BRUSH BRIGADE

Here's to brushing up on hands-on learning—
with brushes, of course!

ideas by Jana Sanderson, Rainbow School, Stockton, CA

BOTTLE-BRUSH PAINTING

Young artists will be thrilled to set aside their regular paintbrushes and experiment with bottle-brush painting. Roll up a sheet of white paper and place it inside an empty Pringles potato crisps can. Have each child dip a bottle brush into diluted tempera paint and then swirl the brush around in the can. Have her repeat the process using another bottle brush and a different color of paint. After she has finished painting, remove the paper from the can and allow the paint to dry. What unique and colorful designs!

VEGETABLE SCRUB

Scrub-a-dub-dub, let's clean dirty vegetables with a vegetable brush! Place a container of dirt and a container of water in an empty water table. Bury real or plastic vegetables—such as potatoes, carrots, or turnips—in the dirt. Invite preschoolers to pull the vegetables from the dirt and then scrub them clean with a vegetable brush. When they have finished scrubbing the vegetables, have youngsters plant them back in the dirt for other children to harvest and then clean.

THE BRUSH-OFF

This brush activity is sure to help little ones' fine-motor skills when they remove lint from cloth. In advance, gather a few lint brushes. Cover several wooden blocks with scraps of fabric and use heavy tape to secure the fabric. Rub the covered blocks with lint collected from the lint trap of a dryer. Instruct children to remove the fuzzy bits from the blocks using a lint brush. Then show youngsters how to clean the lint brushes; encourage them to clean the brushes periodically. The lint's all gone!

BRUSH MATES

Brush up on matching skills with this go-together game. Gather a variety of brushes and corresponding objects that represent how each brush is used. For example, collect a clean toothbrush and a small tube of toothpaste, a hairbrush and a wig, a paintbrush and a watercolor paint set, a bottle brush and a baby bottle, and a vegetable brush and a plastic vegetable. Have each student pair the brushes and objects that go together. We're brushing up on brushes!

NAMELY, NAILBRUSHES

Let's lather up some clean fun with nailbrushes! To prepare, gather a nailbrush, a towel, a container of dirt, and a container of soapy water. Place the dirt and water containers in an empty water table. Have each child who visits the center dig in the dirt with her fingers to get her nails dirty. Then direct her to scrub her fingernails clean with the nailbrush dipped in soapy water. Have her rinse her fingers in the water and pat them dry with a towel. Squeaky clean!

Laundry Label Patterns
Use with "Sorting Laundry" on page 20.

buttons

snaps

zippers

Arts & Crafts for Little Hands

Arts & Crafts for Little Hands

Contrasting Artwork

Improve your preschoolers' scissor skills with this eye-popping artwork! Have each young artist cut pieces of white construction paper and then glue them in the design of her choice onto a sheet of black construction paper. While this artwork is drying, have the child cut pieces from black paper to glue onto a white background. Display all the finished black-and-white art for everyone to admire!

Magnet Painting

Can a magnet make a masterpiece? Of course! Set up your magnet painting station by taping a magnetic wand (magnet side up) to a tabletop. Drop a bit of tempera paint in a child's choice of color onto a thin white paper plate. Then put one or two small metal paper clips on the plate. Have the child hold the plate on top of the magnet and slowly move it around, causing the paper clips to move and spread the paint. After each child has finished painting, remove the paper clips before allowing the project to dry. Wow!

Sarah Bollingmo—Preschool
Sarah's Baby Bear Daycare & Preschool
Red Bluff, CA

Me in the Mirror

Ask your little ones to reflect on their appearance when they create these mirror paintings! Provide a child with a large round mirror and tempera paints to match her skin tone, eye color, mouth color, and hair color. Have her look into the mirror and paint her portrait on the mirror. Then carefully place a sheet of white paper on top of the mirror and rub gently to make a print. What super self-portraits!

Bonnie Martin—PreK
Hopewell Country Day
Pennington, NJ

Jennie

Puffy Painting

Add a touch of texture to your children's artwork when you forgo the tempera paint and try this sticky-smooth substance instead! Mix equal parts of white glue and nonmenthol shaving cream. Create the colors of your choice by dripping in some food coloring or liquid watercolor. Then invite youngsters to paint with fingers, brushes, or mini paint rollers. Little ones will love the puffy effect when their pictures dry!

Kimberly Quale—PreK Head Start
Glendive AEM Head Start
Glendive, MT

35

Arts & Crafts for Little Hands

Footprint Ghosts

Your little ones will want to step right up and create these gorgeous ghosts! Paint the bottom of a child's foot with white tempera paint. Then have him carefully step onto a sheet of black or purple construction paper. When the paint dries, have him use a black marker to add eyes and a mouth to his ghost print. Ooh!

Ann Zelter and Jenny Knoll—Toddlers
Salem Lutheran Preschool
Springville, NY

Preschool Pumpkins

These pumpkins are *cute!* Give each child a small foam ball that has been flattened on one side by pressing it against a table. Have her glue pieces of orange tissue paper all over the ball, being sure to overlap the pieces. When the glue is dry, help the child stick a two-inch piece of green pipe cleaner into the top of her pumpkin to create a stem. Then, if desired, have her draw eyes, a nose, and a mouth on her pumpkin with a black marker. Display these pumpkins for everyone to admire!

Stacy Beman—Toddlers
Plaza Boulevard Child Development Center
Rapid City, SD

"Unbe-leaf-able" Placemats

Create these lovely, leafy placemats to grace Thanksgiving tables in your students' homes this November! Go on a nature walk with your preschoolers and ask each of them to collect several colorful fall leaves. When you return to your classroom, press the leaves between the pages of heavy books for several days. Then have each child lay her leaves on the sticky side of a placemat-size piece of clear Con-Tact covering. If desired, have her add seasonal stickers, seasonal cutouts, or confetti to the design. Then carefully press an identically sized piece of clear Con-Tact covering over the design, and this pleasing placemat is finished!

adapted from ideas by
Sandra Remmert—Two-Year-Olds
First Baptist Nursery School
Savoy, IL
and
Doris Porter
Head Start
Anamosa, IA

Crayon-Melt Trees

These fall trees will look fantastic displayed in your classroom windows! To prepare, cut a tree shape with bare branches from brown construction paper for each child.

To make a tree, lay the branches of a cutout on top of a piece of waxed paper. Have youngsters use pencil sharpeners to make crayon shavings in shades of red, yellow, orange, and dark green on the paper. Encourage the tree's owner to watch at a safe distance as you lay another piece of waxed paper over the top and press a warm iron over the project to melt the crayon and seal the waxed paper pieces together. Cut around the tree branches to create a treetop outline. Then display the trees for all to see!

Pam Sockett—Four- and Five-Year-Olds
Lutheran Home Child Care
Wauwatosa, WI

Turkey Headbands

These headbands will be the hit of your Thanksgiving party! Enlarge the patterns below by 10 percent. Cut them out; then trace them onto construction paper for each child (see materials list). Help each youngster cut out her pieces and then follow the directions below to make a turkey headband. Gobble, gobble!

Materials for one turkey headband:
any color construction paper (tail feathers)
2" x 24" strip of brown bulletin board paper (headband)
two 1" x 12" strips of brown construction paper (legs)
brown construction paper turkey head
two orange construction paper feet
yellow construction paper beak
red construction paper wattle
glue
stapler
pencil
scissors

Directions:
1. Trace a child's hands on construction paper and cut them out.
2. Glue the hand cutouts to the headband.
3. Fit the headband around the child's head and staple the ends.
4. Fold the beak in half.
5. Glue the beak and wattle in place on the turkey head before gluing it to the headband.
6. Accordion-fold the legs. Glue one end of each leg to opposite sides of the headband.
7. Glue the feet onto the free ends of the legs.

Stephanie Drone and Monica Short—PreK, Coquina Elementary, Titusville, FL

- -

Turkey Patterns
Use with "Turkey Headbands" on this page.

head

beak

foot (Cut 2.)

wattle

Arts & Crafts for Little Hands

Shiny Snowflakes

The forecast calls for flurries of flakes when you try this art project! Give each child a piece of aluminum foil and have him lay it shiny side up. Have the child dip the end of a thread spool (resembling a wagon wheel) into white paint. Then have him press the spool onto the foil to make prints. Have him repeat the process, making prints with blue and purple paint too. What a gorgeous snowfall!

Barb Stefaniuk
Kerrobert Tiny Tots Playschool
Kerrobert, Saskatchewan, Canada

Paint Stick Menorah

A quick trip to the hardware store—yes, the hardware store—and you'll be ready to make these menorahs! Hot-glue a small wooden craft spool to the center of a paint stir stick for each child. Have her paint a prepared stick and spool with blue paint. When the paint is dry, use tacky glue to attach nine evenly spaced ⅜-inch hex nuts along the length of the stick (glue one to the top of the spool) to serve as candleholders. When the glue is dry, have each child add Hanukkah stickers to decorate her menorah. Send each child's menorah home with a supply of candles and let the celebrating begin. Happy Hanukkah!

Nancy Goldberg, B'nai Israel Schilit Nursery School, Rockville, MD

Free-form Snowmen

Let your little ones' creativity shine with these cute snowmen! Give each child a sheet of black or royal blue construction paper and access to white tempera paint. Invite him to paint a snowman on the paper, but encourage him to paint any way he wishes. When the paint is dry, determine the spot on the painting you think looks most like a head. Then glue on a construction paper carrot nose and top hat. Use a black marker to add two eyes. Hello, Frosty!

Ann Zelter and Jenny Knoll
Salem Lutheran Preschool
Springville, NY

Seven Candles for Kwanzaa

Your youngsters will love painting with Kwanzaa colors as they create these cool kinaras! In advance, enlist the help of parents in collecting cardboard tubes from paper towels and gift wrap. Cut the tubes to equal lengths. Give each child seven tubes. Have her paint three of them red, three green, and one black to make candles. When the paint is dry, help her glue the seven candles to a strip of poster board as shown. After the glue is dry, have her stuff a bit of orange or gold tissue paper into the top of each tube to make a flame. Happy Kwanzaa!

Shannon Stakley, Decker Family Development Center, Wadsworth, OH

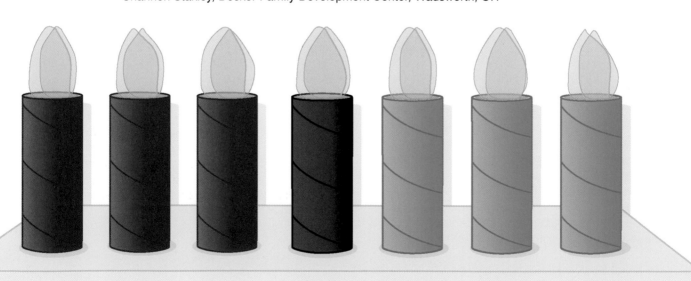

Arts & Crafts for Little Hands

Lovebugs

Welcome Valentine's Day with these colorful critters adorning your classroom! To prepare, cut out the following shapes for each child: a large oval from pink construction paper (body), two smaller ovals from waxed paper (wings), and six thin strips from purple construction paper (legs). Have each child glue a pair of wings to the lovebug's body and then glue on six legs. Invite her to use a red or purple crayon to draw a face on her lovebug. Cute!

adapted from an idea by Cindy Paolucci and Lynn Lavelle
Warren Community Elementary—LEAP Preschool
W. Warren, MA

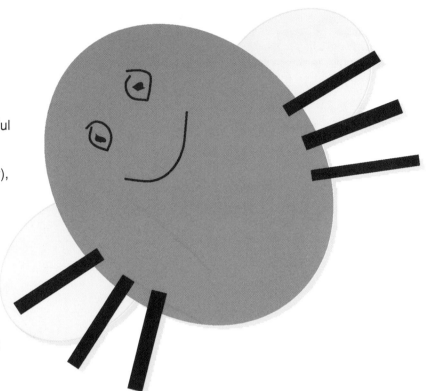

Swirls and Shimmers

Decorate hearts for Valentine's Day or shamrocks for St. Patrick's Day with this fun and fancy technique! Purchase a twist whisk. Have a child dip the whisk into white paint and then bounce it on a red heart cutout or a green shamrock cutout to make spiral prints. Before the paint dries, have him sprinkle on a bit of iridescent glitter. What shimmery seasonal shapes!

Sandy Barker
ECFE–District Program Center
Cottage Grove, MN

41

Peekaboo, See Right Through!

This Valentine's Day project is sure to win your youngsters' hearts! Purchase a class supply of clear plastic sheet protectors. Cut a large heart shape from each one (leaving you with two transparent hearts). Staple the hearts together in the center. Hole-punch the perimeter of the paired hearts; then thread a long length of red curling ribbon through one hole and tie the end in place. Have a child lace the hearts together, leaving a small opening at the top. Remove the staples. Then provide materials to stuff the hearts, such as tissue paper pieces, crinkled gift bag filler, or lengths of curling ribbon in valentine colors. Help each child finish lacing her stuffed heart and tie the ribbon ends. Display this unique heart art for everyone to admire!

Rachel Castro
Albuquerque, NM

Wiggle Painting

Here's a new twist on painting with toothbrushes! Have each child, in turn, use a clean battery-powered toothbrush to paint. Instruct him to dip the toothbrush into paint, turn it on, and wiggle the paint all over his paper!

Lola Anderson
Canby Head Start
Canby, MN

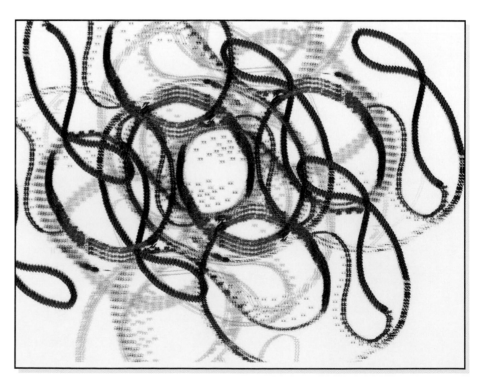

Arts & Crafts for Little Hands

Spoon Tulips

Greet spring with this fun and flowery project! Purchase plastic spoons in one or more tulip colors (you'll need three per child). To make one project, bundle three spoons together and wrap green craft tape around the handles. As you wrap the tape, also secure two silk leaves to the handle stem. Then press some clay into the bottom of a small plastic flowerpot. Stick the stem into the clay; then add a bit of moss on top.

Susan Dzurovcik
Valley Road School
Clark, NJ

"Egg-cellent" Maracas

Use some leftover plastic Easter eggs to make maracas for Cinco de Mayo! To make a shaker, cut a slit in one end of a plastic egg. Insert a wooden craft stick; then secure it with hot glue. Put some rice inside the egg, snap it closed, and wrap clear packing tape around the seam. Then cover the egg with a layer of red, white, and green tissue paper squares applied with diluted white glue. When the glue is dry, get ready to shake these maracas at your classroom fiesta!

Kandi Campbell
St. Columba's CLC
Camarillo, CA

Painting Like Michelangelo

When you teach your preschoolers about the great artists of history, you're sure to want to tell them about Michelangelo. Show them pictures of the ceiling in the Sistine Chapel; then invite them to try their hand at painting from this angle! Tape bulletin board paper to the undersides of your tables and line the floor under them with newspaper. Dress each child in an oversize T-shirt, goggles, and a shower cap to protect her clothing, eyes, and hair. Invite each youngster to lie on her back and paint the paper. Can they imagine and appreciate the effort it must have taken for Michelangelo to accomplish his task? You bet!

Karen Sprous
Grandma's House Child Care Center
Desloge, MO

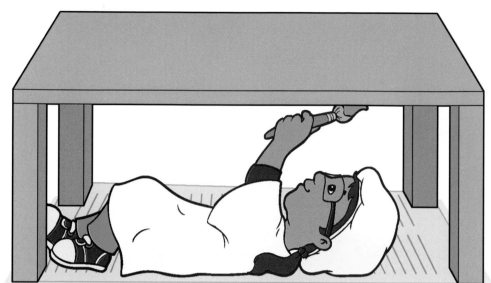

Collage Bouquet

These lovely bouquets could grace your tables at a Mother's Day tea *and* make pretty presents for moms! For each child, cut several flower shapes from colored tagboard. Invite a child to use glitter glue and collage materials to decorate his flowers. Then poke a hole in the center of each flower, insert a green pipe cleaner, and bend the end to secure it as shown. Slip the pipe cleaner stems into an individual plastic water or juice bottle. Then wrap colorful tissue paper around the bottle and tie a length of ribbon or raffia around the bottle's neck to secure it.

Beth Taylor Devlin
Dutch Lane Elementary
Hicksville, NY

"Bee-utiful"!

Your youngsters will be all abuzz about this cute project! To begin, have each child paint a cardboard tube with yellow tempera paint. When the yellow paint is dry, have him add black paint stripes. When that paint is dry, hot-glue a foam ball to one end of the tube. Then have the child poke two short lengths of yellow or black pipe cleaners into the ball for antennae. Instruct him to use a marker to draw a face. Finish the bee by having him glue on waxed paper wings. Buzz, buzz!

Jamie Holly
All Aboard School
Valhalla, NY

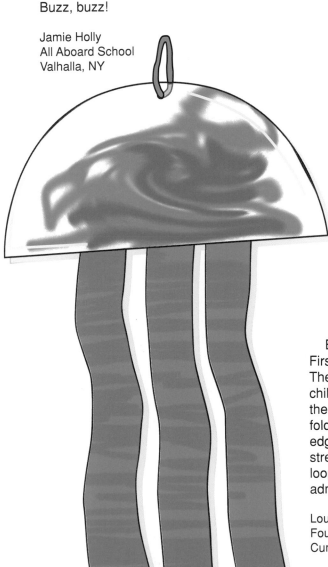

Colorful Jellyfish

Enhance an ocean theme by making these jazzy jellyfish! First, cut out a circle of clear Con-Tact covering for each child. Then peel off the backing to reveal the sticky side. Invite a child to paint with the colors of her choice in the center of the sticky circle, leaving an unpainted edge all around. Then fold over the paper to create a semicircle, and press the edges together to seal in the paint. Tape some crepe paper streamers to the straight side of the jellyfish, and add a yarn loop to hang these ocean critters in your room for everyone to admire!

Louisa Tompkins
Four Corners Early Learning Center YMCA
Cumberland, RI

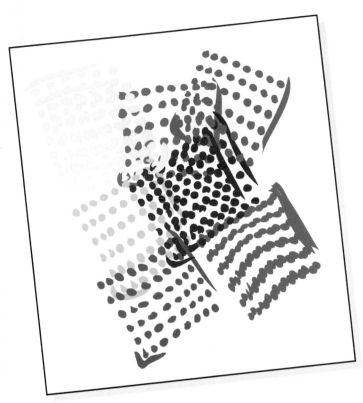

Flyswatter Paintings

Put on your smocks, everybody, because this outdoor art activity is messy but fun! Purchase some inexpensive flyswatters at your local dollar store or discount store. Give each child a flyswatter and a large sheet of construction paper. Squeeze a few dabs of paint onto each child's paper. Then invite youngsters to swat the paint flies. They'll be improving their eye-hand coordination while they create some very cool abstract art!

Katie Kasoff
West Point Child Learning Center
Lansdale, PA

Darling Dragonflies

Send these dragonflies whirring to children's homes to land on their families' refrigerators!

Materials for one:
half of a thick (fuzzy) pipe cleaner
two 3" x 5" pieces of colored plastic wrap
2 hole reinforcers
small piece of magnetic tape
glue

Directions:
1. Bend down two inches of the pipe cleaner and twist it around the rest of the pipe cleaner, creating the dragonfly's head and body as shown.
2. Fold each piece of plastic wrap lengthwise to create the wings.
3. Crisscross the two wings and tuck them under the twisted end of the pipe cleaner. Secure them with a drop of glue if necessary.
4. Attach two hole reinforcers for eyes.
5. Affix the magnetic tape to the back of the dragonfly.

Janet Boyce
Cokato, MN

46

GET MOVING!

Movement Ideas for Preschoolers

A Balance of Friendship

Youngsters build trust and friendship with a simple walk across a balance beam. Have each child choose a friend to help her walk across the balance beam (or a pretend balance beam, a line taped to the floor). As she walks, have her friend hold her hand and offer words of encouragement. When the child reaches the end of the beam, snap a photo of the twosome's accomplishment. Then have little ones switch places. Youngsters will be eager to do this activity again and again!

Deborah Luke—PreK
Fairmont Nursery School
Syracuse, NY

Musically Moving

Any season is the season for music and movement! Simply cut out a class supply of shapes from fabric, felt, or sturdy paper to match the season or your theme. Use apple, pumpkin, or bat shapes for fall; Christmas tree, snowman, or heart shapes for winter; flower, raindrop, or kite shapes for spring; and sun or beach ball shapes for summer. Label the cutouts with geometric shapes, colors, or symbols you have introduced. Position a set of cutouts on the floor. Have each child stand on a cutout. Play music in intervals, having youngsters hop, dance, or walk from cutout to cutout. Each time you stop the music, have each student identify what is on the cutout he lands on.

Deborah Ryan—Child and Family Development Specialist
Early Head Start
Milwaukie, OR

Ants in the Grass

Your adventurous little ants will be ready to scurry through grass! To set up a grassy trail, tape lengths of green paper streamers to the undersides of two tables that have been pushed together. (The paper should nearly touch the floor, and the strips should be spaced several inches apart.) Have your little ants crawl between the blades of grass. For added interest, make ant antennae headbands with black strips of paper, two black chenille stems, and black pom-poms. Go, ants! Go!

adapted from an idea by Marie DePauw—PreK
St. John's Daycare
Excelsior, MN

Beach Ball Fun

This large-motor activity will provide lots of fun! Blow up a beach ball and close the valve. Tie a length of thin elastic to the stem of the valve. Attach the free end of the elastic to a door frame whose door can be left open. (For outside play, tie the free end of the elastic to the monkey bars.) Adjust the height of the ball to suit your students' heights. Invite a pair of children to hit the ball back and forth to one another. With each hit, they will build eye-hand coordination while having a ball!

Nancy Wolfgram—Two-Year-Olds
Kindercare Learning Center #1111
Lincoln, NE

Get Moving!

Movement Ideas for Preschoolers

Mirror Me!

"Mirror me!" is what you'll hear little ones saying when they try a round of this copy game. Stand in front of your students and have them watch and imitate your movements as you move an arm up and down or a leg from side to side. Once youngsters master copying you, pair students, have them stand face-to-face, and ask them to take turns being the leader!

Bat Bounce

Youngsters will go simply batty over these fun bouncing balls! Buy a pack or two of racquetball balls. Use a dark permanent marker to draw bat features on each one as shown. Have students bounce and catch the finished bat balls. Once they get the hang of it, have them count the number of bounces before each catch.

Front view

Side view

50

Tap on a Triangle; Step on a Square

Have your youngsters practice shape recognition as they hop, jump, and tiptoe on these mats just made for moving! Cut four equal mats from a solid-colored shower curtain. On each mat, draw a few different basic shapes you want your little ones to recognize. Gather a small group and give each child a shape mat. Call out directions, such as "Hop on a square" or "March on a circle." What a shipshape way to have fun with movement skills and practice shape recognition!

Pumpkin Roll

Pumpkin, pumpkin, oh so fine—watch him roll around the vine! Invite one child to play the part of a pumpkin and four more children to be the pumpkin vine. Ask these four children to stand in a line, holding hands with their arms extended. Have the pumpkin start at one end of the vine and roll or crawl around and between the children making up the vine until he reaches the opposite end. Then have another child take a turn playing the pumpkin.

Get Moving!

Movement Ideas for Preschoolers

ideas by Ada Goren, Winston-Salem, NC

Rudolph's Workout

Invite each child to wear an antler headband and a red sticky dot on her nose as she follows along with this fun song!

(sung to the tune of "Head, Shoulders, Knees, and Toes")

Hooves, belly, antlers, nose,
Antlers, nose.
Hooves, belly, antlers, nose,
Antlers, nose.
Left hoof, right hoof,   *Child holds up left hand then right hand.*
Strike a pose!   *Child poses as she wishes.*
Hooves, belly, antlers, nose,
Antlers, nose.

Shake Your Flake

There'll be a whole lot of shakin' going on when your children make *these* snowflakes! To make a snowflake shaker, have a child decorate the bottoms of two thin white paper plates with snowflake designs. Tape a craft stick handle to the undecorated side of one plate. Then staple the rims of the plates together, leaving an open space. Put in a couple of milk jug lids; then staple the remainder of the rim. Have each child use her shaker to act out the rhyme below.

Shake your flake high;
Shake your flake low.
Shake your flake to and fro!

Shake your flake to the ceiling;
Shake your flake to the floor.
Shake your flake some more, more, more!

Shake your flake while you're walking;
Shake your flake while you hop.
Shake your flake again, and then we…stop!

Walk, Jump, and Hop Into the New Year

Introduce your little ones to the number for the new year by putting it right on your classroom floor! Use masking tape to form the numbers in 2005 on an open floor space. Then encourage youngsters to move along the lines in various ways. Ask them to walk, hop, tiptoe, or crawl along the lines to form the new year's number. Welcome, 2005!

Iceberg Jump

Calling all preschool polar bears! It's time for a round of Iceberg Jump! To prepare for this fun activity, first label several large white paper icebergs with various letters or numbers. Use clear Con-Tact covering to adhere the labeled icebergs to an open floor area. Space the icebergs so that youngsters can jump from one to another. Then invite three or four students at a time to pretend to be polar bears and jump from iceberg to iceberg as you play some lively music. Stop the music and ask each polar bear to identify the letter or number on her iceberg. Then restart the music for more icy fun and learning!

Frosty Says

Visit your local party supply store to purchase a plastic top hat. Then you'll be ready to play this wintry version of Simon Says! Put on your top hat and introduce yourself as Frosty the Snowman. Give your youngsters movement directions such as "Frosty says, 'Touch your toes'" or "Frosty says, 'Run in place.'" Once your little ones get the hang of the game, invite them to take turns playing Frosty themselves!

Get Moving!

Movement Ideas for Preschoolers

Sandwich Squish

Invite your preschoolers to be both the guests *and* the goodies at this picnic! Begin making a kid sandwich by laying down a gym mat. Have a few youngsters lie down on the mat side by side, with their heads off one end of the mat. Then lay a second mat on top of them. Ask what kind of sandwich they are pretending to be. Peanut butter and jelly? Yum! Oh, but no picnic would be complete without ants! Have a student or two crawl over the legs half of your kid sandwich. Once the giggles subside, make another sandwich with different children as the filling; then watch the ants arrive again! For added fun, play the song "The Ants Go Marching" during this silly scenario!

Who Has the Hearts?

This seasonal guessing game will help your little ones practice throwing and catching a ball. Have youngsters stand in a circle, facing inward. Designate one child to be Cupid. Have her stand in the center, give her a playground ball, and have her close her eyes. Give a few small craft foam hearts to one child in the circle; then have youngsters hold their hands in front of them as if holding the hearts. When everyone is set, have the group say, "Cupid, Cupid, who has your hearts?" Cupid opens her eyes and throws the ball to the child she thinks has the hearts. That child catches the ball. If the hearts fall in the process, Cupid has guessed correctly. If no hearts fall, the child throws the ball back to Cupid. The child who had the hearts is Cupid for the next round.

Pattern Rock

Get students moving in rhythm as they recite patterns! Teach everyone a stomp, stomp, clap pattern and have them perform the movements several times until they get the hang of it. Then say, "Pattern rock, pattern rock!" a few times while stomping and clapping the syllables. Next, pick a pattern to recite to the rhythm, such as red, red, blue, red, red, blue. Have students recite the pattern with you. Then leave off the last word of the pattern and have students fill in the blank. Continue with other patterns that fit the rhythm.

cat, cat, dog, cat, cat, dog
circle, square, circle, square

Shelley Hoster
Jack and Jill Early Learning Center
Norcross, GA

Stepping Stones

Little ones will jump at this chance to practice numbers! To prepare, roll out a long length of blue bulletin board paper to make a creek. Space ten brown paper stepping stones along the length of the blue paper so that children must jump from one to another. Glue the stones in place. Then number the stones from 1 to 10, starting at one end. Invite youngsters to jump from one stone to the next, saying the numbers as they go.

adapted from an idea by Ruth Erb
Discovery Place at St. Matthew Lutheran Church
Hanover, PA

Get Moving!

Movement Ideas for Preschoolers

Fabric Dancing

It's amazing what a simple piece of fabric can do! Give each of your children a ladies' scarf or a piece of fluid fabric. Then suggest that they try to use their fabric pieces as pirates' hats, wings, giant paintbrushes, or whatever else their imaginations can conjure up! Turn on some music and invite youngsters to move to the beat with their scarves or fabric.

Nancy Vogt
Boothbay Head Start
Boothbay, ME

Ice-Cream Relay

These ice-cream cones are guaranteed not to drip! But they will help improve your little ones' coordination! To prepare, gather two small plastic safety cones and two playground balls. Divide your children into two teams and line up each team so that there is about five feet between each child in line. Hand an ice-cream cone—a safety cone turned upside down with the ball on top of it—to the player at the front of each line. Explain that he must hold onto the cone while moving to the child next in line and passing the cone to her. Then she must walk and pass the cone to the next child. The first team to have the cone reach the end of the line is the winner!

Lisa Erdman
Our Savior Lutheran School
Nashville, TN

Color Bowling

This simple twist on soda-bottle bowling ties in basic skills of counting and color recognition. Into each of several clear, empty soda bottles, stuff a different color of tissue paper. Use whatever colors you wish to have students identify. Then set up the bottles and have youngsters bowl them over with a small ball. Once they've knocked down some bottles, have them count how many and tell you what colors they are.

Nancy Jandreau
Kids Corner Day Care
Potsdam, NY

Low, Middle, High

Get little muscles moving and stretching with this fun chant! Repeat the chant a few times as youngsters do the motions. Then try repeating the motions faster and faster.

Bend down low and touch your toes.
Move up a little and touch your middle.
Stretch up high and touch the sky!

Cyndi Smith
Louisville Childcare Center
Louisville, OH

Get Moving!

Movement Ideas for Preschoolers

Spring Winds

Welcome spring's breezes with this movement activity. Give each child a length of crepe paper streamer to use in acting out the lines of this poem.

Spring winds blow high.
Spring winds blow low.
They start out as breezes;
Then they grow and grow!

Round and round they go,
Swaying every treetop,
Sweeping across the grass.
Then, just like that, the winds stop!

Wiggle streamer high.
Wiggle streamer low.
Wiggle streamer slowly.
Wiggle streamer faster and faster.

Wiggle streamer in a circle.
Wiggle streamer back and forth.
Wiggle streamer across the floor.
Drop streamer at feet.

LeeAnn Collins
Sunshine House Preschool
Lansing, MI

Directions Disco

Put on some instrumental disco music and have your youngsters perform the appropriate actions as they say the following chant to reinforce directional words and body awareness.

Over your head.
Under your toes.
Behind your back.
In front of your nose.
On your shoulders.
Beside your hips.
Next to your ears.
In front of your lips.

Wendy Good
Helping Hands Preschool
Medina, OH

Management Tips
& Timesavers

Management Tips & Timesavers

That's the Ticket!

Work on your youngsters' color matching skills as you make the transition from circle time to tables. To prepare, cut small rectangles of colored construction paper that match the colors of the tables (or table labels) in your classroom. Laminate them for durability. At the end of circle time, hand each child a rectangle (a ticket) and have her find a seat at a table of the corresponding color. When everyone is seated, collect the tickets for next time.

Amy Aloi—Preschool Special Education
Bollman Bridge RECC
Jessup, MD

Let's See What's Next...

Post your daily schedule in pictures so your preschoolers can easily figure out what activity comes next. Create a simple picture for each part of your day. Post these on a wall or chalkboard. Then, from red construction paper, cut an outline of a circle that is large enough to frame the pictures. Use Sticky-Tac or magnets to attach the circle over the first picture at the start of the day; then move it along the row of pictures as you move to each subsequent activity.

Charlotte M. Parker, PreK Varying Exceptionalities
Blackburn Elementary
Palmetto, FL

Pattern Trail

This gross-motor activity is a great way to keep little ones busy while their classmates are finishing an activity. In a convenient area of your classroom, lay out a pattern of colored tape similar to the one shown. When a child finishes early, have her start at one end of the trail and jump from one color to the next (feet apart and then together). Have her keep going until everyone is following the pattern trail. Then move the whole group into your next activity.

Nancy O'Toole—Preschool
Ready Set Grow
Grand Rapids, MN

Books, Tapes, and Sticky Dots

Keep your listening center organized with the help of some inexpensive sticky dots! For each book and tape set, place a same-colored sticky dot on the book and on the tape. Place the two together in a large zippered plastic bag. When a child has finished listening to a story, he simply matches the colored dots and stows the items in a bag for the next child to use.

Lauren Bernero—PreK, Early Childhood Department, Jersey City, NJ

Colorful Attendance

Help your little ones recognize their names as you take attendance each day. Begin by cutting a large crayon shape from poster board. Cut out a smaller crayon for each child, and label it with his first name. Attach the hook side of a Velcro strip to the large crayon for each child. Then attach the loop side of a Velcro strip to the back of each smaller crayon. Mount the large crayon on a wall and keep the smaller crayons in a basket nearby. Each day, at arrival time, have a child find the crayon with his name and stick it onto the larger crayon. You'll be able to see at a glance who is in school.

After students have mastered their first names, make a new set of crayons with last names on them.

Julie B. Wilson—Four- and Five-Year-Olds
Laura's Learning Treehouse
Avon, OH

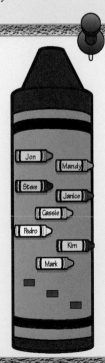

Management Tips & Timesavers

Check This Out!

Do your little ones like to borrow books from your classroom to take home? Here's a way to create a simple checkout system. Choose about a dozen books at a time to display in your checkout library. For each one, make a checkout card by cutting out a picture of the book from a book order form. Glue the picture to an index card. Put a small piece of magnetic tape on the back of each card; then display the cards on a magnetic chalkboard. (Use regular tape if your board isn't magnetic.) Display the books or keep them in a special basket nearby. When a child wants to check out a book, write her name in chalk next to the checkout card. When she returns the book, erase her name. Easy!

adapted from an idea by
Rivki Silverberg—PreK and K
Head Start
New York City, NY

Communication Stickers

Preschool pick-up time can be hectic, and you don't always have a chance to share information about a child's day with his parents. Try this tip to keep in touch! If you need to share information about behavior or boast about a child's great work, jot a few words on a nametag sticker. Then stick the sticker to the child's clothing. Even if you don't get to talk at length with a parent, she can see your note and be sure to ask her child about it.

Mary Gribble—PreK
Country Goose Preschool
River Falls–Prescott, WI

Catch a Bubble

If you need youngsters to be quiet for a bit, try softly singing this song together. Then pretend to blow bubbles through a bubble wand, and have each child pretend to do as the song says. Encourage little ones to keep their bubbles in their mouths and not pop them!

(sung to the tune of "Clementine")

Catch a bubble.
Catch a bubble.
Put it right into your mouth!
Catch a bubble.
Catch a bubble.
Put it right into your mouth!

Jennifer Corkern—Preschool
Hobe Sound Child Care Center
Hobe Sound, FL

Cotton Swab Cleanup

Keep your watercolor paint sets neat and tidy with this tip! After a child uses a paint set, run a cotton swab around the ovals of paint to absorb excess paint and water. If paint colors have gotten mixed, dab a swab on top, and it will absorb the mixed color, revealing the original cake of color beneath.

Leslie Campbell—PreK 4
Jack and Jill Christian Preschool
Fernandina Beach, FL

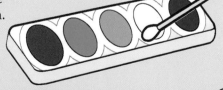

Yoga Transition

If your little ones have trouble with transition times, try some relaxing yoga. Ask students to sit cross-legged on your carpet as you play some soothing music. Give youngsters a few minutes to simply relax and breathe. After all, preschool is hard work, and everyone needs a break!

Linda Haustein—PreK, George Washington School #1
Elizabeth, NJ

Management Tips & Timesavers

Video Boxes to the Rescue!

If your little ones have difficulty putting cards from card games back into their original boxes, try this tip! Ask your local video rental store to donate some of the large plastic boxes they use for videotapes. Cut off the front panel of the card game box and slip it into the clear cover on the video box. Then store the cards inside, and you have an easy-to-open, easy-to-close solution!

Linda Haake
Germantown Elementary
Germantown, IL

Area Markers

If you've ever tried to mark off an area of your classroom by putting strips of masking tape on the carpet, you know it partially peels off and leaves a sticky residue. So use strips of Velcro fastening tape instead! Adhere the hook side of Velcro strips to the carpet to mark off your circle-time area or a particular center. You can vacuum right over it!

Pati Mitchell
Geneva School
Geneva, FL

Squeezy Paint

Don't toss those empty glue bottles! Clean them out and fill them with paint instead. Keep the bottles handy for squeezing out small amounts of paint for projects, or invite youngsters to squeeze out their own paint for blot pictures or marble painting.

Jackie Leagjeld
Creek Day School
Madison, WI

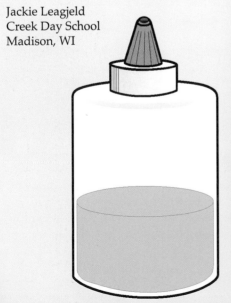

S-T-O-R-Y

Help your little ones make the transition from playtime to storytime with this easy tune!

(sung to the tune of "Bingo")

Let's all clean up and sit right down.
It's time to read a story!
S-t-o-r-y, s-t-o-r-y, s-t-o-r-y,
It's time to read a story!

Jill Jarman, Perryville Elementary, Perryville, KY

Copy 'n' Cut

Make cutting out a large number of patterns easier with this tip! Duplicate the pattern; then staple the copy to a stack of several sheets of paper. Cut out the pattern through all the layers, and you get lots of patterns in a short amount of time. Look—no tracing lines!

Terry Deweese
Children's Ark—Brentwood Christian School
Austin, TX

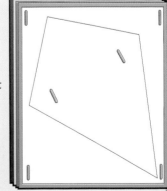

Management Tips & Timesavers

Paint Tub Tip

Need some inexpensive paint tubs for your easel area? How about some *free* ones? To make one, simply poke a hole in the lid of a margarine tub. Then use scissors to enlarge the hole until you can fit a paintbrush into it. Voilà—a covered paint tub!

Pam Arntson, Colfax Elementary
Colfax, WI

Always Be Prepared

Your students' school emergency cards are most likely kept in your school office, but photocopy the cards and keep the copies in a folder. Take the folder along on field trips. You'll have all the information you need in the event of an emergency, including emergency contacts, extra phone numbers, and parent preferences for hospital treatment.

Jean Ricotta
Signal Hill Elementary
Dix Hills, NY

Easing Assessment

Keep a clipboard and some large sticky labels handy to help you make ongoing student assessment easier. Clip a sheet of large labels to the clipboard. Make notes throughout the day with a child's name, the date, and the behavior or skills you observe. Later, simply peel off each label and stick it onto a child's page in an assessment notebook or the student's portfolio.

Heather Kelley
Sulphur, LA

Priya Singh
PS 96
New York, NY

4/7
Brendon counts to ten

Cleanup Crews

Make cleanup less chaotic by assigning a cleanup crew each day. Divide your class into three or four teams and give each team a color name. Each day, have one crew be responsible for cleaning up the room while one teacher or an assistant supervises. Have another adult take the remaining children outside. Fewer children in the room and specific tasks for each crew member will make cleaning the classroom a snap!

Kerri Bailey and Andria Bradley
The O'Quinn School
Mt. Pleasant, SC

Clip the Art

Here's a tip to make displaying student artwork easy! Put a bit of Sticky-Tac adhesive on the back of a spring-type clothespin. Then stick the clothespin to the wall, jaws down. Clip a piece of student artwork in the clothespin for an instant, easy-to-change display!

Melissa Adams
Bright Promises Preschool
Indianapolis, IN

Management Tips & Timesavers

Yarn Cans

Here's a great tip for storing yarn! Put each separate color of yarn ball into a clear tennis ball can. Punch a hole in the plastic lid of the can and thread one end of the yarn through the hole. Your students can easily pull out just as much yarn as they need, and you can easily see when you're almost out of a particular color. You can store several cans in a divided box (check your local grocery store for boxes that hold wine bottles). *Mary Lyons, Oakwood-Windsor Elementary, Aiken, SC*

Alphabet Roundup

Want to signal your little ones that cleanup time is ending? Start saying the alphabet. Explain that by the time you reach z, they should be done cleaning and should be sitting with you in the group area. They'll get the hang of this letter routine in no time! *Stephanie Schmidt, Lester B. Pearson Public School, Waterloo, Ontario, Canada*

Outdoor Painting Time

Painting outdoors is great fun in the warm weather! To make management simple, bring along some clothespins, a towel, and a wagon with two buckets, one filled with soapy water and one with clean water. When youngsters finish painting, clip their artwork to a chain-link fence to dry. When it's time to head inside, have little ones wash and rinse their hands in the buckets of water and then dry them on a towel. *Sarah Booth, Messiah Nursery School, South Williamsport, PA*

UFO Box

Do you and your youngsters sometimes come across stray objects during cleanup time? If you can't remember on the spot where an item or puzzle piece belongs, put it into a box for UFOs, or unidentified found objects. Occasionally go through the box after school and try to put all the items and pieces back where they belong. *Dot Stein, Christian Beginnings Preschool, Prince Frederick, MD*

Double-Duty Dishwasher

Use the dishwasher to wash food—the play food from your dramatic-play area, that is! Put small plastic and vinyl items from your housekeeping area into a fine-mesh laundry bag. Then place the bag on the top rack of your dishwasher. Stop the dishwasher before the drying cycle, and lay out the items on a clean towel to air-dry. *Sheila Shank, St. Paul's Hilltop Christian Nursery School, Torrington, CT*

It's Circle Time

Copy Cats

Youngsters will think this activity is the cat's meow! For each child, make a paper headband with two cat-ear cutouts. Play a version of Follow the Leader by designating a cat leader and having everyone else play the copycats. Invite the leader to choose a cat action, such as purring, cleaning his paws, or meowing. Have all the copycats do the same. After a few kitty-cat moves, instruct the leader to lead the group to line up, wash their hands, or go back to their seats—whatever you need youngsters to do as you head into your next activity!

Deborah Ryan—Child and Family Development Specialist
Early Head Start
Milwaukie, OR

Whose Name Is Hiding?

Familiarize your students with one another's names with this hide-and-seek activity! Each day, choose a child and write his name on several sticky notes. Hide the notes throughout your classroom. Have your preschoolers hunt for the sticky notes and return them to your group area. Then post all of the notes on the wall or chalkboard and discuss the unique qualities of the child's name, such as its beginning letter and its length. Your little ones will know everyone's name in no time!

Dana Sanders—Preschool
Hamilton Crossing Elementary
Cartersville, GA

Carpet-Square Shapes

Reinforce the shapes your preschoolers are learning by arranging your circle-time seating to match! For example, when you are teaching your little ones about rectangles, arrange carpet squares in a large rectangle. Invite the class to look at the shape and then sit on the carpet squares. After your youngsters have mastered the shapes, try using carpet squares to form letters of the alphabet.

Tami Renner—PreK
Flanagan's Preschool
Collegeville, PA

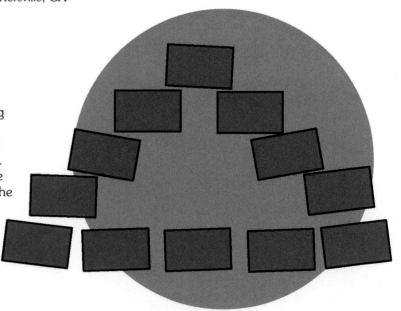

A Friendly Chant

Use this easy chant to help your new preschoolers get acquainted. Invite the child named in the third line to stand up and wave to the group when directed. As a variation, call out "girls," "boys," or the names of teachers or parent helpers in the third line.

Who are all our friends today?
Who is here to learn and play?
Stand up, [child's name], and look around.
Wave hello and sit back down.

Reggie Bender—Preschool
Orchard Park Cooperative Nursery School
Orchard Park, NY

A Colorful Concoction

Stir up some interest in colors with a pot of color soup! To prepare, cut out various simple shapes from different colors of construction paper. Label a box or basket with each color. Then hide the colorful shapes throughout your classroom. At circle time, ask youngsters to hunt for the shapes and sort them by color into the containers. To conclude the activity, dump all the shapes into a large pot and invite little ones to take turns stirring the pot of color soup with a big wooden spoon!

Once youngsters know their colors, relabel the containers to help your students concentrate on the shapes and make a pot of shape soup instead!

Pepper Leclerc—PreK
Merrimack Valley Christian Day School
Lowell, MA

Textured Numbers

Using the sense of touch and identifying numerals

Your youngsters get a feel for number recognition when you try this alternative to a traditional feely box. Use large number stencils to cut numerals from various textured materials, such as sandpaper, felt, burlap, or small-bubble bubble wrap. Glue each cutout to a large index card. At circle time, put one number card in a feely box. Have a child reach into the box and try to identify the number by touch only. Have the youngster verbalize for the group what he feels. Give hints to the child if needed. After he's guessed, reveal the number card and have him check his answer. Then invite another child to try his hand at identifying a different textured number. Easy as 1, 2, 3!

Michelle Bowman—PreK
Noah's Ark
Lima, OH

Pumpkin Faces

Identifying feelings

Try this group-time game to help little ones express and interpret feelings. Make several orange construction paper copies of the pumpkin face patterns on page 78. Draw a different face on each one, expressing a variety of emotions, such as happiness, sadness, anger, or surprise. Put the cutouts into a plastic pumpkin bucket.

At group time, seat students in a circle. Play some music as students pass the pumpkin. Stop the music, and ask the child holding the pumpkin bucket to draw out one pumpkin face. Ask her to show the pumpkin to the group and describe how it is feeling. Then restart the music and continue to pass the bucket until everyone has had a turn.

Sue Fleischmann—Child and Family Specialist
Waukesha County Project Head Start
Waukesha, WI

Roll the Pumpkin

Communicating orally

Use a miniature pumpkin to review concepts or simply give students an opportunity to practice speaking skills. Cut off the stem of a mini pumpkin so that it doesn't interfere when the pumpkin is rolled. Seat students in a circle. Hand the pumpkin to a child and have him roll it to someone else in the circle. Then either ask that child a question to help review skills, such as "What color are Mary's shoes?" or simply ask a question to encourage speaking in complete sentences, such as "What is your favorite food?" Then have that child roll the pumpkin to someone else. Keep the pumpkin rolling until everyone has a turn to speak!

Heather Brown—Preschool
St. John Noah's Ark Preschool, Clarinda, IA

I like spaghetti best.

It's in the Cards
Sorting and identifying numbers

A deck of cards can make your circle time a prime time for reviewing all kinds of skills! Deal a card to each child. Ask everyone with a red card to stand or everyone with a number 4 to touch her toes. To practice sorting, create piles of cards (sorted by number, suit, or color) and ask each child to add her card to the pile she thinks it matches best. Have her explain why she chose that pile. Or, for a different activity, simply practice number recognition by using the numeral cards as flash cards. If youngsters still possess cards when circle time is over, practice seriation—aces line up first, then twos, then threes, etc. The possibilities with playing cards are endless!

Tori Zissman—Four- and Five-Year-Olds
Billy Dalwin Preschool of Temple Emunah
Lexington, MA

Ah-choo!
Identifying letters and developing hygiene skills

Help your preschoolers remember to cover their noses and mouths when they sneeze. To prepare, make a set of alphabet cards with the letters you've covered in class. Also make a number of cards labeled "Ah-choo!" Shuffle all the cards together. Next, demonstrate how a sneeze can spread germs. Hold a colored napkin in front of a spray bottle of water. Say, "Ah-choo!" as you squirt the water onto the napkin. Show the students how the napkin is now covered with drops of water. Good thing you caught that pretend sneeze before it spread all over everyone!

Next, use the cards you made to play a game. Give each child a tissue. Hold up one card at a time and have students identify the letter on it. If you hold up a card that says "Ah-choo!" have each child quickly sneeze into his tissue.

Sue Fleischmann—Child and Family Specialist
Waukesha County Project Head Start
Waukesha, WI

Alphabet Soup

Encourage letter recognition with a hot pot of alphabet soup! Place a large pot or a plastic Halloween cauldron in the center of your circle area. Toss in a set of plastic or foam letters. Then invite each child to take a turn stirring the concoction with a wooden spoon. After he stirs, have him scoop out a letter and identify it. Then, as he returns the letter to the pot, have the group chant the following, substituting his chosen letter in the first line.

[A], [A], in the pot.
Stir it up and make it hot!

Shelley Barney
New Athens Elementary
New Athens, IL

Left Mitten, Right Mitten

Help your preschoolers practice visual discrimination and the concepts of left and right with this marvelous mitten match! Using the mitten pattern on page 106, cut out a pair of mittens from wallpaper samples for each child. Attach magnetic tape to the back of each mitten. Then display the right-hand mittens on a magnetic surface. Pass out the left-hand mittens to your group. Have each child match her mitten to its mate and then attach it to the surface in the correct left-hand position. If she successfully positions the mitten, have the class give two thumbs-up as they say, "Left and right." Instruct her to check her work by placing her hands on the cutouts. If she doesn't position the mitten successfully, have students show a thumbs-down and encourage her to reposition the mitten. On another day, after much practice, display and distribute a mixture of left-hand and right-hand mittens.

Pattie Williams
Boutte Christian Academy
Boutte, LA

Two of a Kind

Here's a seasonal shape-matching activity! Cut a large wreath shape from green poster board. Then cut out or die-cut pairs of identically shaped ornaments from recycled greeting cards. Glue one ornament from each pair on the wreath cutout. Place the remaining ornaments in a holiday cookie tin for storage. At circle time, have each child take a turn drawing an ornament from the tin. Then instruct him to find the same shaped ornament on the wreath and position his ornament on top of its match. This wreath has shaped up!

Julie Maffett
Plantation, FL

Happy New Year!

Celebrate the new year with this fun musical activity! In advance, lay out carpet squares in a circle, one per child. Next to each square, place a rhythm instrument. Then invite youngsters to don New Year's party hats (purchase them at postholiday sales). Have each child stand on a carpet square and chant, "Teacher, Teacher, what time is it?" Answer, "Two o'clock" or any time you wish. Have students take that many steps around the circle and then chant again. When you respond, "It's midnight!" each child picks up the instrument nearest her carpet square, plays it, and shouts, "Happy New Year!"

Laurie Jonas
Trinity Lutheran School
Wisconsin Dells, WI

Snowstorm!

A large supply of white packing peanuts is all you need for this seasonal literacy activity! Use a permanent marker to label a large supply of the peanuts with letters; then pour them all into a box. Invite youngsters to listen to a snow-related story, such as Ezra Jack Keats's *The Snowy Day.* Then open up the box and encourage each little one to pick up a handful of foam snow and toss it into the air! After the snowfall, ask each child to try to find the letter that begins her name. It's a guarantee that little ones will want to do this activity again and again!

Kathy Schlickenmaier
St. Augustine Preschool
Elkridge, MD

71

It's Circle Time

True or False
Understanding true and false

Introduce your preschoolers to the idea of *true* and *false* with some sentences in a seasonal container! Write a number of true statements, such as "I have two hands," and a number of silly false statements, such as "I wear socks on my head." Put the sentences in a seasonal container, such as a heart-shaped candy box during February. Explain to students that true sentences are often ones you could agree with or say yes to and false sentences are ones you might disagree with or say no to. Then have each child, in turn, draw a sentence from the container. Read the sentence aloud and have students tell you whether it is true or false. For each false statement, have students discuss the changes that could be made to make the statement true.

Sue Fleischmann
Waukesha County Project Head Start
Waukesha, WI

The sky is green.

Weather Math
Using tally marks

The forecast calls for including math in your daily weather report! Make a weather chart similar to the one shown, labeled with the appropriate month; then laminate it for durability. Post the chart in your group area. Each day, after a child reports the weather, have her use a marker to add a tally mark to the appropriate row. Review the chart every day for a month by counting the number of days with each type of weather and making comparisions. Post the monthly weather charts side by side and compare them each month.

Linda Haustein
George Washington Elementary #1
Elizabeth, NJ

Voice Patterns
Patterning

Put a twist on patterning practice by having students make patterns with their voices! Try whisper, whisper, loud, whisper, whisper, loud; high, low, high, low; or sad, happy, sad, happy. Help youngsters think of ways their voices can change to imitate the patterns.

Krista Vilbig
Kristagarden
Idaho Falls, ID

Whisper, whisper, loud!

72

The Name Game
Recognizing initial letter substitutions

Emphasize a letter sound and have some fun with this game using students' names! Substitute a letter sound students are familiar with at the beginning of a child's name. For letter *b,* if the student's name is Zachary, you would say, "Bachary." Have students guess whose name was changed and guess what letter made the new beginning sound. After students get the hang of the game, invite them to rename classmates using other familiar letters during play!

Christine Giordano
Y's Owl Nursery School
Warwick, RI

Wiggle That Tooth!
Singing, playing a game

Gather your group for some wiggly, giggly fun with a circle-time song! Have students stand in a circle and pass a white craft foam tooth cutout as you sing the song below. The child holding the tooth when you sing, "Oops!" must sit down in his place. Continue singing and having students pass the tooth until everyone is seated.

(sung to the tune of "The Farmer in the Dell")

My tooth is falling out!
My tooth is falling out!
I'll wiggle, wiggle, wiggle it
Until it comes right out.
Oops!

It's Circle Time

Plate Pals

Use the colorful sectioned animal plates available at your grocery store for a memory-building game! Purchase a package of the plates and sort them by animal so that you have at least one pair of each type. Show each type of animal to the children. (If desired, use only specific types of animals to fit a theme.) Then turn each plate over and place it on the carpet so that the printed side can't be seen. Have children play the game by turning over two plates at a time to try to find a match. Cheer when a match is found and continue on to the next player if one isn't found. Keep going until all the matches are made.

Ellen Conti
Our Lady of the Assumption Nursery School
Copiague, NY

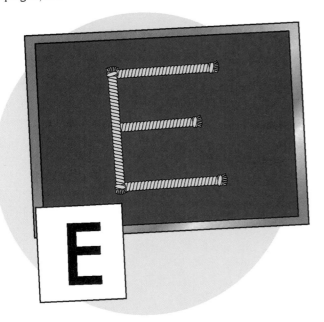

Use Some Yarn!

A few lengths of yarn, a flannelboard, and some flash cards are all you need for giving your students hands-on practice with forming shapes, letters, and numbers. In advance, cut a few different lengths of colorful yarn. At group time, show a flash card of a shape, letter, or number. Put the card away and have a child use one or more yarn lengths to try to form what you've shown.

Amber Baker
Precious Playmates Daycare
Martinsville, IN

"Fan-tastic"

Here's a super fun way to reinforce letter sounds! Bring in a portable fan and set it up to blow on low. While supervising, have one child at a time come up to the fan and make a letter sound that you specify. Students will love hearing the sounds!

Susan Chappell
Lake Jackson Library
Lake Jackson, TX

74

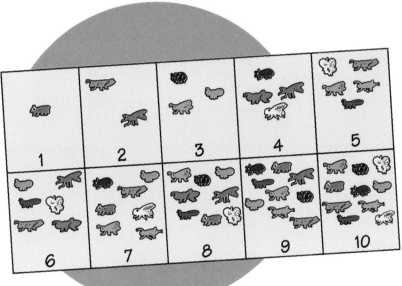

Sticker Counting Chart

Your preschoolers will love helping you create this class counting chart! Label a sheet of chart paper with the numbers 1 through 10 in a grid as shown. Then gather a large supply of stickers to match your current theme, such as farm animals or bugs. For each number, have student volunteers help count out the corresponding number of stickers and place them inside the box. When the chart is complete, use it during circle time to practice counting!

Shelley Hoster
Jack and Jill Early Learning Center
Norcross, GA

Spring Piñata

Here's a unique way to "hatch" a butterfly! Have your preschoolers help make a simple balloon piñata. Blow up a balloon and knot it. Cover it in newspaper strips dipped into a one-part flour and two-parts water mixture. When the balloon is completely covered, except for a small portion near the knot, allow it to dry. Then pop the balloon and remove it. Have youngsters help paint the balloon to resemble a butterfly's chrysalis. Set it aside to dry. Later, when students are not in the room, insert a small toy butterfly inside the piñata; then glue tissue paper over the hole. Hang the piñata and have children take turns smacking it with a stick to break it open. Won't they be surprised to see what's inside!

Corina Damron
Elkton Judy Headstart
Elkton, MD

It's Circle Time

Phone Number Bingo

"Ring, ring!" That's what you'll hear when you play this tasty version of bingo, which reinforces number recognition and learning personal information. To prepare, write each child's phone number on a separate sentence strip. Give each child her strip and a handful of M&M's candies or cereal pieces. Randomly call out numbers from zero to nine. When a child hears a number in her phone number, she covers that digit with a candy or cereal marker. Once she's covered her whole phone number, she calls out, "Ring, ring!" Keep going until everyone has her phone number covered.

Have youngsters keep their cards covered for the next round. Play again the same way, but have youngsters remove the candy or cereal pieces and eat them as they uncover the numbers. The first one to clear her number strip calls out, "Ring, ring!"

Tammy Wetzel, Canterbury Preschool, Mountain Brook, AL

Creative Stories

Put your preschoolers' imaginations to work as they tell stories to their classmates! Gather a collection of interesting pictures from magazines or greeting cards. Each day, post one of the pictures; then invite one child to come up and tell the class a story based on the picture. Jot down the story as it's told; then assemble all the stories into a booklet for everyone to enjoy!

Pam Porritt
St. Margaret Preschool
Otsego, MI

Alphabet Trash

Preschoolers are often fascinated with throwing away trash, so capitalize on this by turning it into a learning experience! Gather a collection of clean trash consisting of soup can labels, candy wrappers, or empty snack bags. Display the trash near a small plastic trash can in front of your group. Then ask a child to come up and identify the first letter on a label and tell a word that starts with that letter. Invite him to throw that trash away in the trash can. Keep going until everyone has participated and the area is clean!

Nancy Foss
Wee Care
Galion, OH

Musical Chairs by the Numbers

Here's a variation of Musical Chairs where everyone wins—and everyone gets practice with identifying numbers! Set up a circle with a class supply of chairs facing outward, just as you would for Musical Chairs. On each chair seat, place a card with a number on it. Play music and have your students walk around the circle. When you stop the music, have everyone sit down in the nearest seat. Ask each child, in turn, to identify the number on her chair. If a child has trouble, ask a volunteer to help her. Then start the music again for another round! Keep going until student interest fades.

Kathy Tingwald
Emmanuel United Methodist Church
Noblesville, IN

Jelly Letters

Looking for a tasty twist on letter formation? Prepare a class supply of toast. Then set up tables with a slice of toast on a paper plate for every child and an alphabet strip in plain view. Provide a few squeeze bottles of jelly and have little ones squeeze as they please to make the letters of their choice on their toast! Then invite them to eat up these alphabet creations.

Teresa Farrow
Surrey Child Care Center
Hag, MD

Pumpkin Face Patterns
Use with "Pumpkin Faces" on page 68.

KIDS IN THE KITCHEN

KIDS IN THE KITCHEN

Put on your apron and step into the kitchen—with your kids, of course! What's on the menu? A generous portion of learning opportunities served up with a batch of fun. Savor the following hands-on activities, perfectly measured for pre-school success and teacher ease. Learning has never been so delicious!

Here's what to do:
- Collect the necessary ingredients and utensils using the lists on one of the recipe cards below.
- Follow the teacher preparation guidelines for that activity.
- Photocopy the step-by-step recipe cards on page 81 or 82.
- Color the cards; then cut them out.
- Display the cards on a bulletin board or chart in your snack area so that students can see the title card and directions for the recipe you've selected.
- Discuss the directions with a small group of children.
- Have the children wash their hands; then let the fun begin!

Firefighter's Ladder

Ingredients for one:
graham cracker (four sections)
frosting
9 pretzel sticks

Utensils and supplies:
paper plate for each child
plastic knife for each child

Teacher preparation:
Arrange the ingredients, utensils, and supplies near the step-by-step recipe cards (page 81).

Jana Sanderson—PreK
Rainbow School
Stockton, CA

Cheesy Spiderweb

Ingredients for one:
string cheese stick
½ green grape
8 pretzel stick halves

Utensils and supplies:
black paper plate for each child

Teacher preparation:
- Cut grapes in half.
- Break pretzel sticks into halves.
- Arrange the ingredients, utensils, and supplies near the step-by-step recipe cards (page 82).

Ada Goren
Winston Salem, NC

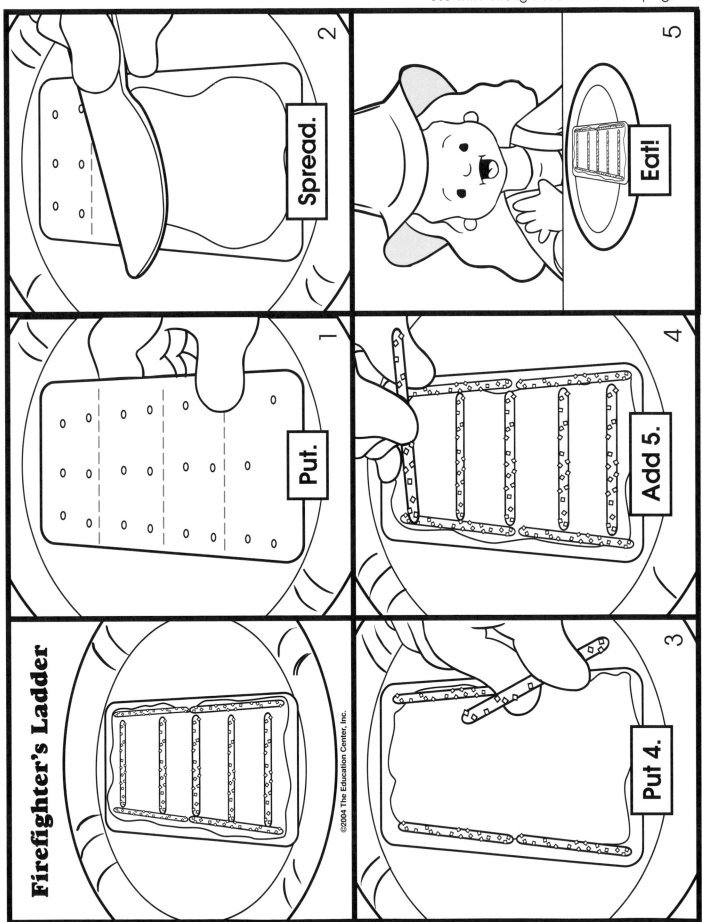

Firefighter's Ladder

Put.

Spread.

Put 4.

Add 5.

Eat!

1

2

3

4

5

Recipe Cards
Use with "Cheesy Spiderweb" on page 80.

Cheesy Spiderweb

Put. — 2

Pull. — 1

Eat! — 5

Add 8. — 4

Add 1. — 3

KIDS IN THE KITCHEN

Put on your apron and step into the kitchen—with your kids, of course! What's on the menu? A generous portion of learning opportunities served up with a batch of fun. Savor the following hands-on activities, perfectly measured for preschool success and teacher ease. Learning has never been so delicious!

Here's what to do:

- Collect the necessary ingredients and utensils using the lists on one of the recipe cards below.
- Follow the teacher preparation guidelines for that activity.
- Photocopy the step-by-step recipe cards on page 84 or 85.
- Color the cards; then cut them out.
- Display the cards on a bulletin board or chart in your snack area so that students can see the title card and directions for the recipe you've selected.
- Discuss the directions with a small group of children.
- Have the children wash their hands; then let the fun begin!

Santa Mix

Ingredients for one:
M&M's Minis candies (elf noses)
small pretzels (reindeer antlers)
Kix cereal (Santa's buttons)
o-shaped cereal (reindeer food)

Utensils and supplies:
bowl for each ingredient
tablespoon for each ingredient
paper cup for each child

Teacher preparation:
- Pour each ingredient into a separate bowl and add a spoon.
- Arrange the ingredients, utensils, and supplies near the step-by-step recipe cards (see page 84).

Anne Arceneaux
Ward School
Jennings, LA

Bagel Snowman

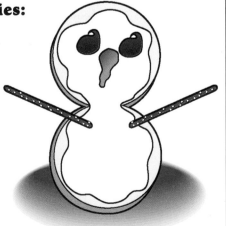

Ingredients for one:
mini bagel
cream cheese
Cheez Doodles snack
2 pretzel sticks
2 mini chocolate chips

Utensils and supplies:
plastic knife for each child
paper plate for each child

Teacher preparation:
- Slice bagels.
- Arrange the ingredients, utensils, and supplies near the step-by-step recipe cards (see page 85).

Lola Anderson
Canby Head Start
Canby, MN

Recipe Cards

Use with "Santa Mix" on page 83.

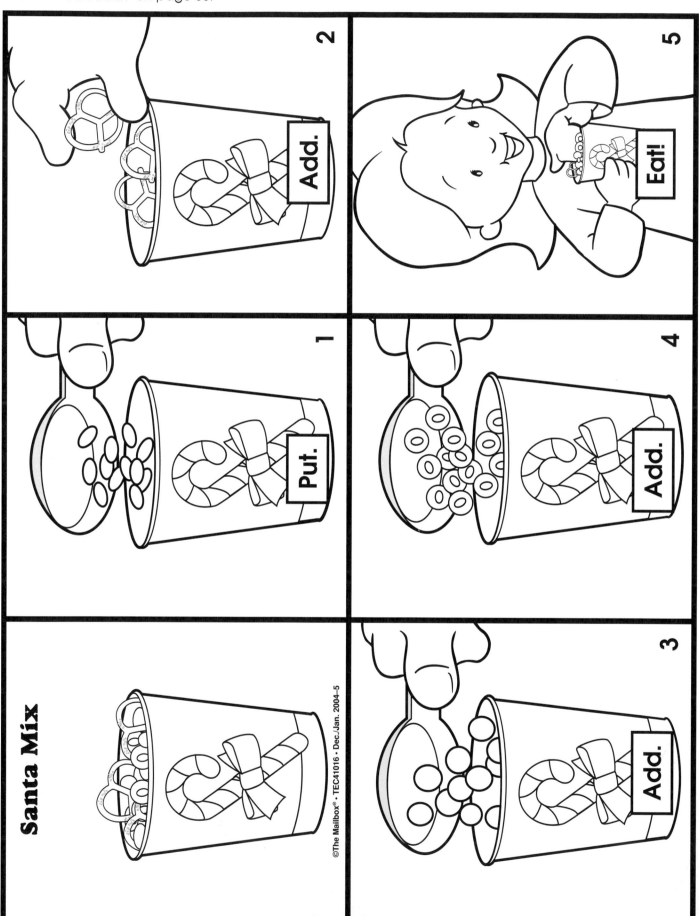

Santa Mix

Put.

Add.

Add.

Add.

Eat!

©The Mailbox® • TEC41016 • Dec./Jan. 2004–5

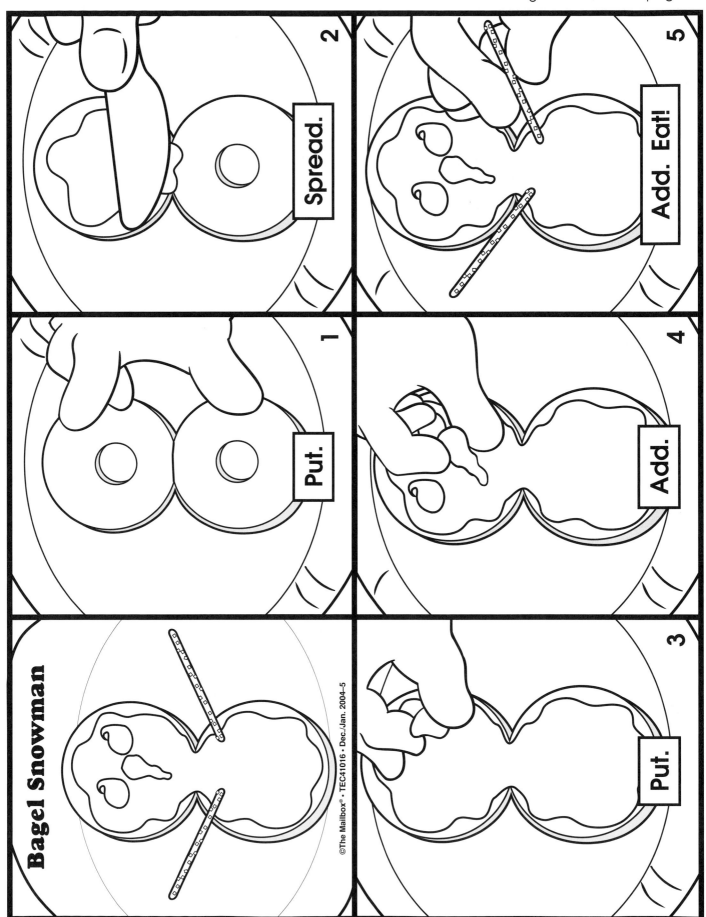

Bagel Snowman

1 Put.

2 Spread.

3 Put.

4 Add.

5 Add. Eat!

©The Mailbox® • TEC41016 • Dec./Jan. 2004–5

KIDS IN THE KITCHEN

Put on your apron and step into the kitchen—with your kids, of course! What's on the menu? A generous portion of learning opportunities served up with a batch of fun. Savor the following hands-on activities, perfectly measured for preschool success and teacher ease. Learning has never been so delicious!

Here's what to do:
- Collect the necessary ingredients and utensils using the lists on one of the recipe cards below.
- Follow the teacher preparation guidelines for that activity.
- Photocopy the step-by-step recipe cards on page 87 or 88.
- Color the cards; then cut them out.
- Display the cards on a bulletin board or chart in your snack area so that students can see the title card and directions for the recipe you've selected.
- Discuss the directions with a small group of children.
- Have the children wash their hands; then let the fun begin!

Groundhog Grub

Ingredients for one:
banana half
3 mini chocolate chips (eyes and nose)
2 almond slices (ears)

Utensils and supplies:
3 oz. Dixie cup for each child
(garden scene on the side)

Teacher preparation:
- Cut bananas in half.
- Pour each ingredient into a separate bowl and add a spoon.
- Arrange the ingredients, utensils, and supplies near the step-by-step recipe cards (see page 87).

Itty-Bitty Bunny

Ingredients for one:
pear half
3 M&M's Minis candies (2 eyes and a nose)
2 almond slices (ears)
small marshmallow (tail)

Utensils and supplies:
paper plate for each child

Teacher preparation:
- Drain pear halves.
- Arrange the ingredients, utensils, and supplies near the step-by-step recipe cards (see page 88).

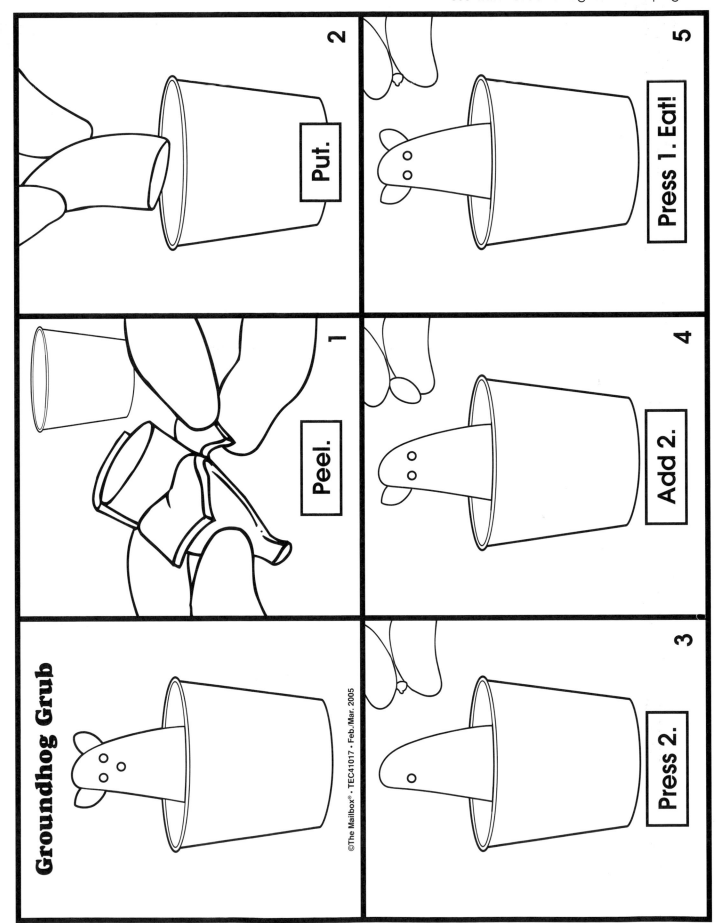

2 Put.

5 Press 1. Eat!

1 Peel.

4 Add 2.

Groundhog Grub

3 Press 2.

©The Mailbox® • TEC41017 • Feb./Mar. 2005

Recipe Cards

Use with "Itty-Bitty Bunny" on page 86.

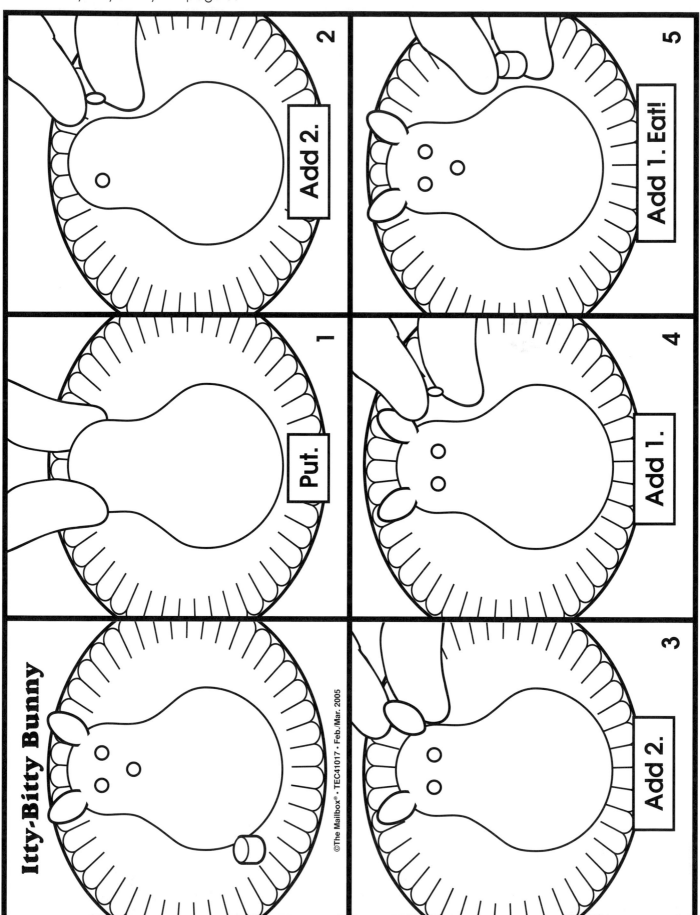

2 — Add 2.

1 — Put.

Itty-Bitty Bunny

5 — Add 1. Eat!

4 — Add 1.

3 — Add 2.

KIDS IN THE KITCHEN

Put on your apron and step into the kitchen—with your kids, of course! What's on the menu? A generous portion of learning opportunities served up with a batch of fun. Savor the following hands-on activities, perfectly measured for preschool success and teacher ease. Learning has never been so delicious!

Here's what to do:
- Collect the necessary ingredients and utensils using the lists on one of the recipe cards below.
- Follow the teacher preparation guidelines for that activity.
- Photocopy the step-by-step recipe cards on page 90 or 91.
- Color the cards; then cut them out.
- Display the cards on a bulletin board or chart in your snack area so that students can see the title card and directions for the recipe you've selected.
- Discuss the directions with a small group of children.
- Have the children wash their hands; then let the fun begin!

Beautiful Butterfly

Ingredients for one:
hot dog eighth (body)
hot dog bun half (wings)
2 chow mein noodles (antennae)
colorful ketchup (red, green, or purple)

Utensils and supplies:
paper plate for each child

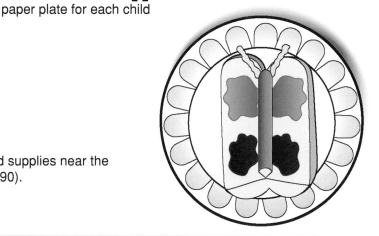

Teacher preparation:
- Cook the hot dogs.
- Cut the hot dogs in eighths.
- Cut the hot dog buns in half.
- Arrange the ingredients, utensils, and supplies near the step-by-step recipe cards (see page 90).

Dana Smith, Donaldsonville Primary School
Donaldsonville, LA

Roaring Lion

Ingredients for one:
mini bagel half (head)
flavored cream cheese
chow mein noodles (mane)
2 M&M's Minis candies (eyes)

Utensils and supplies:
paper plate for each child
plastic knife for each child

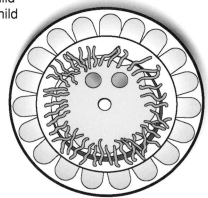

Teacher preparation:
- Cut the bagels in half.
- Toast the bagels if desired.
- Arrange the ingredients, utensils, and supplies near the step-by-step recipe cards (see page 91).

Amy Rudolph
Lafayette Head Start
Lafayette, IN

Recipe Cards
Use with "Beautiful Butterfly" on page 89.

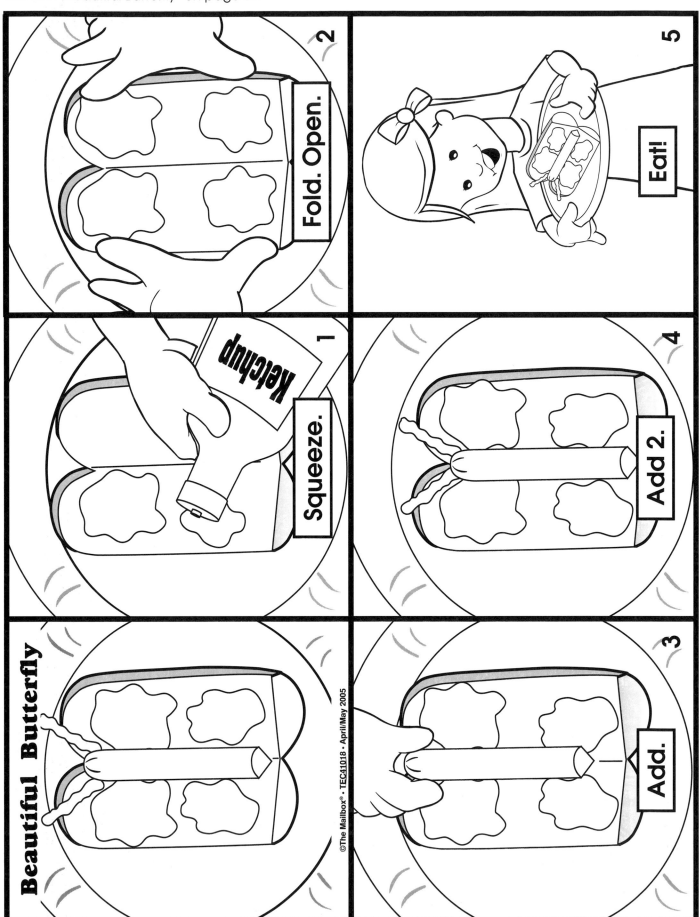

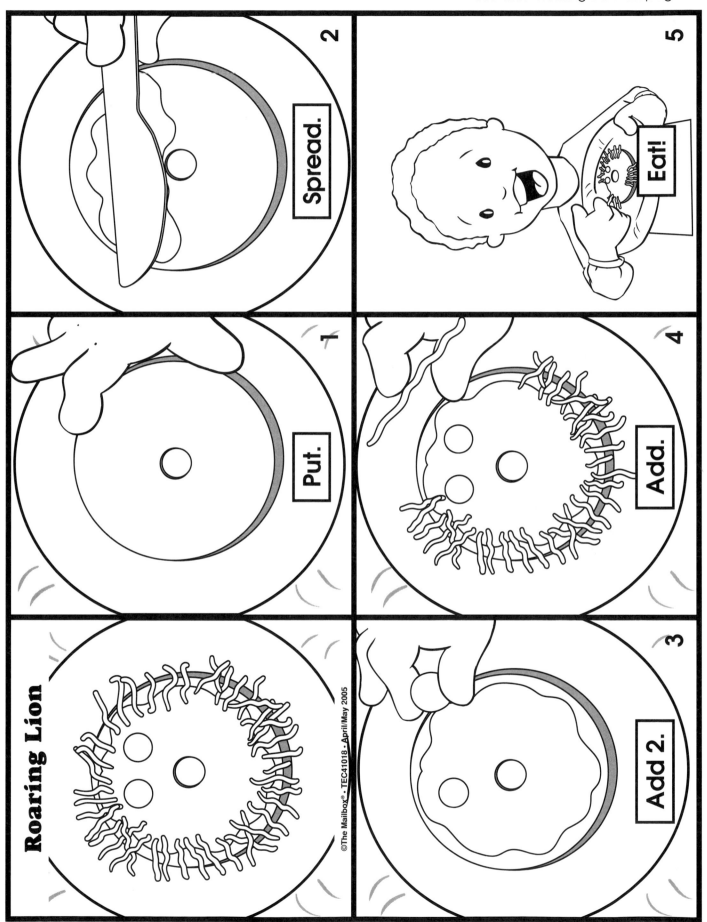

2 Spread.

5 Eat!

1 Put.

4 Add.

Roaring Lion

3 Add 2.

KIDS IN THE KITCHEN

Put on your apron and step into the kitchen—with your kids, of course! What's on the menu? A generous portion of learning opportunities served up with a batch of fun. Savor the following hands-on activities, perfectly measured for pre-school success and teacher ease. Learning has never been so delicious!

Here's what to do:

- Collect the necessary ingredients and utensils using the lists on one of the recipe cards below.
- Follow the teacher preparation guidelines for that activity.
- Photocopy the step-by-step recipe cards on page 93 or 94.
- Color the cards; then cut them out.
- Display the cards on a bulletin board or chart in your snack area so that students can see the title card and directions for the recipe you've selected.
- Discuss the directions with a small group of children.
- Have the children wash their hands; then let the fun begin!

Strawberry Parfait

Ingredients for one:
angel food cake
strawberries
whipped topping

Utensils and supplies:
clear plastic cup for each child
plastic spoon for each child

Teacher preparation:
- Slice cake.
- Wash and cut strawberries. Stir in a small amount of sugar if desired.
- Arrange the ingredients, utensils, and supplies near the step-by-step recipe cards (see page 93).

Roxanne LaBell Dearman
Western NC Early Intervention Program for Children Who Are Deaf or
    Hard of Hearing
Charlotte, NC

A Simple S'more

Ingredients for one:
2 graham cracker squares
chocolate frosting
marshmallow cream

Utensils and supplies:
paper plate for each child
plastic knife for each child

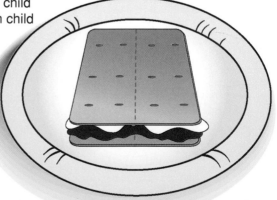

Teacher preparation:
- Arrange the ingredients, utensils, and supplies near the step-by-step recipe cards (see page 94).

Denielle Albertowicz
Quality Time Child Care
Chicopee, MA

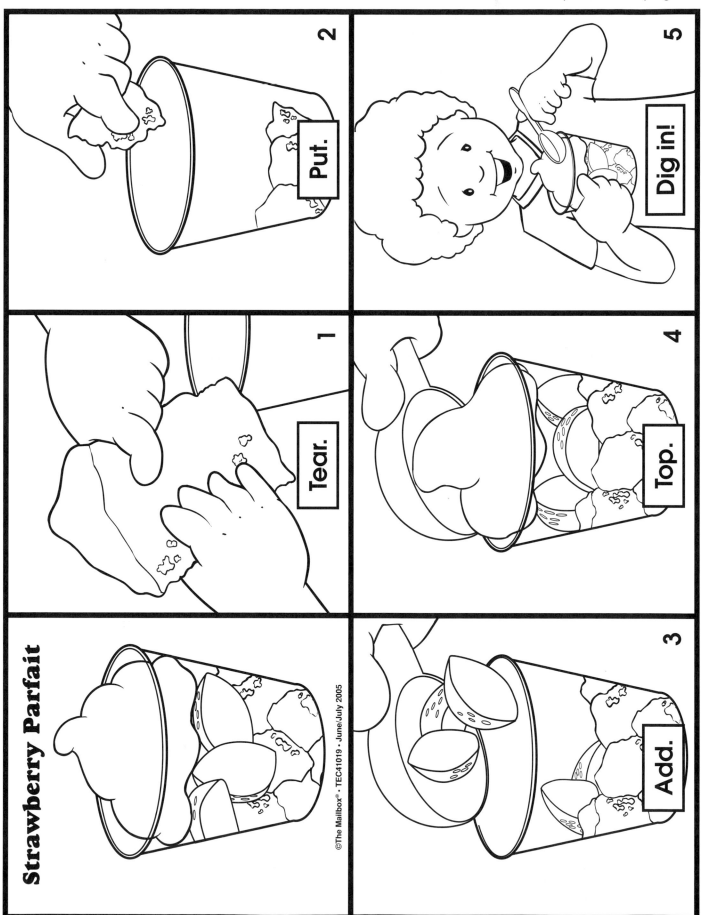

Strawberry Parfait

2 — Put.

1 — Tear.

5 — Dig in!

4 — Top.

3 — Add.

©The Mailbox® • TEC41019 • June/July 2005

Recipe Cards

Use with "A Simple S'more" on page 92.

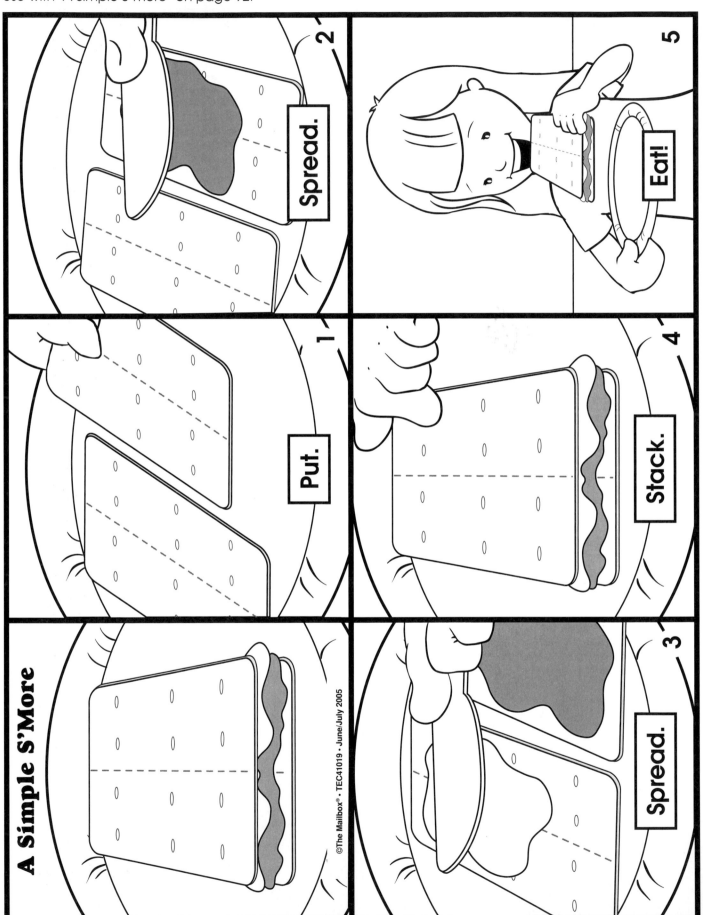

LEARNING CENTERS

Learning Centers

A Placemat Palette
Dramatic Play

Build youngsters' color-matching skills with the help of the plastic dishes in your housekeeping area! For each color of dishes, make a placemat by tracing around the plate, cup, and utensils on coordinating construction paper as shown. Cut out the paper dishes and glue them to a sheet of white construction paper; then laminate the finished placemats. Put these on the table in your dramatic-play area and ask children to set the table by matching the dishes to the placemats.

Cathy Consford—Director
Buda Primary Early Learning Center
Buda, TX
and
Angie Kutzer
Audrey Garrett Elementary School
Mebane, NC

Bountiful Bales
Block Center

Enhance a farm theme in your block area by feeding the toy animals bales of hay and straw! Simply cut green and yellow kitchen sponges into small rectangles. Invite youngsters to haul the hay in wagons, stack it into haystacks, count the number of bales, or practice one-to-one correspondence as they feed one bale to each toy cow or horse.

Karen Tubbs—Preschool
Malad Headstart
Malad, ID

What a Feeling!
Sensory Center

Stimulate your preschoolers' senses with this bubbly idea! Securely tape bubble wrap (in different sizes if desired) inside your sensory table. Pour on some washable liquid paint or sweet-smelling lotion. Watch little hands explore this slippery, bumpy sensation! Add a little water to the table if the bubble wrap begins to dry out. Keep paper towels or a few old bath towels on hand for a quick cleanup before youngsters head to the sink.

Candy Rickner—PreK
Head Start
Vinita, OK

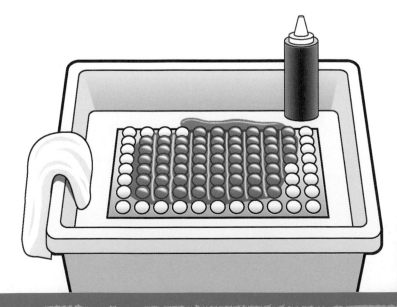

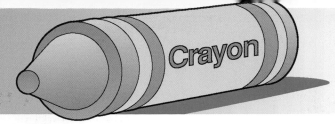

Searching for Lids
Sand Table

Introduce your young students to the magic of magnets with this sand table activity. Bury a supply of metal juice can lids in your sand table. Then equip youngsters with magnetic wands and challenge them to find the hidden lids without digging!

Rhonda Urfey—Junior Kindergarten
Allen A. Greenleaf School
Waterdown, Ontario, Canada

Pot Scrubber Toss
Gross-Motor Area

Here's a colorful game that's easy and inexpensive to make! Visit your local discount store and buy a pack of colorful plastic pot scrubbers and a plastic dishpan. Put the dishpan on the floor; then mark the floor a short distance away with a piece of tape. Invite preschoolers at this center to stand behind the tape and toss the pot scrubbers one by one toward the dishpan, trying to land one inside!

Denise Wrege—Preschool
Building Bridges Child Care
Muskogee, OK

Cupcakes and Candles
Play Dough Center

Celebrate a birthday any day with this fun play dough activity! Stock your play dough table with muffin pans in different sizes, cupcake liners, play dough, and birthday candles. Encourage your young bakers to make play dough cupcakes, adding candles to each one for festive flair! Don't miss out on opportunities for counting and comparing at this center as you discuss with children the sizes of the cupcakes made in each pan, the number of cups in each pan, or the number of candles in each cupcake.

Shelley Hoster—PreK
Jack and Jill Early Learning Center
Norcross, GA

Learning Centers

Scarecrow Bingo
Game Center

Use an adorable scarecrow to help your little ones practice colors or shapes! Make a scarecrow card similar to the one shown and copy it to make a supply of bingo cards. Program each scarecrow with patches in various colors and/or shapes as shown. Then create a simple spinner showing either corresponding colors or shapes, whichever you wish youngsters to practice.

Each child in a small group takes a scarecrow card. She takes a turn spinning and then uses a construction paper square to cover a patch that matches the color or shape of her spin. The first one to cover all her scarecrow's patches is the winner!

Nancy Morgan
Care-a-Lot Daycare In-Home Daycare and Preschool
Bremerton, WA

Scarecrow Bingo

Pizza Bakers
Dramatic Play

Transform your dramatic-play into a pizza kitchen with some fun props! Cut several pizza crusts from tan craft foam, large circles of sauce and small pepperoni circles from red craft foam, and shredded cheese from yellow and white tissue paper. Assemble one or two pizzas and glue the parts together. Then cut your pretend pizzas into slices. Set out the assembled pizzas and some unassembled pizza ingredients so your pizza bakers can make, bake, and serve pizzas for their customers!

Cheryl Cicioni—Preschool
St. Anne Preschool at St. John Neumann
Lancaster, PA

Ghost Hunt
Math Center

Hide some ghosts in your sensory table for a frighteningly fun find! First, partially fill your sensory table with white foam packing peanuts. Take out a handful and use a marker to add eyes and a mouth to each one to make ghosts. Then stir the ghosts back into the peanuts in the table. Next, cut out several ghost shapes from white paper and label each one with a number no larger than the number of foam peanut ghosts.

Have a child at this center choose a ghost card, identify the number on it, and then try to find a matching number of ghosts hidden in your sensory table. What "boo-tiful" math!

Jo Montgomery—PreK
John C. French School
Cuero, TX

Letter Webs
Literacy Center

Preschoolers are bound to get caught up in this fun letter-matching activity! Make a few copies of a web gameboard like the one shown. Program each copy with various letters you've introduced to your students. Then make a set of matching letter cards. Place the web gameboards, the letter cards, and a supply of plastic spiders in your literacy center.

Youngsters can play this game alone or in pairs or small groups. Place the letter cards in a stack facedown. Each child takes a gameboard. He draws a letter card from the stack. If he sees that letter on his web, he covers it with a spider. Play continues until all the letters on a child's gameboard are covered.

Beverly Holak—Preschool
Riverside Elementary
Riverside, NJ

Poppin' Indian Corn
Fine-Motor Center

Add a seasonal twist to a sensory tub that will get those little fingers working! Purchase or ask parents to donate cobs of Indian corn in different sizes. Gently twist each cob to loosen the kernels. Then put the cobs in a sensory tub. Have little ones pick and pop the kernels off the cobs and into the tubs. Ask youngsters to check the floor and return any stray kernels to the tub before leaving this center!

Cathy Patterson—Preschool
Westerville Learning Center
Columbus, OH

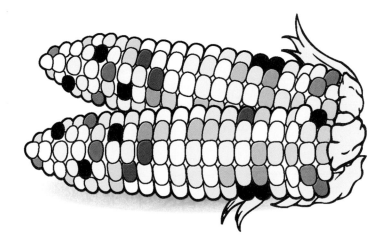

Fine-Feathered Turkeys
Play Dough Center

Invite your preschoolers to make gorgeous gobblers at your play dough table! Give each child some play dough (or clay), and have her shape it into a round turkey body with a head. Then provide her with a variety of craft feathers, and have her stick them into the dough to make tail feathers for her bird. What colorful Thanksgiving turkeys!

Monica Saunders—Preschool
Hazelwild Educational Foundation
Fredericksburg, VA

Learning Centers

Cool Blocks
Block Center

Brrr! There's a blizzard in your blocks center with this idea! Wrap small, medium, or large cardboard brick blocks or soft blocks in white bulletin board paper. Then encourage youngsters to build snow forts or icebergs for some frosty fun. Encourage snowman building by adding craft foam snowman features backed with Sticky-Tac to the center. Then have pre-schoolers create snow families among the snow forts. Cool!

Laura Anderson, Partin Elementary
Oviedo, FL

Peppermint Play Dough
Play Dough Center

Add a seasonal scent to your play dough area when you mix up a batch of this dough. Add candy molds, cookie cutters, rolling pins, and four-inch pieces of waxed paper to the center so little ones can wrap up their peppermint creations. To turn your play dough center into a candy cane factory, make two batches of dough—one with and one without food coloring. Show children how to make candy canes by twisting strands of red and white dough together. Now that will create some "excite-mint"!

2 c. flour	2 tbsp. vegetable oil
1 c. salt	4 tsp. cream of tartar
2 c. water	red food coloring
2 tsp. peppermint extract	

Combine all the ingredients in a large pot. Cook over low heat, stirring until dough forms and pulls away from the sides of the pot. Remove the dough from the heat and allow it to cool before using.

Becki Yahm, First Lutheran Children's Programs
Portland, ME

Feed the Penguin
Game Center

Fishing for a fun way to teach color recognition? Try having your pre-schoolers feed colorful fish to a penguin! Use black and white construction paper to make a penguin on one side of a cardboard box. Make a slit in the box where the penguin's mouth should be; then glue an orange beak above and below the slit. Next, cut out a number of fish from various colors of construction paper. Have pairs of children take turns feeding the fish to the penguin, identifying the color of each one before slipping the fish into its mouth. On another day, label a supply of fish cutouts with shapes, letters, or numbers and encourage youngsters to name them before feeding the penguin. Mmm!

Susan Foulks, University City UMC Weekday School
Charlotte, NC

Counting Snack Mix
Math Center

Math is mighty tasty at this counting center! On a table, place four bowls, each with a different trail mix food, such as fish-shaped crackers, various cereals, or oyster crackers. Add a spoon to each bowl and then place a large die in front of each snack. Also, give each child a cup.

Have each child roll the die in front of the first bowl, count the dots on top of the die, and put the corresponding number of food pieces from the bowl in her cup. Have her repeat this process with the other bowls until she has added each type of food to her cup. Then, for all her work, invite her to munch on her snack mix. One, two, three, yum!

Tami Johnson
Epworth Cooperative Preschool
Midland, MI

Mitten Match
Fine-Motor Center

Here's a visual-discrimination activity with an added pinch of fine-motor skills! To prepare this center, use the mitten patterns on page 106 to trace several pairs of mittens onto wallpaper samples. Glue the mittens to tagboard, laminate them for durability, and then cut them out. Next, string a clothesline within children's reach. Clip one mitten from each pair on the line, spacing them out. Put the remaining mittens and a supply of clothespins in a basket nearby. Have each youngster who visits the center find the mate for each hanging mitten and clip it next to its mate on the line. It's a match!

Katherine Zorn
Parkminster Preschool
Rochester, NY

White as Snow
Sensory Center

Invite your little ones to explore the color white as they dig into some pretend snow. Fill your sensory table with white packing peanuts (snow). Bury several white items in the snow, such as a white crayon, a golf ball, cotton balls, a white sock, a coffee filter, a white plastic egg, or a toy snowman. Provide each child who visits the center with a pair of mittens or gloves to wear and a basket for collecting the white items he finds. If desired, provide each child with a recording sheet depicting the items you've hidden. Have him use a pencil to mark each item he finds. After he finds all the items, have him bury them for another child to find. It's "snow" much fun!

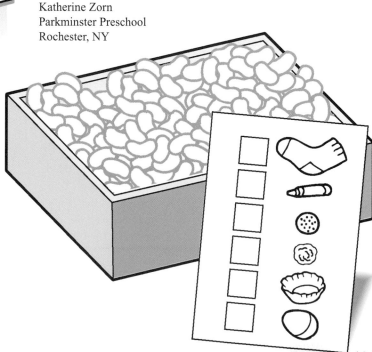

Deb Jacox, Busy Bees Preschool
Lincoln, NE

Learning Centers

Letters in My Name
Literacy Center

Focus on letter sorting with this delicious activity! To prepare, create a simple T chart like the one shown. Label the chart and then make a class supply. Place the charts at your literacy center, along with a plastic bag of Alpha-Bits cereal for each child and sentence strips with children's names. Have a child find his name strip and then refer to it as he sorts the cereal letters onto the chart. After all of his cereal pieces have been sorted, invite him to eat all the letters for a yummy snack!

Catherine Brubaker
Girard Head Start
Coldwater, MI

A Sticky Situation
Sensory Center

Step right up and try this sensory experience for your youngsters' feet! Tape a three- to four-foot piece of Con-Tact paper to the floor sticky side up. Invite your preschoolers to take off their shoes and socks and walk across the sticky paper. If desired, invite them to jump, crawl, or tiptoe across the paper too. Stupendously sticky!

Erica Avila
Wee Care Learning Center
Festus, MO

Spring Patterns
Math Center

Eggs and bunnies will soon be hiding in the grass when you set up this patterning center! To prepare, fold a supply of 9" x 4" green paper strips in half lengthwise. Unfold the strips and fringe-cut along one long edge up to the crease. Place in the center the prepared strips and a supply of egg and bunny stickers. Have each child who visits the center place egg and bunny stickers along a strip on the uncut side to create a simple AB pattern. (Prepare sample patterns for youngsters to use as a guide.) Have the student refold her strip. Now you see them; now you don't!

adapted from an idea by Cindy Carswell
Central Methodist Preschool
Fitzgerald, GA

Space Place
Dramatic Play

Simulate looking at a nighttime sky with this easy idea. Purchase two black plastic tablecloths at your local party supply store. Before opening the packages, use a pushpin to poke holes all over the folded tablecloths. Then open them up and spread the cloths over a table, making sure the cloths touch or nearly touch the floor on all sides but don't overlap. Invite two youngsters to crawl under the table and look at the legion of stars the pinholes create where light shines through. Add a few toy telescopes and toy space shuttles to complete this super space place!

Krista Mayer
Holy Trinity Children's Center
Lenexa, KS

Taking Care of Teeth
Science Center

Make some oversize teeth to help your youngsters practice brushing and flossing! Cut off the bottom sections of four 16-ounce soda bottles (teeth). Spray-paint the insides of the bottle bottoms with white spray paint. After the paint has dried, turn the teeth over and hot-glue them to a strip of pink craft foam (gums). Then provide youngsters with toothpaste, toothbrushes, and water as well as lengths of yarn for flossing. Now take care of those teeth!

Erica Glass-Terhune
Salem Lutheran Preschool

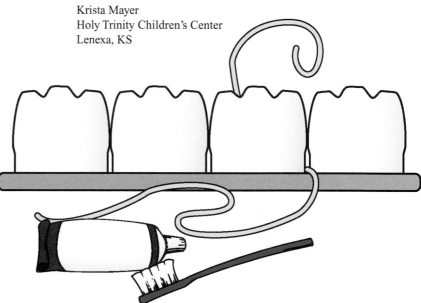

Telephone! It's for You!
Dramatic Play

A collection of old telephones will delight your preschoolers and encourage lots of learning! Assemble a selection of old phones, such as a rotary phone, a push-button phone, a cell phone, and a cordless phone. Make a class phone book by placing a picture of each child in an album with her name and phone number below it. Encourage each youngster to refer to the phone book and pretend to call a friend.

For more fun, add a few notepads and pencils to the center for taking messages.

Rose Cox
Riverdale Hansel Headstart
Goshen, IN

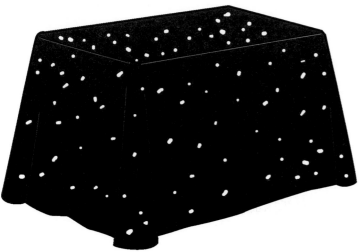

Carley
123-4567

Learning Centers

Watermelon Seeds
Games Center

Here's a game that will give your youngsters practice with counting and comparing quantities. Make four watermelon slices from red and green construction paper. Also cut out a supply of black construction paper seeds. Invite a group of four students to the center and have each student take a watermelon slice. Ask one child to roll a die, count the dots, and place the corresponding number of seeds onto her slice. Have each of the other players, in turn, do the same. At the end of the round, ask youngsters to compare their slices. Who has the most seeds? The least? Do any players have an equal number of seeds? For more practice, have the students repeat the game.

Jessica Lloyd
Children's World Learning Center
Grayslake, IL

Fossil Fun
Science Center

Add to a dinosaur exploration with some fossil-forming fun! Put some damp sand (fine beach sand works best) in a disposable bowl. Invite a child to press a shell or a plastic dinosaur into the sand to make an impression. Remove the shell or the toy and pour plaster of paris into the impression. Allow the plaster to dry for a couple of days. Then have the child remove the hardened plaster and use a clean paintbrush to carefully brush away the sand. Ta-da! A fossil!

Lisa Boquist
Catherine Creek Preschool
Union, OR

Patriotic Patterning
Math Center

Red, white, and blue—that's the perfect pattern at this fun center! Provide each child with a 1½" x 22" strip of white bulletin board paper and a large supply of red, white, and blue 1½" construction paper squares. Have each child glue the squares onto his strip in an ABC pattern. When he's finished, size the strip to fit his head and staple the ends. Have each youngster wear his headband while singing a favorite patriotic tune!

adapted from an idea by Susan Luengen
Makalapa Elementary
Honolulu, HI

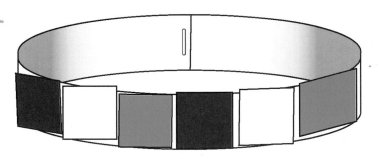

Rubber Stamp Rebus Stories
Writing Center

Inspire your young writers to create new stories with the help of some rubber stamps! Gather a collection of interesting stamps to put in your writing center. Have a child choose a few stamps around which he can build a story. Then have an adult helper write as a child dictates a story, letting the child fill in some of the key words by stamping the images on the paper. Invite the authors to share their stories with the class at group time!

Jennifer Schear
Clover Patch Preschool
Cedar Falls, IA

I went to my friend's 🏠. She gave me a ⊙ and a 🎂. We went to play.

Laundry on the Line
Dramatic Play Center

Introduce the idea of evaporation with a laundry center in your dramatic-play area. Set up a clothesline and a plastic tub of sudsy water. Invite youngsters to wash and rinse doll clothes and clip them on the line. Ask them to predict what the clothes will feel like when they return to school the next day. Follow up by having them feel the dry clothes. Ask them what happened and where they think the water went. Then invite them to do the washing and drying all over again!

Lorrie Motylinski
Rutherford Child Care Center
Rutherford, NJ

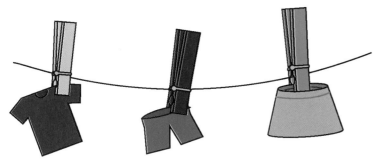

It Begins With a...
Literacy Center

Review letter sounds at the end of the year with this interactive bulletin board. To begin, post several die-cut letters in no particular order on a bulletin board or wall space within youngsters' reach. Add three or four pieces of self-adhesive Velcro fastener near each letter. Then cut out three or four magazine pictures or pictures of clip art for each letter. Add the other half of the Velcro fastener to each picture. Then put all the pictures in a bag near the board.

A child at this center pulls a picture from the bag, decides which letter it begins with, and attaches it near that letter. *S* is for sun!

Leigh Ann Peter
Buttonwood Preschool
Lumberton, NJ

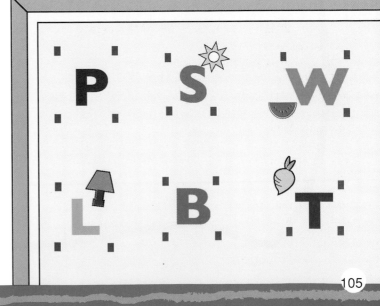

Mitten Patterns
Use with "Left Mitten, Right Mitten" on page 70 and "Mitten Match" on page 101.

OUR READERS WRITE

Our Readers Write

Bag o' Pumpkin

Here's a "sense-ational" way for your little ones to observe color mixing! For each child, put a spoonful of yellow and a spoonful of red tempera paint into a zippered plastic bag. Have her squish the bag and watch as the colors mix to create orange. Finish the fun by using a black marker to draw a jack-o'-lantern on each child's bag.

Melissa Weimer—Preschool Hearing Impaired
Stepanski ECC
Waterford, MI

There's a Spider on You!

Practice body part recognition with Raffi's fun version of "There's a Spider on the Floor." Give each child a plastic spider to touch to the parts of his body as the song indicates. Then extend the fun by taking a full-length photo of each child. Tape a plastic spider to one end of a length of yarn. Tape the free end of the yarn to the back of the photo. Then have each youngster touch the spider to the body parts in the photo as you play the song again!

Betsy Fuhrmann—PreK, Dodds School, Springfield, IL

Preschool Is a Scream!

Give your preschoolers a chance to put on their scariest faces for this Halloween display! Take a photo of each child making a scary face. Trim each photo to fit behind an orange jack-o'-lantern die-cut. Then staple a die-cut over the photo at the top to create a lift-up flap. Mount all the scary jack-o'-lanterns on a bulletin board with paper vines and leaves and the title "Preschool Is a Scream!" Invite guests to lift the flaps to view your Halloween cuties!

Cary Howes and Shelley Slack—PreK
New Athens Elementary
New Athens, IL

My Own Special Leaf

This fall, have each child adopt a leaf on a tree near your classroom. For each child, cut a 20-inch length of string. Label a piece of masking tape with the child's name and stick the tape to the center of the string. Have the child choose one special leaf on the tree. Tie one end of the string to the leaf's stem and the other end to the nearest branch. Check daily and watch for the excitement when a child finds that "his" leaf has fallen!

Iola Coulter—Director/Teacher
Barnyard Pals Preschool
Portage, OH

Our Readers Write

Magic Reindeer Chow

Help little ones mix up a batch of Magic Reindeer Chow to leave for Santa's reindeer! Mix together a canister of oatmeal and a small container of brightly colored sugar crystals. Have each child take a turn stirring the mixture; then help him scoop some into a snack-size plastic bag. Attach a note to the bag telling moms and dads to sprinkle the chow on their lawns on Christmas Eve!

Kendi Morris, Beale Elementary School, Gallipolis Ferry, WV

Magic Reindeer Chow

Soapy Science

Watch your youngsters' delight when they make their very own soap to take home! To make soap, pour three cups of Ivory Snow detergent (or three cups of grated Ivory bar soap) into a large bowl. (One batch will make six soaps.) Add one to 1½ cups of warm water and a few drops of food coloring. Mix with your hands until the concoction reaches the consistency of play dough. Then rub a bit of vegetable oil onto a child's hands. Give her a bit of the soap mixture and invite her to shape it as she wishes. Push the end of a knotted length of string into the soap shape; then allow it to dry overnight on waxed paper. Happy hand washing!

Chalene McGrath, Discovery Elementary School, Brigham City, UT

Gift Bag Tag

If you're planning on sending home one or more child-made ornaments this season, attach this poem to a gift bag and stow the ornaments inside.

Angie Burns, Quinlan ISD, Quinlan, TX

Here is a gift from me to you,
Made with glitter and made with glue.
Open it up and you will see
Something special for our tree!

Here is a gift from me to you,
Made with glitter and made with glue.
Open it up and you will see
Something special for our tree!

Holiday Magnet Bottle

Add a holiday twist to your discovery area when you make a jingle-bell bottle! Fill a clean, empty plastic soda bottle two-thirds full of salt. Drop in a few jingle bells, add hot glue to the lid, screw the lid on tightly, and then shake. Place the bottle in your discovery area, along with a magnetic wand. Then get your students looking and listening for those bells!

Rachel Garman
Tri-County Cooperative Preschool
Wooster, OH

Border Patterns

Use seasonal or thematic bulletin board borders for patterning practice! Simply cut apart the images on a length of border. Then get your preschoolers patterning! Snowflake, snowpal, snowflake, snowpal,…

Pat Davidson, Padonia International, Cockeysville, MD

Pool Painting

These oversize paintings make neat sheets of gift wrap! Place a large sheet of newsprint or a large piece of bulletin board paper in a child's small plastic swimming pool or a large plastic storage container. Dip two or three golf balls into different colors of paint and then drop the balls into the pool. Have three or four children pick up the pool and tilt it back and forth to make the golf balls roll over the paper. Cool!

Cindy Daraskavich, Auburn Co-Op Preschool, Auburn, WA

Friendship Salad

Celebrate Martin Luther King Jr. Day by making a friendship salad! Ask each youngster to bring in fruit (precut or whole) to add to a fruit salad. Help your class prepare the salad, stressing hand washing and kitchen safety. You might also talk about each type of fruit and which one each child likes or dislikes. Serve the finished salad at snacktime and watch your little ones beam with pride as they eat the snack they've created together!

Beverly A. Lanham, Carlisle Community Nursery School, Carlisle, PA

The Feel of Foil

Try this twist on fingerpainting for a sensory delight! Give each child a piece of aluminum foil and a few colors of fingerpaint. Talk about how the foil feels as little fingers slip and slide across it. Colors will look bright on this shiny surface, making it fun for the eyes too! Or, for another twist, spray a bit of cooking spray onto foil. Then let fingers slip and slide away!

Shelley Hoster
Jack and Jill Early Learning Center
Norcross, GA

Lunches to the Limit!

Whenever students bring Lunchables lunches (or similar prepackaged tray lunches) to school, save the divided plastic trays and put them to use in your classroom! Use them as paint trays, sorting trays, planters, or holders for collage materials, or use them in math lessons involving manipulatives.

Suzanne Godfrey, FCCDC, Madison, FL

A Card for Mom

Here's a different kind of fingerpainting that makes an adorable Mother's Day card! To begin, fold a sheet of white construction paper in half to make a card. Paint a child's four fingers and part of the palm yellow; then make a print in the top corner of the card to resemble a sun as shown. Create a flower with a green fingerprint for the stem, green thumbprints for the leaves, a yellow fingerprint for the flower's center, and six fingerprints in the child's choice of colors to create the flower's petals. When all the paint is dry, write the child's Mother's Day message inside the card.

Melinda Clark, Mindy's Daycare & Preschool, Fairplay, CO

Sidewalk Chalk

Who knew making sidewalk chalk was so easy? To make four large sticks, collect four empty cardboard tubes. Wrap duct tape over one end of each tube; then set the molds on a foil covered surface. Next, combine two cups of water with two cups of plaster of paris. Stir in approximately two tablespoons of wet or dry tempera paint to tint the mixture. (Or divide the mixture into smaller portions and tint each portion a different color.) Set the mixture aside for a few minutes to thicken; then pour it into the molds. When the chalk is firm, peel away the cardboard tubes. In one or two days the chalk will be completely dry and ready to use!

Laurie Sprouse, Young Ideas Preschool, Newton, IA

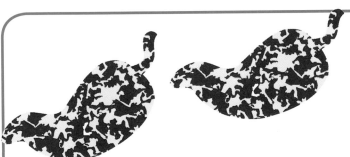

Chili Pepper Prints

Spice up your Cinco de Mayo celebration with this art project! Cut a few sponges into chili pepper shapes. Then pour some red tempera paint into a shallow pan and stir in a small amount of corn syrup to make a glossy paint. Have youngsters make prints with this red-hot technique!

Windy Ford, NTBC Weekday School, Columbia, SC

Baby Shoe Flowerpot

Looking for a creative Mother's Day gift? This one is a shoe-in! Ask each family to send in one of its preschooler's baby shoes (any size will work, but the shoe must have a closed toe). Explain that the family will get the shoe back but that it will be altered. Spray-paint each shoe with gold paint. When it is dry, stuff the shoe with florist's foam. Then have the child poke artificial flowers into the foam. Add a bow and a florist's pick holding a special card. Cute!

Eileen Sproule, Hermiston Christian School, Hermiston, OR

A Gift That Makes "Scents"

Make these sweet-smelling gifts for dads for Father's Day! To begin, use cookie cutters to trace shapes (a class supply) onto stiff felt; then cut the shapes out. Punch a hole at the top of each cutout and add a loop of yarn. Next, mix some men's cologne and water in a bowl. Have each child dip a felt cutout into the water and then hang the shape to dry.

Next, copy and cut out two construction paper cars per child (pattern on page 114). Staple the scented shape at the top of one copy. Then have a child color the other copy and staple the two together as shown. On the inside left of each card glue a copy of the poem shown. After removing the air freshener from the card and placing it in his car, each dad will be reminded of how special he is to his child.

Joyce Trammel and Joan Newcomb
Emanuel's Child Development Center
Catonsville, MD

I made this present just for you
For this Father's Day.
When you get into the car,
You'll smell it right away.

Every time you take a drive
To travel east or west
You'll smell this scent and always know
I think you are the best!

Doughnuts for Dads

Honor dads with a special day at preschool! Invite dads, grandpas, and uncles to join your students for a special presentation. Have each youngster draw a picture of his dad or another male role model and dictate something about that person. On your Doughnuts for Dad day, invite each child to share his drawing and thoughts. Then have your students sing some songs or recite a poem about dads before showing their fathers around the classroom and enjoying doughnuts and juice together.

Amber Murray, Christ the King School, Des Moines, IA

Graduation Goodies

Make the snacks at your preschool graduation extra special! Print congratulatory messages on sticker labels on your computer. Then stick the labels onto snack-size candy bars for your young graduates to enjoy!

Sarah Booth, Messiah Nursery School, South Williamsport, PA

You did it, graduate!
It's true!
We're so very proud of you!

Texture Tools

Get creative with your classroom painting activities by making your own unique brushes! Gather items that can be clipped into a clothespin or taped onto a wooden craft stick, such as pom-poms, rubber bands, plastic wrap, sponges, or aluminum foil strips. Secure each type of painter in a clothespin; then add tape to keep it in place. (Or tape items securely onto a wooden craft stick.) Invite your young artists to experiment with these fun painting tools. They may even come up with some other items they'd like to use as paintbrushes!

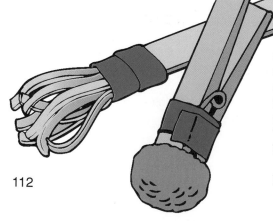

Melissa Weimer, Stepanski ECC, Waterford, MI

Bug Viewer

Invite your little ones to take a closer look at creepy-crawly critters with these homemade bug viewers! Gather a few plastic frosting containers (or similar containers with removable plastic lids). Remove each label and then cut a hole in each lid. Cover the top of the open container with netting; then replace the lid. Decorate the outside of the canister with bug stickers and puffy paint designs.

When a child wants to do a little bug-watching, capture a critter in the canister and put on the netting and lid. Be sure to release the bug after a short visit!

Sharon Semas, Head Start Silver Lake, Kingston, MA

New Life for Old Markers

Get the most from your markers with this tip! When your classroom markers dry out, give children small cups of water. Have them dip the markers into the water and watch as they keep going, and going, and going!

Wendy Sullivan, Huffer Memorial Children's Center, Muncie, IN

Thank You, Helpers!

Say thank you to your classroom helpers with this creative card! On the front of a blank folded card, print the poem shown. Inside, tape a packet of flower seeds on the right side of the card and include a note of personal thanks on the left side.

Sarah Booth, Messiah Nursery School, South Williamsport, PA

Thank you for your help this year.
You're so kind and full of cheer!
People like you should be grown from seeds,
So teachers could harvest your many good deeds!

Friendship Rings

Send your preschool graduates off to kindergarten with a reminder from the old rhyme "Make new friends, but keep the old. One is silver and the other's gold." Give each child a gold plastic ring and a silver ring (such as those used for wedding decorations). Tell youngsters to wear the gold rings on their first day of kindergarten to help them remember their old friends at preschool. Ask each of them to give his silver ring to a new friend at his new school!

Casey Burks, La Petite Academy, Rocklin, CA

Individual Rain Sticks

Each of your students can shake her own rain stick with this simple idea! Cover a potato chip canister with construction paper; then have each child decorate the outside with craft foam cutouts and marker drawings. Next, instruct her to roll a piece of aluminum foil into a snake shape. Staple one end to the inside lid of the canister. Pour some rice into the can; then secure the lid with tape. Give the canister a shake to hear the rain!

Heather Campbell, HCDS, Pennington, NJ

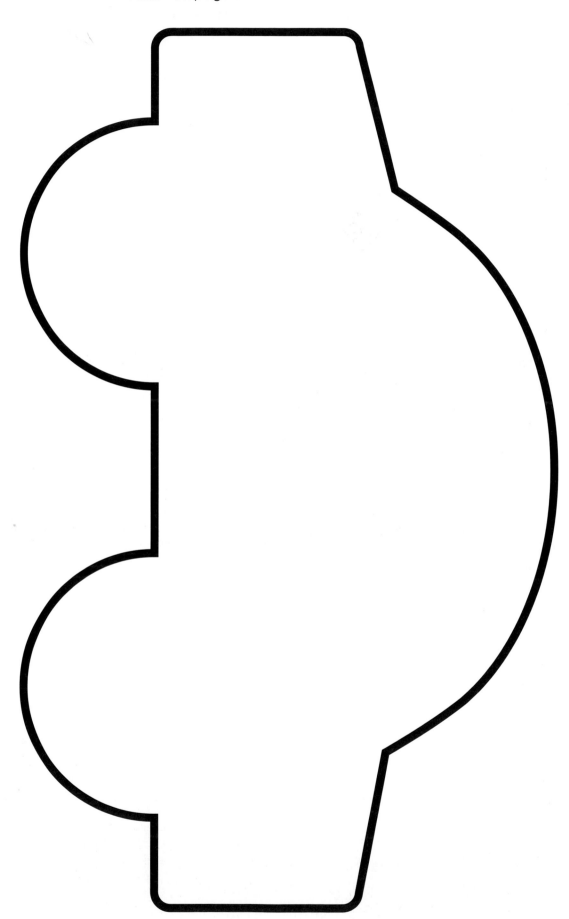

SCIENCE EXPLORATIONS

Science

Skin—the Great Protector

Little ones learn what an important purpose our skin serves with this demonstration.

STEP 1

Invite a small group to join you at a table. Have each youngster look at the skin of her arm and talk about its importance.

STEP 2

Cover the bowl of water with plastic wrap to simulate skin, and use a rubber band to secure it in place. Explain to students that the plastic wrap is like our skin because it protects the water in the bowl as our skin protects the inside of our bodies.

STEP 5

To demonstrate a cut, use a rock to make a small hole in the plastic-wrap skin. Ask students what they do when they get boo-boos. Have a child wipe the cut with a towel, and instruct another youngster to place a bandage over it.

STEP 6

Repeat Step 3 to show that our skin and a bandage can help keep germs and dirt out of our bodies. After wiping away the dirt, have youngsters check the water in the bowl for dirt particles.

Explorations

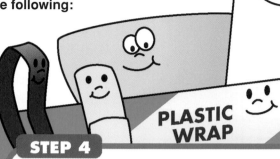

To demonstrate the purpose of our skin, you will need the following:

bowl with water   damp towel
plastic wrap   rock
large rubber band   bandage
dirt

STEP 3

Have a student put some dirt on the plastic-wrap skin. Did the skin protect the water inside? You bet!

STEP 4

Invite another child to use a damp towel to gently wipe the dirt away, simulating washing dirty skin.

Did You Know?

Check out the thickness of a sheet of paper. The outermost layer of our skin is about that thick over most of the body.

What Now?

Rewrap the bowl with plastic wrap and secure it with a rubber band. Invite youngsters to test the plastic-wrap skin with paint or markers. Is it paintproof and markerproof? Yes!

Science

Seeds, Seeds, Seeds!

Little ones learn about seeds with this exploration.

by Sue Fleischmann—PreK
Holy Cross School, Menomonee Falls, WI

STEP 1

Invite a student to join you at a table. Have youngsters investigate a small pumpkin and an ear of corn, looking for their seeds. (Cut open the pumpkin to reveal the seeds.)

STEP 2

Corn has lots of seeds!

Pumpkin seeds are slimy!

Invite each child to use a hand lens to look more closely at the seeds. Invite the children to discuss what they observe.

STEP 5

Explain that different fruits and vegetables have different seeds, and each seed can create a new plant. Save and dry some of the seeds for planting in the spring.

STEP 6

Repeat Steps 1 through 5 with another type of food, such as an apple, a cucumber, or a squash.

Explorations

To investigate and compare corn and pumpkin seeds, you will need the following:

ear of corn in its husk
small pumpkin
knife (teacher use only)
hand lenses
spoons

STEP 3

Have students work together to remove the seeds.

STEP 4

Instruct little ones to compare the seeds, noticing their sizes, shapes, and numbers.

Did You Know?

Each ear of corn has approximately 18 rows of kernels. That's a lot of seeds for potential new plants!

What Now?

Have a seed taste test. Purchase shelled toasted pumpkin seeds and canned corn. Heat the corn. Give each child a small sample of each. Seeds are yummy! What other seeds could your students sample? Beans, peas, sunflower seeds,…

Science

In Touch With the Sense of Touch

Youngsters build language skills as they explore the sense of touch with this investigation.

Rough! Cold! Prickly!

Invite a small group to join you at a table. Lead youngsters to discuss the sense of touch and how it might feel to touch something. Encourage the use of descriptive language such as *smooth, rough, prickly, warm, cold,* or *soft.*

Away from students' view, place the pinecone or small pine branch on the tray and cover it with the towel. Then position the tray in the center of the table. Invite each child to reach under the towel to feel the items. Have him describe what he observes as he touches the items. Write students' observations on a chart.

Repeat the activity with the other item. Then have each youngster hold and observe the items and then share any other descriptions with the group. Explain that when two senses are used to observe an object, we can notice more details about it.

Place different items on the tray and put the towel over them. Invite youngsters to repeat the exercise to explore and describe the items they feel.

120

Explorations

To investigate the sense of touch, you will need the following:
pinecone
small pine branch with pine needles (Choose other items common to your area if pinecones and pine branches are not available.)
tray
towel
chart paper
marker

STEP 3

I think it's a pinecone!

Have each child predict what he is feeling. Record student responses on a chart.

STEP 4

We were right!

Remove the towel and talk about the item. Review the chart to see whether predictions were correct.

Did You Know?

Second to the tip of the tongue, fingertips and the tip of the nose are some of the most touch-sensitive areas on our bodies.

What Now?

Transform a center into a touch station. Fill several bowls with different items such as ice, cotton balls, rice, sand, cornstarch, and shredded paper. Encourage youngsters to visit the center. Have them close their eyes, touch each bowl's contents, and then describe what they feel. Fun!

Science

Moving Air Helps Make Bubbles!

Your preschoolers will walk, run, and jump at the chance to make bubbles with body movements.

by Jana Sanderson, Rainbow School, Stockton, CA

STEP 1

Pour bubble solution in a bowl and add bubble wands. Invite youngsters to practice blowing bubbles. Discuss other ways that they could make air go through the wands to make bubbles without using their mouths.

STEP 2

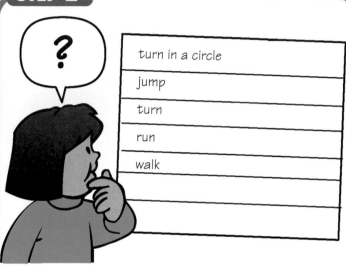

Add students' responses to a copy of the chart on page 128.

STEP 5

Ask children to help you count the number of stickers for each movement and record the totals.

STEP 6

Have youngsters determine which motion had the most success making wind for bubbles.

Explorations

To explore making bubbles, you will need the following:

bubble solution
bubble wands
chart paper
marker
sticky dots
bowl

STEP 3

Have each student try out each of the movements listed on the chart while holding a wand dipped in solution.

STEP 4

Invite each child to add a sticky dot to the chart beside each movement that he thought was successful in making bubbles.

This Is Why

Wind helps create bubbles. The body movements that create a steady breeze make bubbles. Quick movements make too much wind, thus popping the solution on the wand before the bubble is formed.

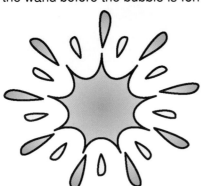

What Now?

Invite students to find other ways to produce wind to make bubbles.

Suggestions:
fanning wand with paper or a book
sliding down a slide
riding a teeter-totter
riding a tricycle
swinging
riding a rocking horse

123

Science

Going, Going, Gone! Water Absorption

Preschoolers get drawn into this observation of water absorption.

STEP 1

Place a cotton ball, a tissue, a sheet of construction paper, a paper towel, a piece of cloth, a sheet of copy paper, a piece of plastic, a piece of wood, a piece of plastic wrap, and a piece of aluminum foil on a table. Have students study the items.

STEP 2

Talk about absorption and have students guess which materials will absorb water droplets well and which ones will not. Have youngsters divide the materials into the two groups.

STEP 5

Engage students in reevaluating the groups. Allow youngsters to re-sort the materials as needed.

STEP 6

Have students test their predictions, making sure each child has an opportunity to test an item.

Explorations

To explore water absorption, you will need the following:

cotton ball
tissue
sheet of construction paper
paper towel
piece of cloth
piece of plastic

sheet of copy paper
piece of plastic wrap
piece of aluminum foil
piece of wood
container of water
eyedroppers

STEP 3

Invite a youngster to choose a material from one group and use an eyedropper to drip water on it. After a short time, have students describe what happened.

STEP 4

Ask a different child to choose a material from the other group; then tell her to drip water on it. Have students describe what happens.

This Is Why

Some materials act like sponges. Absorption happens when the water is drawn into the material and becomes distributed throughout.

What Now?

Invite students to find out just how much water a cotton ball can hold. Invite each child to add drops of water to a cotton ball until it's saturated. Then invite the child to squeeze the water from the cotton ball into an empty cup. They'll be surprised how much water that little puff of cotton can absorb!

Science

Cheesy Changes

What happens to a cheese-topped chip when it's heated by the sun? Your little scientists will say, "Melted cheese, please!" when they discover the answer.

by Lucia Kemp Henry, Fallon, NV

STEP 1

Gather a small group of students at a table. Put a large plain tortilla chip on a paper plate and sprinkle it with a thin layer of finely grated cheese. Have students describe how the cheese looks.

STEP 2

Have youngsters predict what will happen if a hair dryer is used to blow warm air on the chip. Then set the dryer on medium heat and direct the warm air toward the cheese. (Be careful not to blow the cheese off the chip.)

STEP 5

Have each child place her bowl in direct sunlight. Help each student use a block to prop her bowl at an angle, if needed, so that the sun shines directly inside the bowl. Have youngsters check their bowls often to observe any changes.

STEP 6

When the cheese has melted, have each child remove the plastic from his bowl. Encourage youngsters to discuss how the cheese has changed.

Explorations

To explore heating and melting, you will need the following:

small hair dryer
plain tortilla chips
finely grated cheddar cheese
paper plate

foil-lined paper bowls
clear plastic wrap
rubber bands
block

STEP 3

Have youngsters observe what happens to the cheese. Introduce the words *heat* and *melt* as you discuss the observed changes. Invite students to suggest other ways to melt the cheese on the chip.

STEP 4

Give each child a foil-lined paper bowl. Have her place a chip in the bottom and top it with a small amount of cheese. Help each child cover the bowl with plastic wrap; then use a rubber band to keep the plastic in place.

This Is Why

When a substance is heated, its molecules begin to move faster, changing the way it looks or feels and in some cases making the substance melt.

What Now?

Extend the exploration on another day by placing an ice cube and a tablespoon of ice cream in separate bowls. Put the bowls in the sun and observe the changes. Youngsters will see that heating makes various substances look different when they melt.

Recording Chart

Use with "Moving Air Helps Make Bubbles!" on page122.

turn in a circle	jump	turn	run	walk		

SONGS & SUCH

SONGS & SUCH

A Pocket-Chart Poem

Welcome your students to a new year with this poem featuring their names! Write each verse on a long paper strip and display it in a pocket chart. (Add or delete verses, depending on your class size.) Write each child's name on an individual sticky note and use the names to fill in the blanks in the poem. Invite your preschoolers to pop up when they hear their names in the poem. Mix up the names periodically to keep little ones interested and to improve name recognition.

I know this will be a wonderful year!
I'm so glad _____, _____, and _____ are here!

You know that it just wouldn't do
If _____, ____, and _____ weren't here too!

Coming to school wouldn't be such a ball
If _____, _____, and _____ weren't here with us all!

It would be hard to start our day
If _____, _____, and _____ weren't here to play!

At school the fun just never ends,
With _____, _____, and _____ as our preschool friends!

Elizabeth Farella—Pre-Nursery
Kiddie Junction
Levittown, NY

I know this will be a wonderful year!
I'm so glad Sara, Greg, and Ivy are here!

Find a Friend

Use this simple tune to encourage your new preschoolers to make friends.

(sung to the tune of "This Old Man")

Find a friend;
Say, "Hello!"
Help to make your friendship grow.
Be good to friends, and they'll be good to you.
Find new friends; keep old ones too!

Linda Gordetsky
Palenville, NY

Five Terrific Preschoolers

Ask your little ones to hold up the corresponding number of fingers as they recite each line of a poem that's all about them!

Five terrific preschoolers standing in a row.
The first one said, "We are friends, you know."
The second one said, "We are alike; it's true."
The third one said, "But there's no one exactly like you."
The fourth one said, "We all shine in different ways."
The fifth one said, "We grow more special every day!"

LeeAnn Collins—Director
Sunshine House Preschool
Lansing, MI

SONGS & SUCH

Leafspeak

After teaching this little song, take your youngsters on a walk through some crunchy fall leaves. They'll be asking to sing the song again!

(sung to the tune of "Clementine")

Leaves are falling; leaves are falling
From the trees down to the ground.
Some are orange and some are yellow.
Some are even red and brown!

They are swishing; they are crackling
When I go out for a walk.
They are saying, "It is autumn!"
In their leafy kind of talk!

Days of the Week!

This peppy addition to calendar time is sure to put a spring in your little ones' steps! Have youngsters march in a circle as they recite this version of the days of the week.

There's Sunday and there's Monday.
There's Tuesday and there's Wednesday.
There's Thursday and there's Friday,
And then there's Saturday!
The days of the week. Yahoo!

Suzan Hill—Three-Year-Olds
6th and Izard Day School
Little Rock, AR

Heather McCarthy—Toddlers
Jack N Jill Childcare
Quincy, MA

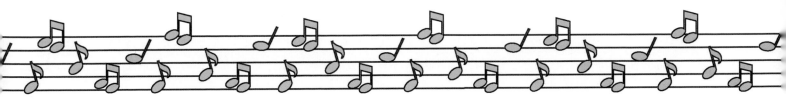

Big Orange Pumpkins

This little ditty takes pumpkins from seeds to festive jack-o'-lanterns!

(sung to the tune of "The Itsy-Bitsy Spider")

Pumpkins start as fat seeds
Planted in the ground.
Then they push up vines
That wiggle all around.
Soon pumpkins grow.
They're big and orange too.
Then you carve a jack-o'-lantern
That lights up and says, "Boo!"

Deborah Garmon
Groton, CT

Five Little Train Cars

Choo, choo! All aboard this little train rhyme!

Five little train cars all in a row,
The first one said, "Which way will we go?"
The second one said, "Down the track."
The third one just said, "Clickety-clack."
The fourth one said, "We have a job to do."
The fifth one said, "I'm following you."
"Choo, choo," said the engine strong and bright,
And the happy little train chugged out of sight!

Shelley Hoster—PreK
Jack and Jill Early Learning Center
Norcross, GA

SONGS & SUCH

Autumn

Welcome autumn with this catchy tune!

(sung to the tune of "Old MacDonald Had a Farm")

Autumn time has come at last. Yes, oh yes, it has!
And while it's here we'll have a blast!
Yes, oh yes, we will!
With a pumpkin here and a scarecrow there,
Watching leaves drifting in the air.
Autumn time has come at last. Yes, oh yes, it has!

Sarah Hibbett
Henderson, TN

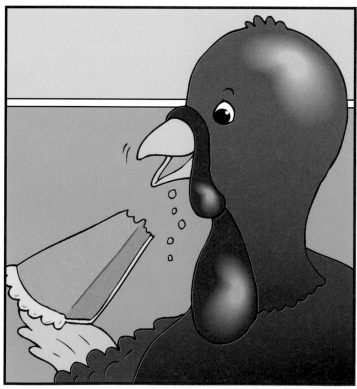

Thanksgiving Day

Teach your youngsters this song to celebrate
Thanksgiving Day.

(sung to the tune of "Sing a Song of Sixpence")

Come and join the party
On Thanksgiving Day.
We will eat some turkey;
Some of us will play.
We're feeling oh so stuffed,
But before we say goodbye,
Let's gather round the table
And have some pumpkin pie!

Linda Gordetsky
Palenville, NY

Hanukkah Time

Sing this little song to brighten the Hanukkah holiday!

(sung to the tune of "Up on the Housetop")

Menorah in the window shining bright,
Hanukkah time is here tonight.
Time to give and time to share
With friends and family everywhere.
Hanukkah, what a sight!
Hanukkah is here tonight.
Menorah in the window shining bright,
Hanukkah time is here tonight!

Randy McGovern
Twin Oaks Country Day School
Freeport, NY

Trimming the Tree

Have youngsters help decorate your classroom Christmas tree as they sing this song! For additional verses, substitute *shiny stars, candy canes,* and *icicles* for *Christmas lights.*

(sung to the tune of "She'll Be Comin' Round the Mountain")

We'll be trimming our tree with [Christmas lights].
We'll be trimming our tree with [Christmas lights].
We'll be trimming our tree
For the whole wide world to see.
We'll be trimming our tree with [Christmas lights].

LeeAnn Collins
Sunshine House Preschool
Lansing, MI

SONGS & SUCH

Martin Luther King Jr.

Dr. Martin Luther King Jr. is honored when your students sing this song!

(sung to the tune of "You Are My Sunshine")

You are a hero
To many people.
And of your praises,
We love to sing.
You said we should be
Kind to each other.
Your name is Martin Luther King!

Linda Gordetsky
Palenville, NY

Body Parts Boogie

You'll hear giggles galore when youngsters move body parts high and low and then fast and slow while singing this fun song!

(sung to the tune of "The Hokey-Pokey")

I stretch my body high.
I stretch my body low.
I move my body really fast,
And I move it really slow.
My body's made of parts; each is special—this I know.
Watch as I move it so!

I move my hands up high.
I move my hands down low.
I move my hands really fast,
And I move them really slow.
I use my hands to clap, and I use my hands to touch.
Watch as I move them so!

I move my tongue up high.
I move my tongue down low.
I move my tongue really fast,
And I move it really slow.
I use my tongue to lick, and I use my tongue to taste.
Watch as I move it so!

I move my nose up high.
I move my nose down low.
I move my nose really fast,
And I move it really slow.
I use my nose to breathe, and I use my nose to smell.
Watch as I move it so!

I move my eyes up high.
I move my eyes down low.
I move my eyes really fast,
And I move them really slow.
I use my eyes to blink, and I use my eyes to see.
Watch as I move them so!

I move my ears up high.
I move my ears down low.
I move my ears really fast,
And I move them really slow.
I use my ears to listen, and I use my ears to hear.
Watch as I move them so!

Karen Briggs, The Early Childhood Center
Marlborough, MA

I'm a Little Groundhog

Use this song to help your little ones remember what the groundhog's shadow means. In advance, duplicate the groundhog puppets on page 144 onto tan construction paper so that you have one per child. Cut out the puppets and attach each one to a craft stick handle. Have each child make a hole by holding one arm in front of him as if he were holding a beach ball. Have him hold his puppet in the other hand as he performs the actions in the song.

(sung to the tune of "I'm a Little Teapot")

I'm a little groundhog
On Groundhog Day.
I peek from my hole
On a winter day.
If I see my shadow,
In I go!
Winter's going to stay, I know.

I'm a little groundhog
On Groundhog Day.
I peek from my hole
On a winter day.
If I see no shadow,
Out I'll stay.
Spring will soon be on its way!

Heather Graley
Grace Christian School, Blacklick, OH

Wash Your Hands

Keep germs at bay this winter by using this happy tune at hand-washing time!

(sung to the tune of "Row, Row, Row Your Boat")

Wash, wash, wash your hands.
Wash the germs away!
Watch the suds go down the drain
So germs do not stay!

Charlene McGrath
Discovery Elementary
Brigham City, UT

SONGS & SUCH

Oh, My Darlin' Valentine

February is the month of love, so celebrate with this heartfelt song!

(sung to the tune of "Clementine")

February is a short month,
28 days or 29.
In the middle is a love day.
Won't you be my valentine?

Oh, my darlin', oh, my darlin',
Oh, my darlin' valentine!
In the middle is a love day.
Won't you be my valentine?

Linda Gordetsky
Palenville, NY

FEBRUARY

S	M	T	W	T	F	S
		1	2	3	4	5
6	7	8	9	10	11	12
13	14	15	16	17	18	19
20	21	22				
27	28					

We like your smile!

Our Valentine

Your little ones are sure to love this song full of compliments! To begin, choose a child to sing to and ask your students to think of two things they like about this person. Then fill in the blanks with those two things as everyone sings! Repeat the song until every child has been the subject of this little ditty.

(sung to the tune of "You Are My Sunshine")

[Child's name] is our valentine,
Our special valentine.
What a great kid in every way!
We like your _____ and
We like your _____, so
Be our valentine today!

Linda Gordetsky

Spring Is Here

Welcome the warm season with this happy song!

(sung to the tune of "If You're Happy and You Know It")

If you look, you'll see spring is all around!
See flowers coming up from underground.
See the blossoms on the trees,
Hear the buzzing honeybees.
If you look, you'll see spring is all around!

Deborah Garmon
Groton, CT

I Love the Earth

Take note of Earth Day by teaching your preschoolers this earth-friendly tune.

(sung to the tune of "This Old Man")

I love the earth.
The earth loves me.
We must live in harmony.
If you care for animals, plants, and oceans too,
The earth will be a friend to you!

Cheryl Calchera
The Flying Goose
Cortlandt Manor, NY

SONGS & SUCH

Rain Cloud

'Tis the season for rainy days! Help your youngsters make these crafty rain clouds and use them to act out the song that follows. To make a cloud, cut a paper plate into a cloud shape; then glue cotton balls onto it. Tape silver or blue tinsel strands or ribbon lengths to the bottom of the back of the cloud to resemble rain. Then sing away!

(sung to the tune of "I'm a Little Teapot")

I'm a fluffy white cloud in the sky.   *Hold up cloud.*
Watch me as I drift on by.   *Make cloud "drift."*
When I'm full of water, then I say,   *Hold arms out to sides to indicate "full."*
"It's time for another rainy day!"   *Stoop down and shake rain side to side.*

The Rainbow Song

Here's a colorful tune just right for singing in the rainy months of spring!

(sung to the tune of "Did You Ever See a Lassie?")

Did you ever see a rainbow, a rainbow, a rainbow?
Did you ever see a rainbow light up the gray sky?
With red, orange, and yellow,
And green, blue, and purple,
Did you ever see a rainbow light up the gray sky?

Cheryl Scheurer
St. Joan of Arc ELC
Arvada, CO

A Tune for Moms

Mothers will love this song sung by your class at a Mother's Day tea. Or, if you don't have a gathering planned for Mother's Day, record the class singing the song on inexpensive cassette tapes and send them home as gifts!

(sung to the tune of "I've Been Working on the Railroad")

We all really love our mothers!
We think they are the best!
They are better than all others,
And we never let them rest!

We appreciate their hard work,
All the things they do.
We just think our moms are super!
Hey, Mom, I love you!

Oh, Mom, don't you know?
Your child loves you so!
We wish you a happy Mother's Day!
Mom, I think you are
My favorite shining star!
Happy, happy Mother's Day!

Beverly Lushbaugh
Turtle Rock Preschool
Irvine, CA

Adapt these songs for youngsters who don't have a mom at home.

Someone Special

Have your youngsters recite this poem for their moms. It's sure to be a hit!

I know of someone special
Who tucks me in at night,
Who teaches me to comb my hair
And dress myself just right.
She hugs me when I'm angry
And helps keep me calm.
I bet you know already;
I'm thinking of my mom!
Mom, I want to let you know,
On this Mother's Day,
That I really love you so!
You're great in every way!

Soraya Rosario
The Children's First Learning Center
New York, NY

SONGS & SUCH

It's Red and Sweet

What would summer be without watermelon? Teach your little ones this poem about one of summer's favorite foods!

In summertime
It's really fine
To slurp the best
Fruit from the vine.

It's red and sweet.
It can't be beat!
It's watermelon—
What a treat!

Linda Gordetsky
Palenville, NY

The Letter-Writing Song

Give your youngsters paper and pencils. Then model writing each letter on the board as you sing this song together.

(sung to the tune of "The Farmer in the Dell")

We can write a [b].
We can write a [b].
Use your pencil and write with me!
Oh, we can write a [b].

Keely Peasner
Midlands Kiddie Korral
Tacoma, WA

Fireworks!

Get ready for Independence Day by teaching your preschoolers this delightful ditty about fabulous fireworks! If desired, provide drums or have students bang their hands on the table as you sing "boom" and "bang"!

(sung to the tune of "This Old Man")

Fourth of July,
Fourth of July—
Time for fireworks in the sky
With a boom, bang, boom, bang
Dazzling surprise!
See the sparkle before your eyes!

Colleen Dabney
Williamsburg, VA

Graduation Chant

Parents are sure to get a kick out of this military-style chant when your preschoolers recite it at a preschool graduation! Lead the class in the following chant.

Leader	Class
I don't know, but I've been told	*Echo.*
Kindergarten is the place to go!	*Echo.*
I've learned my numbers and ABCs.	*Echo.*
Now I'm smart as I can be!	*Echo.*
Sound off!	One, two.
Sound off!	Three, four.
Bring it on down!	One, two, three, four.
	One, two…three, four!

Melisa Horsfield
Bright Beginnings Child Care
Fort Payne, AL

144

STORYTIME

Storytime

Lunch

Written and illustrated by Denise Fleming

This is an amusing story about a cute little mouse who is so hungry he decides to eat a large and very colorful lunch. The clever illustrations give the reader a small glimpse of each food the mouse eats before revealing the food on the following page.

Before You Read

Turn storytime into feast time with this appetizing activity! Gather two of each kind of fruit and vegetable from the story. Place one of each food in a picnic basket. Cut the remaining fruits and vegetables into bite-size pieces, cook the pieces if necessary, and put them in separate resealable plastic bags. Place a large tablecloth on the floor and have students seat themselves around it. Give each child a paper plate. Introduce each fruit or vegetable and talk about its color. After you've explored all the foods, offer youngsters a sample of each one. Then discuss the ones they like. Is there a class favorite?

Robin McClay—PreK and K
St. Joseph Institute for the Deaf
Chesterfield, MO

After You Read

If you were a hungry mouse, what would you eat? After reading the story, have each child tell you! Give each child a copy of page 158, watercolor paints, and cotton swabs. Instruct him to paint spots on the mouse in corresponding food colors to show his lunch choices. Then have him dictate what he ate. Bind the completed pages into a class book titled "Hungry Mice."

Robin McClay

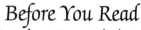

MOUSE'S LUNCH

If **Jon** were a mouse, **he** would eat **carrots, grapes, blueberries, and corn.**

Rosie's Walk

Written and illustrated by Pat Hutchins

This tale lends itself to teaching little ones about positional words as Rosie the hen walks over, around, under, and through the barnyard. A fox follows her every move and so will your little ones!

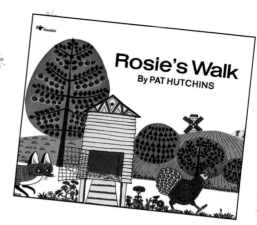

Before You Read

Get your preschoolers thinking about positional words with beanbag hens! Give each child a beanbag and have her hold it in different positions as you sing the song below. Substitute the underlined phrases with *under my chin, around my foot, between my knees, behind my ear,* and *over my head.* Encourage youngsters to suggest other ways the hen could walk around their bodies.

(sung to the tune of "The Wheels on the Bus")

The hen on the farm walks [across my arm],
[Across my arm],
[Across my arm].
The hen on the farm walks [across my arm] all around the barnyard.

Robin McClay—PreK and K
St. Joseph Institute for the Deaf
Chesterfield, MO

After You Read

Who's ready for a walk, Rosie style? Your preschoolers! Set up an obstacle course that resembles Rosie's barnyard. Demonstrate how to follow the course while walking on two feet like Rosie or on four feet like the sneaky fox. Use the suggestions below for setting up your course.

- **across** the yard—Use a balance beam or tape on the floor. Have youngsters walk forward, backward, and sideways.
- **around** the pond—Place a blue towel at the end of the balance beam. Have students walk around the towel.
- **over** the haystack—Tape brown bulletin board paper over the seat of a small chair. Have students step over the chair's seat.
- **past** the mill—Have students do forward somersaults on a mat past a bookshelf or table.
- **through** the fence—Have students crawl through a play tunnel or create a tunnel with a blanket.
- **under** the beehives—Have students crawl under a table and then hurry back to their henhouses (seats).

Robin McClay

Storytime

Pumpkin Pumpkin

Written and illustrated by Jeanne Titherington

Jamie plants a pumpkin seed in the spring, watches it grow all summer, and carves a jack-o'-lantern from the resulting giant pumpkin. He saves six seeds for spring planting. Soft, realistic pencil drawings invite the reader into this story.

Before You Read

It's orange, it's large, and it's bumpy, but how does it grow? Find out what your little ones know about pumpkins with this simple activity. Gather youngsters in your reading area and show them a pumpkin. Invite students to take turns feeling the pumpkin and noticing its shape, color, and size. Have youngsters describe how and where they think pumpkins grow. Discuss the possibilities and then invite youngsters to keep an eye on the pumpkin while they listen to this story all about how a pumpkin grows!

After You Read
Sequencing a story

Proper story sequence is just a step away with this interactive retelling! In advance, make a copy of the pumpkin sequencing cards on page 159 and an extra copy of the pumpkin seed card. Color and laminate the cards if desired. Scatter the cards on a table and invite students to help you put them in order. Next, model how to use the book's illustrations to check the card sequence. Invite a pair of students to point to the first card; then reread the story as you prompt them to point to the appropriate cards. Repeat with several pairs of students, encouraging youngsters to recite the story with you. Before you know it, your preschool pumpkin professors will be able to sequence and retell the story in just a few easy steps!

The Night Before Thanksgiving

Written by Natasha Wing
Illustrated by Tammie Lyon

Oh, what a Thanksgiving feast is in store for this extended family! Join in this lighthearted tale as the meal is prepared, the family arrives, and everyone enjoys each other's company—and leftovers—the next day!

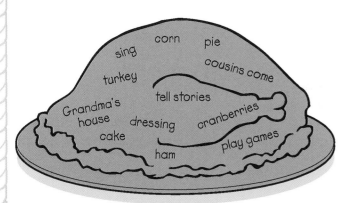

Before You Read

A huge platter of roast turkey is sure to get youngsters' attention! Cut a large turkey-and-platter shape from tan bulletin board paper and display it in your reading area. Gather students and discuss the upcoming holiday. Encourage each youngster to share a favorite Thanksgiving food or tradition as you record his thoughts on the cutout. When everyone has had a turn, invite students to settle in for the story.

After You Read

Graphing

Which students host Thanksgiving guests? This simple graph makes it easy to find out! Use electrical tape to make a large two-column graph on a vinyl tablecloth; then program sheets of white construction paper as shown. Give each child a small white paper plate and instruct her to write her name on it. Read the question aloud and then invite each child to tape her plate to the appropriate side of the graph. Discuss the graph results as a class. Mount the completed graph on a bulletin board for an eye-catching display.

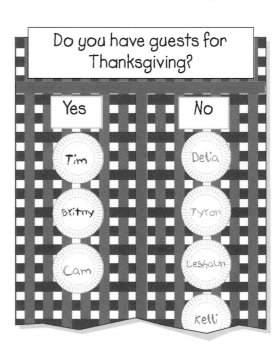

Storytime

Time to Sleep
Written and illustrated by Denise Fleming

Bear sniffs a change in the air and knows it's time for winter sleep. She tells Snail that it's time for their long winter nap, and soon other woodland animals know they must get ready for their seasonal snooze too. Vibrant illustrations and appealing characters are sure to keep little ones wide awake and interested for this story!

ideas by Lucia Kemp Henry, Fallon, NV

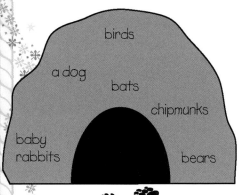

birds
a dog
bats
chipmunks
baby rabbits
bears

Before You Read

Introduce this bear bedtime story by having your little ones track a make-believe bear to its cozy cave! First, cut brown and black bulletin board paper, as shown, to make a cave. Tape the cave to a wall in your story area. Next, cut a supply of bear pawprints from black paper. Use clear Con-Tact paper to attach the prints to the floor, making a path that winds from your classroom door to the cave. Before youngsters enter the classroom, tell them that there are mysterious tracks on the floor! Encourage each child to follow the tracks to the cave and then have a seat. Have students guess what kind of animal might sleep inside the cave. Record each child's response on the cave. Then invite them to listen to the story to find out exactly who sleeps inside!

After You Read

Though the talking animals in the story are pure fantasy, their discussions about sleeping away the winter are based on what happens in nature. Highlight winter's sleep with this puppet and song activity. To make a bag puppet, trim three inches off the open end of a brown paper lunch bag for each child. Make a copy of the bear patterns on page 175. Have her color the patterns brown and cut them out. Assist each child in folding the head and gluing it to the sides of the bag bottom. Then help her glue the legs and the tail to the bag. Invite each child to move her puppet as she sings the song to the right.

(sung to the tune of "Are You Sleeping?")

Good night, Brown Bear. Good night, Brown Bear.
Time to sleep. Time to sleep.
"I must tell my friend. I must tell my friend.
Then I'll sleep. Then I'll sleep."

Good night, Brown Bear. Good night, Brown Bear.
Time to sleep. Time to sleep.
"Next, I'll find a warm cave. Next, I'll find a warm cave.
Then I'll sleep. Then I'll sleep."

Good night, Brown Bear. Good night, Brown Bear.
Time to sleep. Time to sleep.
"I will snore softly. I will snore softly.
I'm asleep. I'm asleep."

Goodnight Moon

Written by Margaret Wise Brown

Illustrated by Clement Hurd

A cuddly bunny goes through its bedtime routine, relaxing and settling down to sleep. The young bunny says good night to almost everything in its room (and some beyond!) before falling fast asleep. The rhythmic text and sweet pictures in this simple storybook are sure to make little listeners feel calm, cozy, and maybe even a little bit sleepy!

ideas by Lucia Kemp Henry, Fallon, NV

Before You Read

Get ready for this bedtime tale by stimulating interest with a guessing game. Gather together a small inflated red balloon, a mitten, a small plush bear, a brush, a sock, and a dark-colored pillowcase. Hide the items in a large paper grocery bag. To begin, secretly place one item inside the pillowcase. Have each child, in turn, feel the object hidden in the pillowcase. When each child has had a turn, ask the group to guess the item. When all the items have been identified, ask students to decide what the objects might have to do with bedtime. Then invite little ones to settle in as you read the story. Encourage them to look for the items from the activity in the story and decide whether their bedtime predictions for each were correct.

After You Read

The sleepy bunny soothes itself to sleep by saying good night to the familiar things in its friendly bedroom. Invite your little ones to talk about some of the familiar and comforting things in their own bedrooms. Do they have a special picture to look at before they fall asleep? Do they listen to calming music or listen to a story? After your discussion, have each child draw a picture of a special bedtime object. Make a caption for each picture, copying the following sentence for each child: "[Child's name] says, "Good night, _____." Use the child's dictation to complete the sentence. When the projects are completed, bind them together between construction paper covers to make a class bedtime book titled "We All Say Good Night!" In turn, send the book home with each child for some special overnight bedtime reading. Good night!

Sydney says, "Good night, pillow."

Storytime

Mud!
Written by Wendy Cheyette Lewison
Illustrated by Bill Basso
The children in this story have lots of fun playing in mud on a sunny afternoon, covering themselves in the sticky stuff from head to toe. The vibrant illustrations draw the reader into the story.

Before You Read
Mix up a batch of mud to get youngsters thinking about this story. Half-fill a gallon-size resealable plastic bag with dirt. Show the bag to youngsters and ask them what they think will happen if you add water to the dirt. Add some water; then invite youngsters to help you squish the bag to make mud. Encourage students to talk about their experiences with mud, and record their responses on a puddle shape cut from tan bulletin board paper. Introduce the book's title and have youngsters think about their list of muddy experiences as they listen to the story.

After You Read
These muddy masterpieces take inspiration from the story. Pour the mud from "Before You Read" into a pan. Give each child a sheet of white construction paper. Have him fingerpaint with the mud or use a brush to paint a muddy picture. After the mud has dried, have him dictate to you a sentence or two about his picture. Display the pictures on a bulletin board and title the display "Marvelous Mud Masterpieces."

I stepped in mud. See my toes!

Kent

Clifford's First Valentine's Day

Written and Illustrated by Norman Bridwell
Puppy love is evident in this sweet Clifford story in which a young girl recalls some sticky situations her red dog gets into on his first Valentine's Day.

ideas by Jana Sanderson, Rainbow School, Stockton, CA

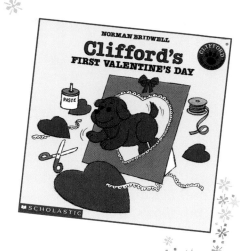

Before You Read

Get little ones thinking about Valentine's Day by naming red things. When a heart is named, invite youngsters to play this big-hearted game. Have each child move away from your group area while you use four ten-foot lengths of red yarn to make four heart shapes on the floor. Play music and invite your preschoolers to dance around the hearts. When the music stops, instruct youngsters to carefully step into a heart shape. Remove the four hearts from the floor. Make two larger hearts, using two lengths of yarn for each one. Play the music again. When the music stops, once again instruct little ones to step into a heart. Remove the hearts from the floor and make one large red heart from the four yarn pieces. Play the music one last time while the children dance around the shape. When the music stops, invite everybody to step inside the giant red heart, which is large enough for our friend Clifford, the big red dog. Have youngsters have a seat inside the heart to listen to the story.

After You Read

There will be big excitement for making valentines after reading this story. Have each child help fingerpaint a large red heart. When the paint is dry, mount the heart on a wall and write "Special Delivery!" off to the side. Take a picture of each child standing in front of the big red heart while holding a satchel. Glue the photographs to blank postcards (available at the post office). Address each child's postcard and help him write a Valentine's Day message to his family. Then attach a postcard postage stamp. Drop the postcards in the mail to send these sweet Valentine's Day wishes on their way!

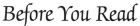

Special Delivery!

Storytime

In the Tall, Tall Grass
Written and Illustrated by Denise Fleming

This colorful book treats students to a caterpillar's-eye view of the critters that live in the tall, tall grass. The rhyming text and vibrant words are used to describe animals like bees, hummingbirds, ants, and bats as they go about their busy day.

ideas by Lucia Kemp Henry, Fallon, NV

Before You Read

Spark students' curiosity about the animals they'll see in the story with this imaginative idea. To prepare, draw grass shapes on a 9" x 12" sheet of green construction paper, as shown, and cut them out. Glue a jumbo craft stick to the straight edge of the grass. Ask your youngsters to sit in a circle; then show them the cover of the book. Discuss what kinds of animals the child in the illustration might see other than the caterpillar. Then invite each youngster to hold the grass puppet, pretend to look through it, and imagine what kind of animal she would like to discover in the tall, tall grass. Have each child share her selected animal by inserting its name in the chant below. After each student has had a turn, encourage youngsters to listen for their animal pick during the story.

Class: What could [child's name] see in the tall, tall grass?
Child: I could see a [animal's name] in the tall, tall grass!

After You Read

Can your little ones hum, flap, scurry, and snap just like the critters in the tall, tall grass? Try this movement activity to find out. Review the animals in the book and how each one maneuvers; then demonstrate a simple way to mimic each animal's movements. Next, take youngsters to a grassy area outside. Read each line of descriptive text from the book; then invite the group to move around the area just like the critter you've described. Use the movements shown as a guide.

Book Text	Movements
Crunch, munch, caterpillars lunch.	*Pretend to munch.*
Ritch, ratch, moles scratch.	*Scratch the ground.*
Dart, dip, hummingbirds sip.	*Pretend to sip through a straw.*
Skitter, scurry, beetles hurry.	*Crawl quickly.*
Strum, drum, bees hum.	*Buzz.*
Zip, zap, tongues snap.	*Stick out tongue.*
Crack, snap, wings flap.	*Flap arms.*
Hip, hop, ears flop.	*Use hands to show ears flopping while hopping.*
Pull, tug, ants lug.	*Pretend to carry something heavy.*
Stop, go, fireflies glow.	*Flash hands.*
Slip, slide, snakes glide.	*Pretend to slither.*
Lunge, loop, bats swoop.	*Pretend to fly in circles.*

It Looked Like Spilt Milk

Written and Illustrated by Charles G. Shaw

This clever book about cloud shapes will have little ones eager to head outside to take a look at the sky. What shapes will they see? Just like the vibrant illustrations in the book, the sky's the limit!

ideas by Lucia Kemp Henry, Fallon, NV

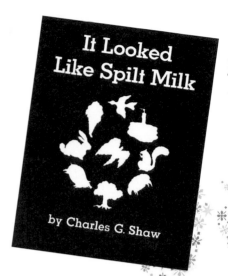

Before You Read

Here's a flannelboard activity that will help your little ones become very clever cloud watchers! Copy page 160 on white construction paper and cut out each cloud shape. Glue torn cotton balls to each cloud; then prepare each one for flannelboard use. Cut out a simple white construction paper cloud shape of similar size, glue on torn cotton balls, and prepare it for the flannelboard. Display the regular cloud shape on the flannelboard. Recite the first line of the rhyme and then ask students to make the sound of blowing wind. When you recite the second line, whoosh the cloud away and replace it with an animal-shaped cloud as you recite its name. After you've displayed all four critter-shaped clouds, encourage youngsters to lie back and pretend to be looking up at the clouds while you read the story.

The wind blows a puffy white cloud way up high.
Whoosh! Now it looks like a [rabbit] in the sky!

After You Read

Now that students' imaginations are soaring, invite each youngster to create some fluffy, puffy art. Have each child use a brush to dab white tempera paint on blue construction paper, making a cloud shape similar to his favorite animal or object. When the paint is dry, have him tear cotton balls and glue pieces to the painted shape. Then ask students to stand in a circle. Have each child, in turn, hold his dried cloud picture above his head while the group recites the rhyme.

Look at that little white cloud way up high.
[Child's name]'s fluffy cloud looks like a [kitten] in the sky!

Storytime

Round the Garden
Written by Omri Glaser
Illustrated by Byron Glaser and Sandra Higashi

A garden comes full circle in this clever book, which starts with a single tear. The vibrant illustrations and simple text introduce youngsters to science concepts focused on precipitation and plant growth.

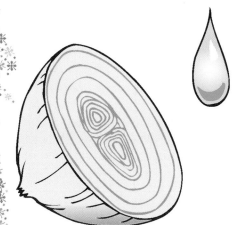

Before You Read
Youngsters may shed a few tears, but they won't be tears of sadness when you introduce this book with a sliced onion. To begin, ask students what types of things can be found in a garden. Record students' responses on an onion-shaped chart. Review the list and then talk about what plants in a garden need in order to grow. Lead youngsters to talk about the need for water. Show students an onion and then cut it in half. Take a sniff and really ham it up, forcing your eyes to tear or pretending to cry. Point out your tears and ask students whether they think a tear could water a garden. After a discussion, invite each child to sniff the onion if he chooses. Pass out some tissues and then settle down for the story.

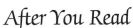

After You Read
Your little ones will be ready to grow a garden after listening to this story. Gather a paper cup for each child, potting soil, seeds, and a container of water with a small opening, such as a ketchup bottle with a pointed tip. Have each child scoop soil into her cup and then poke several seeds into the dirt. After the seeds have been planted, instruct her to use the water container to drip some tears onto the soil to water her seeds. Each day, have students drip new tears into their cups. Before they know it, those tears will help grow their gardens!

New Shoes, Red Shoes

Written and Illustrated by Susan Rollings

She sees low shoes and high shoes, sparkly shoes and magic shoes, but the little girl in this story thinks the best shoes are her new, shiny, red shoes. The colorful illustrations and descriptive language will have every preschooler looking at her own shoes.

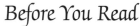

Before You Read

Nearly everbody wears shoes, and your preschoolers will be eager to show off their footwear with this fun activity featuring shoes! Have on hand a pillowcase or a bag. Have each child remove his shoes. Instruct each student to place one shoe from his pair in a line with his classmates' shoes and put his other shoe in a pile next to you. Secretly place one of the shoes from the pile in the pillowcase. Invite a child to put his hands in the pillowcase and feel the shoe. Then have him stand next to the shoe in the line that he thinks is the mate. Reveal the shoe in the bag to check his guess. If he guesses correctly, have him secretly choose the next shoe to put in the bag. If he guesses incorrectly, instruct him to return to his seat, and let another student have a turn. I feel a flip-flop!

After You Read

This class book has youngsters exploring descriptive ways to tell about their shoes. Trace each child's feet on a sheet of paper. Then instruct her to color the shapes to resemble her shoes. To finish her page, have her describe her shoes and write her dictation along the bottom of the page. Bind the pages between construction paper covers and title the book "Preschool Shoes."

Katie's shoes are blue with green sparkles.

Mouse's Lunch

If _____ were a mouse, _____ would eat _____.

©The Education Center, Inc. • *The Mailbox*® • TEC41014 • Aug./Sept. 2004

Note to the teacher: Use with "After You Read" on page 146.

158

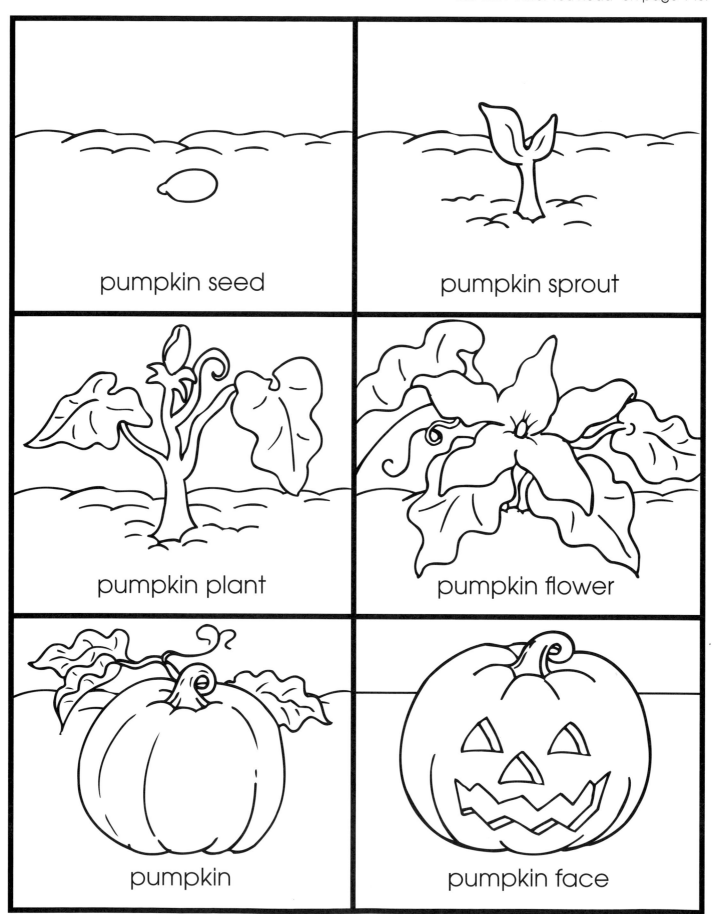

pumpkin seed

pumpkin sprout

pumpkin plant

pumpkin flower

pumpkin

pumpkin face

Cloud Shape Patterns
Use with "Before You Read" on page 155.

BOOK UNITS

The Kissing Hand

Written by Audrey Penn
Illustrated by Ruth E. Harper and Nancy M. Leak

Leaving a loved one can be difficult for a child. It certainly is for the little raccoon named Chester when he has to leave his mother to go to school. But Chester's loving mother gives him a kissing hand so that he will always have her love with him. Going to school doesn't seem as scary now that he has his mother's love right in the palm of his hand.

ideas contributed by Heather Miller—PreK, Creative Playschool, Auburn, IN

A Kiss on the Hand

Making a prediction, dictating thoughts to be recorded
Spark some interest in this story with this prereading activity. Draw a large hand outline on a sheet of chart paper. Cut out a red heart from construction paper and label it "The Kissing Hand." Glue the heart to the center of the hand outline. Show students the cover of the book and lead them to understand that the characters shown on the cover are a mother and her child. Ask youngsters to tell you what they think the story will be about. Write each student's response around the hand. Then share the sweet story with students. After reading, revisit the chart to see which predictions were correct. Then let each child share what special things his parents, grandparents, or caregivers would do to help him feel better in the same situation. Write students' responses on the hand. Post the chart and refer to it when a youngster is feeling a little blue. A reminder of a loved one just might be the pick-me-up a little one needs!

Wastebasket Worries

Using language to discuss feelings
Preschoolers can experience a whole sea of feelings when starting school. Help ease their worries with discussions and then toss those worries in the trash! After reading the story, have students brainstorm a list of reasons why they were and Chester is anxious about starting school. Write each child's worry on a piece of paper and then have students line up. Position a wastebasket a few feet from the group. Have each child crumple his paper and then toss it toward the wastebasket until he makes it in. Encourage little ones to cheer as each worry makes it into the trash!

I don't know anyone.

162

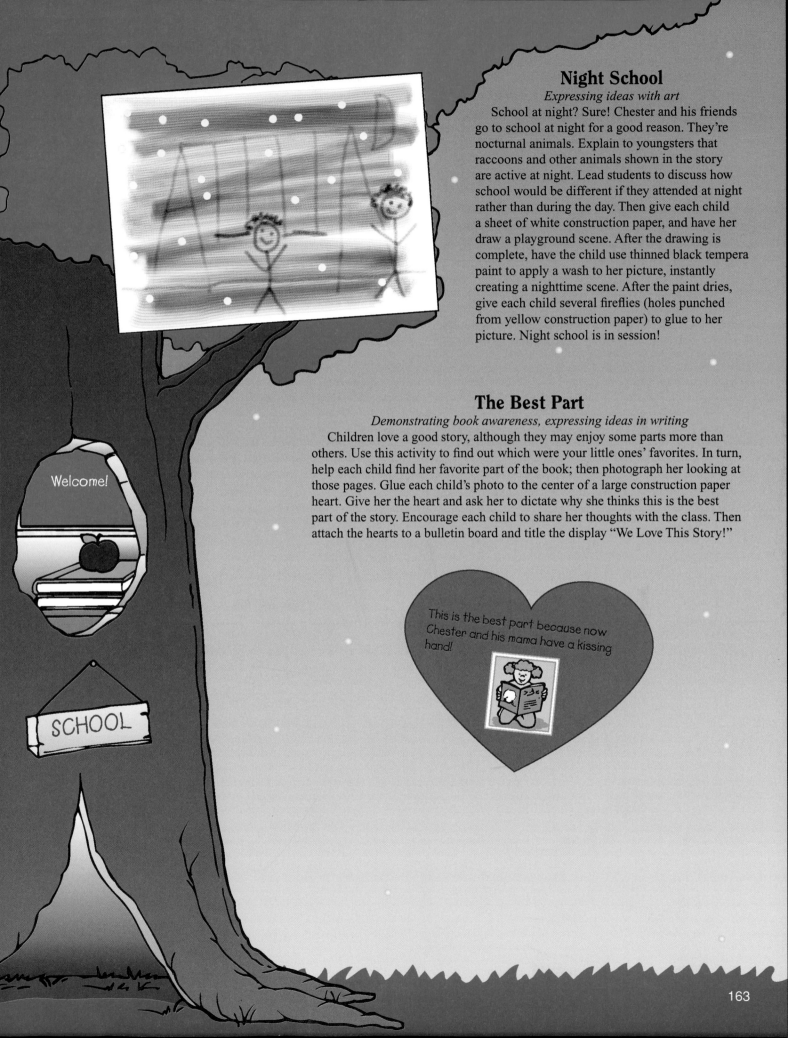

Night School

Expressing ideas with art

School at night? Sure! Chester and his friends go to school at night for a good reason. They're nocturnal animals. Explain to youngsters that raccoons and other animals shown in the story are active at night. Lead students to discuss how school would be different if they attended at night rather than during the day. Then give each child a sheet of white construction paper, and have her draw a playground scene. After the drawing is complete, have the child use thinned black tempera paint to apply a wash to her picture, instantly creating a nighttime scene. After the paint dries, give each child several fireflies (holes punched from yellow construction paper) to glue to her picture. Night school is in session!

The Best Part

Demonstrating book awareness, expressing ideas in writing

Children love a good story, although they may enjoy some parts more than others. Use this activity to find out which were your little ones' favorites. In turn, help each child find her favorite part of the book; then photograph her looking at those pages. Glue each child's photo to the center of a large construction paper heart. Give her the heart and ask her to dictate why she thinks this is the best part of the story. Encourage each child to share her thoughts with the class. Then attach the hearts to a bulletin board and title the display "We Love This Story!"

This is the best part because now Chester and his mama have a kissing hand!

THE VERY HUNGRY CATERPILLAR
by Eric Carle

The Very Hungry Caterpillar

Written and Illustrated by Eric Carle

Join a ravenous caterpillar as he eats his way through the days of the week. By Saturday he has eaten so much he has a tummyache. But the caterpillar knows what to do. He eats a leaf and spins a chrysalis, and two weeks later he emerges as a beautiful butterfly!

ideas by Suzanne Moore, Irving, TX

Caterpillar Lotto

Children delight in playing this lively lotto game featuring the foods the caterpillar eats in the story. To prepare the game for two players, make two white construction paper copies of the gameboards on pages 166 and 167. Color the pages so that the same foods are the same colors. Laminate the pages; then cut out the food pictures from one copy of each page to make playing cards. To play, give each player a gameboard, shuffle the cards, and then place the cards facedown in a stack. The first child takes a card from the top of the stack. If he has a matching food on his board, he puts the card on top of it. If he does not have a match, he returns his card to the bottom of the pile. Play alternates between players until both students have covered their boards. Lotto!

Feed the Caterpillar

Youngsters have fun feeding this always hungry caterpillar. In advance, make a copy of pages 166 and 167. Color the pictures, laminate them, and then cut out the food picture cards (or use the cards made for "Caterpillar Lotto" on this page). Next, create a caterpillar by covering a cylindrical oatmeal or raisin container with green construction paper. Cut a mouth in the plastic lid and glue construction paper eyes and antennae to the lid to create a caterpillar face. To play, have each child mix up the food cards and then retell the story by slipping each food card into the caterpillar's mouth in order. Munch, munch!

Where Will You Fly?

This simple bulletin board project will really spark students' imaginations. Ask children to brainstorm where the butterfly goes after the book ends; accept all student suggestions. Next, have each child cut several colors of tissue paper into small pieces. Then have her fill a snack-size resealable plastic bag with the pieces. Seal her bag and then twist a pipe cleaner around the middle of the bag to create antennae. Staple each child's butterfly to a piece of 9" x 12" blue construction paper. Then have the child draw to show where the butterfly might go. Write her dictation on her paper. Mount the completed projects on a bulletin board titled "Where Will You Fly?"

The butterfly will fly to the park.

Macy

Making Changes

Revisit *The Very Hungry Caterpillar* with your students, pointing out some of the stages of a butterfly's life cycle. Explain that a butterfly starts out as an egg, becomes a caterpillar, forms a chrysalis, and then becomes a butterfly. Then set up this simple art center to reinforce the sequence of a butterfly's life cycle. In advance, dye a supply of large pasta shells with dye made by mixing brown food coloring paste with rubbing alcohol. (You can also combine red and green food coloring to make brown, but the color will not be as vibrant.) You'll also need to dye a supply of bow-tie pasta red, yellow, and blue in the same way. Stock a center with a class supply of colored paper plates, each of which has been divided into four sections. Also supply glue, dry orzo, and uncooked rigatoni, along with the dyed pasta. Explain that the orzo represents the egg, the rigatoni represents the caterpillar, the large shell represents the chrysalis, and the bow-tie pasta represents the butterfly. Make a sample of the completed project to display for correct sequencing of the life cycle. Then have each student glue the items representing the different stages of the life cycle in sequential order on her plate. Ah, the life of a butterfly!

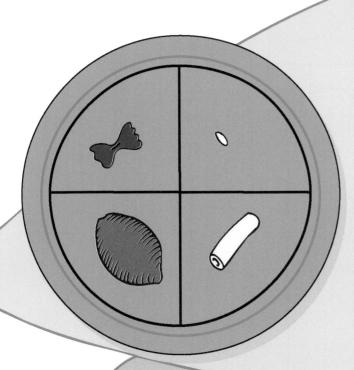

Caterpillar Snack

Students are ready to munch when they make and eat this fun caterpillar snack! Provide each child with a scoop of canned fruit cocktail and a straw. Have him use the straw to pierce each fruit piece, making a hole just like the ones the caterpillar makes. Then invite each child to eat his fruity snack!

Caterpillar Lotto

strawberry	plum	pear	apple
pickle	ice cream	cake	orange

©The Mailbox® • TEC41018 • April/May 2005

Note to the teacher: Use with "Caterpillar Lotto" and "Feed the Caterpillar" on page 164.

Caterpillar Lotto

pie	leaf
lollipop	watermelon
salami	cupcake
cheese	sausage

©The Mailbox® • TEC41018 • April/May 2005

Note to the teacher: Use with "Caterpillar Lotto" and "Feed the Caterpillar" on page 164.

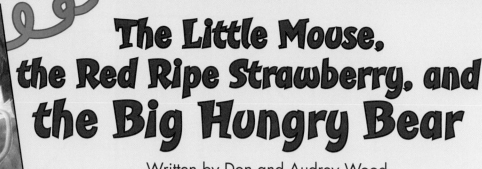

The Little Mouse, the Red Ripe Strawberry, and the Big Hungry Bear

Written by Don and Audrey Wood
Illustrated by Don Wood

Your little ones will delight in this sweet story as a mouse tries one thing after another to save its delicious strawberry from a big hungry bear. In the end, the mouse is tricked into sharing its strawberry with the narrator. After hearing the story, your students will be ready to share some strawberries with each other!

ideas by Roxanne LaBell Dearman, Western NC Early Intervention Program for Children Who Are Deaf or Hard of Hearing, Charlotte, NC

Strawberry Sequence
Sequencing a story

After sharing the story with students, engage them in this small-group sequencing activity. You will need two red craft foam strawberry cutouts, a Velcro fastener, a brown construction paper dirt mound, a length of chain, a pair of disguise glasses, and a plastic knife. Attach the hook side of a piece of Velcro fastener to one berry cutout and attach the loop side to the other cutout so that the two cutouts will stick together. Discuss with students the different ways the mouse protects its strawberry. Then guide youngsters to use the props to retell the story. When it's time to share the strawberry, use the plastic knife to "cut" the strawberry into two pieces. Place the items in a center and encourage each child to retell the story using the props. Nice sequencing!

Bear's Berry
Following directions, playing a game

The mouse hides the strawberry, and youngsters will too when they play this fun game. Cut out a small red construction paper strawberry. Have students sit in a circle. Give each child a paper cup and have her turn it upside down on the floor. Then choose one child to be the bear. While the bear covers her eyes, have the class pass the strawberry around the circle. After a short time say, "Stomp! Stomp! Sniff! Sniff!" to indicate that the bear is coming. At this time, have the child left holding the strawberry hide it under her cup. Then tell the bear to uncover her eyes as the group says, "Bear, Bear, who has your berry?" Instruct the bear to name classmates' names. As a name is called, the child lifts her cup to show whether she has the berry. When the berry is found, that child becomes the new bear and the game continues. Stomp! Stomp! Sniff! Sniff!

Mr. Strawberry Head
Using fine-motor skills, reenacting part of a story
One way the mouse tries to hide the strawberry is by disguising it with a big nose and glasses. Give your preschoolers a chance to act out this part of the story by placing Mr. Potato Head parts and red play dough at your play dough center. Demonstrate for youngsters how to form a strawberry shape from the play dough and then disguise it by pressing the facial parts into the dough. Where's the strawberry?

Sharing a Story
Writing
The mouse is eager to share its strawberry, and your little ones will be too when they complete this writing activity. Program a paper plate as shown for each child. Have him dictate an ending to the sentence as you write his response on the plate. Instruct him to draw a picture to illustrate his dictation. Then give each child a red construction paper strawberry cutout. Have him cut the berry in half, glue one piece to his plate, and then write his name to complete the project. Let's eat!

I will share my strawberry with Grandma.
Kevin

Two Halves Make a Whole
Counting, matching numerals to sets
This simple game shows youngsters that two halves make a whole. In advance, cut out six red construction paper strawberry shapes. Write a different number from 1 to 6 on each cutout. Draw the corresponding number of seeds on the back of each berry; then laminate the berries for durability. Cut each berry in half and place the pieces at a center. Have each child position the halves to create six whole berries, making sure the numbers are formed correctly and the sets match the numbers. Now that's a whole lot of fun!

Red Leaf, Yellow Leaf

Written and Illustrated by Lois Ehlert

Lois Ehlert's striking book takes its readers through the life of a sugar maple tree—from seed to beautiful fall leaves!

ideas by Roxanne LaBell Dearman—Preschool
Western NC Early Intervention Program for Children Who Are Deaf or Hard of Hearing
Charlotte, NC

Tree Parts
Reading for information

There's more to trees than leaves and trunks! Youngsters learn this as they listen to the story. Before reading the book, ask your little arborists to name as many parts of trees as they can. List them on chart paper as they are named. As you read the story, have students listen for the tree parts that were named and for any different parts heard in the story. Revisit the chart and add to it any new tree parts that students learned while listening to the story. What a "tree-mendous" way to discover the wonderful world of trees!

Trees
leaves
bark
trunk
branches

Tree Tale
Sequencing, story retelling

After reading the story, give your little ones a chance to retell the tale of the sugar maple tree. Ahead of time, make a class set plus one of the sequencing cards on page 172. Color, laminate, and cut out one copy of page 172. Gather a small group of students and have them match the sequencing cards to the corresponding pictures in the book. Discuss with youngsters each season the tree experiences. Then have the group put the cards in order. Give each child her own copy of page 172 to color and then cut out. Encourage students to take their season sequencing cards home to retell the story.

Favorite Fall Fun
Story extension, completing a sentence

The narrator of the story says that fall is his favorite time for you to come visit his tree. Then he asks whether you can guess why. Allow little ones to guess. Extend this idea of fall fun into a class book. Give each child a paper programmed as shown. Provide each child with small yellow and red tissue paper squares and glue. Have him crumple the tissue paper squares and glue them on and under the tree as desired. Then instruct him to dictate why he likes fall to complete the sentence on his paper. Invite each child to share his page with the class; then bind all the pages into a class book. Your students will not want to "leaf" this class book alone!

I like fall because I get to play in the leaves.

Tree Treats
Following directions

The character in the story hangs treats on his tree for birds in the winter. Have children make similar treats for birds near your school. Provide each child with a bagel half, a plastic knife, birdseed, and peanut butter. Help each child tie a string through the hole in his bagel for hanging. Have him spread peanut butter on one side of the bagel. Next, instruct him to sprinkle birdseed on the peanut butter. Hang the feeders on a nearby tree. Mmm! Treats for the birds!

Sneaky Squirrels
Following directions, group chant

The sneaky squirrels in this story steal some of the sugar maple seeds. Can your class help find them? Play this game and find out! Make a sugar maple seed cutout from tagboard and a construction paper leaf for each child. Seat students on the floor and place a leaf cutout in front of each child. Choose a child to be It. Have one child place the seed beneath his leaf as It shields her eyes. Have the group chant, "Squirrel, Squirrel, where's your seed?" Invite It to guess who has the seed. As children are named, instruct them to lift their leaves to show whether the seed is hidden beneath. The child with the seed will now be It. Continue to play for a desired length of time. Those sneaky squirrels!

Winter

Spring

Summer

Fall

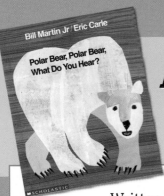

Polar Bear, Polar Bear, What Do You Hear?

Written by Bill Martin Jr.
Illustrated by Eric Carle
This classic picture book introduces readers to animal sounds around the zoo and to the critters that create them. Little ones will love listening to the growling, roaring, snorting sounds in the story. Then your girls and boys will be ready to make their own kinds of critter noise!

ideas by Lucia Kemp Henry, Fallon, NV

Talk Like the Animals
Recalling story characters, oral language
Polar Bear and the other zoo animals make lots of interesting sounds, from roars to bellows! Invite little ones to recall each animal character and repeat the word in the text describing its sound. Then review each animal illustration as you invite youngsters to make the animal's sound. Have students compare one animal's sound when two different children make it. Then challenge youngsters to vary a specific animal's sound by making it loud, soft, long, or short. Hmm, what will you hear when little ones make polar bear sounds in your ear?

Gael

Ooh, ooh, ooh!

Polar Bear's Animal Pals
Recalling story characters, exploring art
Review and discuss the animal illustrations in the book with youngsters. Then invite each child to do an easel painting of her favorite story animal. Next, ask each child to share her painting with the class. Encourage her to make sounds to represent what her animal might sound like. Write the sound phonetically on her paper. Display each child's animal on a bulletin board titled "What Do You Hear at the Zoo?" When the board is complete, point to each animal and have youngsters make the appropriate sound. Now that's a zoo where sounds abound!

173

Polar Bear Puppets
Following directions

Since Polar Bear is the title animal of the story, he makes a great puppet character to enhance students' oral language experiences. To make a puppet, give each child a white copy of the bear patterns on page 175. Help each youngster cut out the puppet pieces. Assist her in folding the head and gluing it to the sides of a white paper lunch bag as shown. Have each child glue the legs and the tail to the bag. Invite each child to stretch white cotton balls to make fur and glue it to the sides of the bag. Direct little ones to use their puppets for "What Does Polar Bear Hear?" on this page or to use them as they retell the story.

What Does Polar Bear Hear?
Using oral language

Polar Bear will hear more than growls with this imaginative activity, which focuses on the /b/ sound! Have students sit in a circle with their polar bear puppets from "Polar Bear Puppets" on this page. Hold up a bear puppet of your own and chant, "Polar Bear, Polar Bear, what *B* word do you hear?" Pretend to whisper in your puppet's ear; then have it answer you by saying, "I hear a teacher whispering [*balloon*] in my ear." Next, have the group chant, "Polar Bear, Polar Bear, what do you hear?" Prompt each child, in turn, to whisper in her bear's ear and imitate her bear by saying, "I hear [child's own name] whispering [*bell*] in my ear." Invite each child to whisper a different *B* word to her bear. Record each youngster's word on a bear-shaped chart.

Sensory Table Sounds
Making observations, motor skills

If Polar Bear were in the Arctic and not in the zoo, he'd be listening for sounds around him in the land of ice and snow. To give students a similar sense-filled experience, hide a large jingle bell, a baby rattle, a small tambourine, and a squeaky dog toy in your sensory table under a layer of quilt batting (snow) and bubble wrap (ice). Invite a small group of students to join you at the table and pretend to be polar bears listening to sounds coming from under the ice! Ask a volunteer to put his hands under the layers and feel to find an object without looking. Then ask the child to shake or squeeze the object without lifting the ice and snow, while the group listens. Prompt youngsters to discuss what the object might be. Then have the child take it out from under the layers to check their guesses. Continue this process until each item has been explored. Sounds cool!

Bear Patterns

Use with "Polar Bear Puppets" and "What Does Polar Bear Hear?" on page 174 and "After You Read" on page 150.

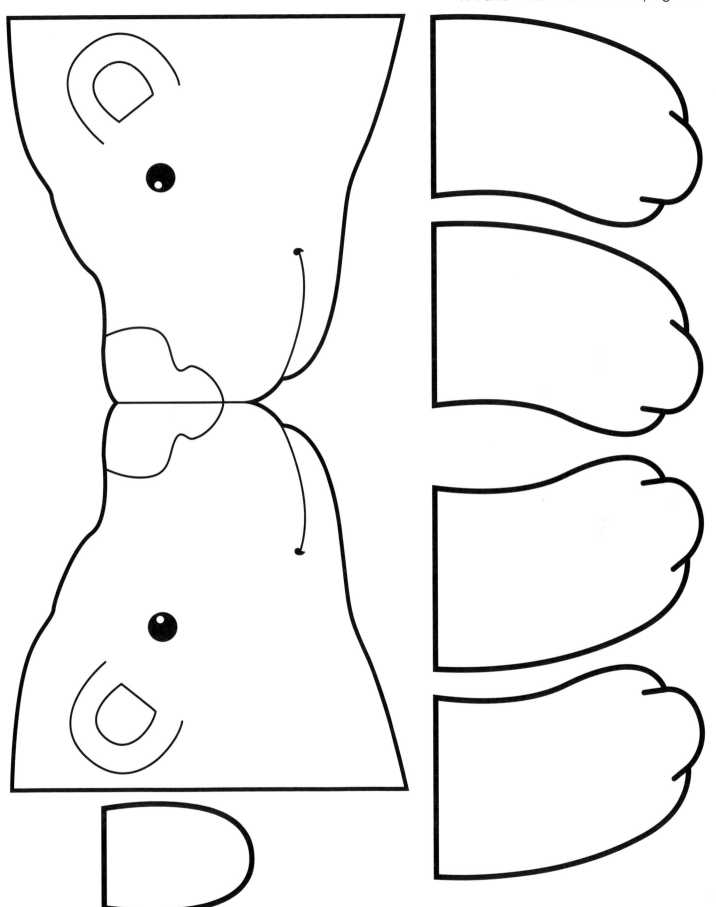

The Wind Blew

This rhyming story follows a wild wind that blows through a village snatching whatever object catches its fancy. The wind leads everyone to the edge of town, keeping their belongings just out of reach. Then, tiring of the game, the wind drops the items for owners to sort before whisking out to sea.

ideas by Janet Boyce, Cokato, MN

Wild Wind

Retelling a story

Grab a parachute and items from the story to blow up a wild wind. Gather the following items: a parachute, an umbrella cut from craft foam, a soft sponge ball (balloon), a craft store top hat, a shirt, a handkerchief, a newspaper, letters, two scarves, a wig, and a kite and flag cut from craft foam. Gather students around the parachute and begin to shake it gently. Retell the story together, tossing the story elements onto the parachute as youngsters recall each one. After all the props are on the parachute, have students shake it wildly. Have the wind drop all of the items by lowering the parachute to the floor. Breezy fun!

The Blowing Wind

Sequencing story events

This sequencing idea will have youngsters thinking about what item the wind catches next in the story. To prepare, make a copy of the sequencing cards on page 178. Color and cut out the cards. Purchase a Mylar helium balloon with a long string. Position the balloon at the front of your reading area. As you read the story, have a volunteer choose the corresponding sequencing card and then use a paper clip to barely clip it to the string. Continue in this manner until all of the cards have been clipped to the string. At the end of the story when the wind mixes up the items and releases them, twirl the string to allow the cards to fall to the floor. Encourage youngsters to retell the story using the cards.

Blow, Wind, Blow!

Using eye-hand coordination

Youngsters blow up a storm with this eye-hand coordination activity! Give each child a feather and have her hold it as high as she can. Instruct her to drop the feather and watch it float to the floor. Next, have youngsters drop their feathers and try to catch them on the way down. Progressively add difficulty to this exercise by having youngsters clap before catching the feather or blow it to keep it in the air. Blow, wind, blow!

What Did the Wind Blow Away?

Using visual discrimination

After reading the story, play this visual memory game with students. Make a copy of the sequencing cards on page 178 or use the set made for "The Blowing Wind" on page 176. Choose four cards and place them in front of a small group of students for them to look at. Cover the cards with a sheet of newspaper. Pretend that a gust of wind blows by; secretly remove one of the cards from under the paper. Show students the remaining cards and have them guess which card was removed. After several rounds, add extra cards to the mix for an added challenge.

Follow the Wind

Following directions

Little ones will be eager to fall in line and follow the leader with this activity. Carry the balloon purchased for "The Blowing Wind" on page 176 and have youngsters line up behind you. Take students outside and pretend to be the wind, leading them around, over, between, and under obstacles on the playground. Talk about each direction as students complete it. End the game by pretending to let the wind carry the balloon out to sea!

Sequencing Cards

Use with "The Blowing Wind" on page 176 and "What Did the Wind Blow Away?" on page 177.

CENTER UNITS

Munch a Bunch of Lunch Centers

Ring the lunch bell! This collection of lunch-related center ideas is sure to get your little ones hungry for preschool learning!

ideas contributed by Jana Sanderson, Rainbow School, Stockton, CA

❊ Math Center ❊
Lunch of All Sorts

Sorting by food type

Sorting lunch yummies is fun and engaging for little ones! Gather three lunchboxes. On the inside of each box, attach a picture of a different food type—fruit, sandwich, or drink. Seal the pictures with clear Con-Tact covering. Next, gather play foods or food pictures cut from magazines for sorting. Store the foods or pictures in a small picnic basket. To use the center, spread out a blanket and invite youngsters to name the foods as they sort them into the appropriate lunchboxes. What's in your lunchbox?

❊ Gross-Motor Area ❊
A "Soup-er" Lunch

Hand-eye coordination, exploring real-life experiences through pretend play

One bowl of split pea soup coming right up! Fill your empty water table with dried green split peas and add a few props, such as bowls, ladles, and spoons. Using the utensils, a visiting student ladles out several bowls full of split pea soup, while being careful not to spill a single pea!

❋ Games Center ❋
Ham and Cheese, Please!

Identifying colors, coloring to match

Hungry for a color-awareness activity for your little ones? This game is sure to whet your appetite! Photocopy the booklet pages on pages 184 and 185. Cut each page section apart and then glue the sections together where indicated. Make a tagboard copy of the spinner on page 185 and then color it as shown. Attach a paper clip with a brad to complete the spinner. Working with a small group, provide each child with the prepared booklet pages to use as a game strip and crayons (pink, green, yellow, orange, and brown). Invite each child, in turn, to spin the spinner, name the color and the ingredient, and then color the appropriate sandwich ingredient on his strip to match. When strips are completely colored, assist each child in accordian-folding his game strip to create a sandwich booklet. Encourage each child to take his booklet home and discuss the colors of each ingredient with his family. Yum!

❋ Art Center ❋
Sack Lunch

Fine-motor skills, art expression

Fun is served when your youngsters decorate these lunch bags! They'll not only look good, but they'll smell nice too! To make fruit paint, pour a packet of sugar-free fruit-flavored drink mix in a cup. Mix in two tablespoons of water. Make several kinds of paint using different fruit scents. Provide each child with a white lunch bag, a paintbrush, and access to the fruit paints. Have each child smell a paint and determine the fruit smell. Then have her paint the corresponding fruit on her bag. Encourage her to continue decorating her bag until it's covered with fruity paintings. Send the bags home with youngsters to use to bring their next day's snacks or lunches to school!

Play Dough Center

Play Dough Cuisine

Fine-motor skills, exploring real-life experiences through play

Your play dough center will be bustling with little lunch chefs. Add some new utensils to this center, such as plastic pizza cutters, mini rolling pins, cookie cutters, and mini muffin tins. Also add plates, cups, napkins, and silverware to the center. Invite youngsters to visit the center to play restaurant. Have the cooks take orders and prepare play dough food while the patrons pretend to eat and then pay. After some time of play encourage youngsters to switch roles and play again. I'll have a play dough pizza, please!

Literacy Center

Order Up!

Matching like symbols

Visual-discrimination skills are sure to stack up during this sandwich-matching activity! Make four copies of the booklet pages on pages 184 and 185. Color each set of the patterns on the booklet pages as desired and then cut them out. Label each set with a different letter or symbol. Then label each of four paper plates with a different corresponding symbol. Place the plates and sandwich patterns at the center. A child matches the symbols on the sandwich patterns to make a complete sandwich and then puts it on the correct plate. After she shows her work to an adult, have her mix up the sandwich fixings to ready the center for the next student!

Tacos, Burritos, and More

Exploring real-life experiences through pretend play

Spice up your dramatic-play center by setting up a taco stand. Stock your center with tortillas (tan felt circles), meat (small brown pom-poms), cheese (shredded orange paper), lettuce (green felt strips), and tomatoes (spool-painted felt circles, cut in half). Also include spoons, bowls, plates, tongs, and waxed paper squares for wrapping tacos. Invite your preschoolers to spoon ingredients onto the felt tortillas and either fold for tacos or roll for burritos to serve customers. To prepare the center for the next participants, have the child return each ingredient to its original container. Olé for flavorful fun!

Dry Versus Fresh

Recognizing similarities and differences

Here's a fresh idea for stimulating your preschoolers' senses and adding variety to their lunchboxes. For each child, put a dried banana chip, a raisin, a piece of candied pineapple, and a dried apple ring on one half of a plate. On the other half, put a banana slice, half a purple grape, a pineapple tidbit, and an apple slice. Instruct youngsters at the center to observe, feel, and smell each food item. Next, have each child match his fresh fruit pieces with his dried fruit pieces. Have students at the center discuss the similarities and differences between each pair of foods. Then invite each child to munch on his fruity foods.

Booklet Pages
Use with "Ham and Cheese, Please!" on page 181 and "Order Up!" on page 182.

1

©The Education Center, Inc. • *The Mailbox*®

2

Glue page 3 here.

3

4

Glue page 5 here.

5

Ask me to name the color of each ingredient in my sandwich booklet.

6

Spinner Pattern
Use with "Ham and Cheese, Please!" on page 181.

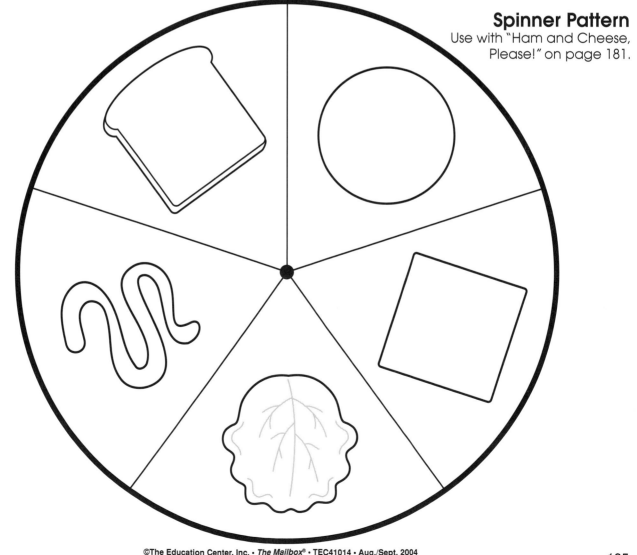

Sensational Snowmen

When it's cold outside, nothing's hotter for your centers than snowmen! Youngsters will warm up to these fun centers in no time!

ideas by Suzanne Moore, Alvin, TX

Snowman Match

These sassy snowmen will perk up your flannelboard center and reinforce letter-matching skills too. To prepare, make six copies of the snowman and hat patterns on page 189. Color each snowman's buttons and hat and label each pair with a matching letter as shown. Laminate the patterns and then cut them out. Attach a piece of self-adhesive felt to the back of each pattern to ready it for flannelboard use. Place the patterns in a basket near a flannelboard. Invite a pair of children to the center. In turn, have each child draw a snowman and hat from the basket. Instruct him to look at the letter on each pattern and determine whether they match. If they do, have him attach the patterns to the flannelboard. If they don't match, instruct him to return the patterns to the basket. Have his partner check his work and then switch roles.

Build It

There's no snow required for this clever snowman-building activity! In advance, stuff several small, medium, and large white plastic bags with newspaper or packing peanuts. Use permanent markers to draw faces on the small bags and to draw buttons on the medium-size bags. Then invite youngsters to don their mittens and get busy pretending to roll and stack the snowballs to build snowmen. Building snowmen couldn't be more fun!

186

Colorful Snowmen

Who said snowmen have to be white? In advance, stock your art center with a supply of large round coffee filters and three bowls of water tinted with food coloring (red, blue, and yellow). Give each child three coffee filters and have her stack and then fold them several times. Instruct her to dip each corner of the filters into a different bowl of colored water. Help her unfold the filters and lay them on paper towels or newsprint to dry. Encourage students to name the colors they see on the filters. They'll be surprised to discover colors other than red, yellow, and blue. Explain to little ones that when two colors mix, a new color is made.

After the filters have dried, cut one of each child's filters into a smaller circle. Have each student glue her filters into a snowman shape on a 12" x 18" sheet of construction paper. Stock the center with plenty of craft materials to complete these colorful snow characters, such as crayons, pom-poms, sticky dots, crepe paper, construction paper scraps, and glue. Mount the completed projects on a bulletin board titled "Colorful Snowmen."

Copycat Snowmen

No two snowmen are alike—except the ones you'll find created by students at this center. In advance, cut two large snowman shapes from poster board. Stock your blocks center with the snowman shapes. To play, pair students and have one child use blocks to make a face on his snowman cutout. Then have him add blocks to represent buttons. Next, encourage his partner to duplicate the snowman, using the same number and colors of blocks. Have the two students clear their snowman shapes and start again, this time with the other child designing the snowman to be copied. Snowman twins—cool!

Snowy Dough

Brrr! It's cold outside! Bring some of the coldness into your classroom with this chilly play dough idea. Begin by mixing up a batch of your favorite play dough; then knead in some iridescent glitter. Chill the play dough in the refrigerator before placing it in your play dough center. Encourage your little ones to roll the dough into balls to make snowmen. Stock the center with rolling pins, plastic snowman cookie cutters, craft sticks (snowman arms), and craft foam facial feature cutouts.

Snowmen—Beach Style

No snow? No worries! Simply dampen the sand in your sand table and provide various sizes of ice-cream scoops along with craft sticks and twigs, and encourage students to create snowmen—beach style! Have each child gently use the point of a pencil to "draw" facial features on her snowman. For added interest, provide miniature straw hats, found at your local craft store, and lengths of ribbon to serve as snappy scarves for these sandy snowmen.

Just Add Eyes

Your little ones will really enjoy throwing themselves—and a couple of black pom-poms—into this easy-to-create center. Begin by drawing a large snowman on bulletin board paper and then taping it to the floor in a corner of your classroom. Add facial features to the snowman, using orange vinyl tape for the nose and black tape for the mouth and buttons, but do not add eyes. Stock the center with two black jumbo-size pom-poms (eyes). Have each child stand on a designated spot and toss each pom-pom eye onto the snowman. If he misses, have him try one more time before passing the eyes to the next child. Fun!

Bunnies and Baskets

Hop to it and try these super seasonal ideas for your classroom centers!

by Ada Goren, Winston-Salem, NC

Craft Center
Bunny Headbands
Following directions

A few centers will be even more fun if your youngsters wear bunny headbands as they play. Make them easily by duplicating the bunny patterns on pages 194 and 195. Color, cut out, and laminate the bunny cutouts; then staple each one to a sentence strip headband.

Reading Area
Read to Your Bunny
Reading

Encourage youngsters to read aloud to some bunny friends when you give your reading area a quick face-lift! Replace your usual bookshelves or boxes with pretty Easter baskets full of books! Then add a number of appealing stuffed bunnies to the area. Invite a child to pick out a rabbit and a book and read aloud to her new bunny buddy!

Sensory Center
Don't Put All Your Eggs in One Basket!
Matching colors

Use a *few* baskets instead! To set up this color-sorting center, partially fill your sensory tub or table with plastic Easter grass. Then hide plastic eggs of a few different colors in the grass. Collect a basket to match each egg color, or simply tie a matching colored ribbon to the handle of a basket for each color. Encourage a child at this center to find the eggs and put each one in its corresponding basket. When he's found them all, he can hide them again for the next egg seeker.

Math Center
"Eggs-ploring" Capacity
Understanding capacity
All you need for this center are at least three Easter baskets in various sizes and a large supply of plastic eggs. Encourage youngsters to predict how many of the eggs will fit in each size basket. Which basket will hold the fewest? The most? Have your little ones fill the baskets and count the eggs that fit in each one.

Block Center
A Hopping Good Hunt!
Problem solving, sorting
Prepare for an egg hunt in your classroom by sticking egg and bunny stickers to some of the wooden blocks in your collection. Put the stickered blocks in a special basket. Have one child at the center put on a bunny headband (see "Bunny Headbands" on page 190) and play the part of the Easter Bunny. Have her hide the "eggs" by placing the special blocks sticker side down among others on the floor. Then have other children hunt for them and collect them in their own baskets. After all the special blocks are found, have everyone work together to sort the bunnies and eggs into two piles. Then put all the special blocks back in a basket for the next Easter Bunny to hide.

Art Center
Bunny-Tail Painting
Following directions
You've painted with brushes and sponges, but how about bunny tails? Use this fun technique to create some beautiful Easter egg art! For each child, cut a large egg shape from white construction paper. Put an assortment of powdered tempera paint colors on separate paper plates. Then clip several cotton balls (bunny tails) with clothespins. Have a group of children sit at a table; give each child an egg shape. Lightly mist each child's egg with water from a spray bottle. Then have each youngster dip a bunny tail into powdered tempera paint and shake or tap it against her finger to sprinkle the paint all over her egg shape, redipping as necessary. She may repeat the process with one or two other colors of paint. Allow these creations to dry before displaying them for your proud preschoolers!

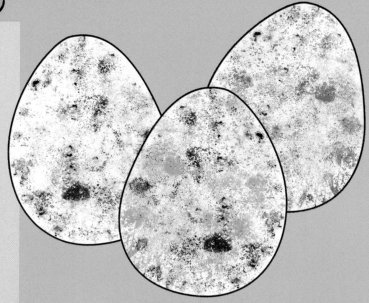

Literacy Center
"Ears" to You!

Matching letters, matching uppercase and lowercase letters
Have your little bunnies practice matching letters with this activity! To prepare, make several copies of the bunny head pattern on page 195. Program each set of ears with letters your preschoolers have studied. Or, for older preschoolers, program the ears with matching uppercase and lowercase letters. Cut out the bunny heads and cut off the ears; then store them in a basket at your literacy center. Have a child lay the bunny heads on a tabletop and then find a matching set of ears for each bunny.

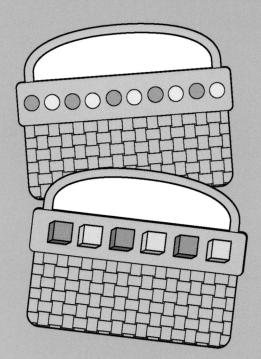

Manipulative Area
Basket Patterns

Patterning
A tisket, a tasket, let's make some pretty baskets! Invite your youngsters to create some beautiful baskets as they practice patterning with manipulatives. To prepare, make several copies of the basket pattern on page 196. Color the baskets, cut them out, and laminate them for durability. Put the baskets in your manipulatives area along with a variety of manipulatives, such as colored wooden cubes or flower counters. Ask a child at this center to choose a manipulative and create a simple AB pattern along the basket rim.

For a take-home activity, simply make a class supply of the basket pattern. Have each child color a basket and then create a rim pattern with spring-themed stickers or pastel sticky dots.

Dramatic Play
Easter Bunny's Egg Factory

Using imagination through play
Put your little bunnies to work at the Easter Bunny's egg factory! Transform your dramatic-play area into the Easter Bunny's workshop by adding numerous baskets, play dough for molding eggs, bunny- and egg-shaped candy molds from your local craft store, paper and crayons for drawing and coloring egg designs, a play phone for taking egg orders, and paper and pencils for creating lists of good boys and girls who should receive baskets. Then ask the factory workers to don bunny headbands (see "Bunny Headbands" on page 190) and get to work!

Games Center
Roll and Deliver
Counting

Invite a pair of preschool bunnies to practice counting as they deliver eggs! First, stock two large Easter baskets with an equal number of plastic eggs. Place the baskets at your games center, along with a die and a large box or tub partially filled with Easter grass. To play the game, each child takes a turn rolling the die. She identifies the number rolled and "delivers" a corresponding number of eggs by taking them from her basket and putting them into the box or tub. The first player to deliver all her eggs wins! Add to the fun by having students wear bunny headbands (see "Bunny Headbands" on page 190) as they play. And for even more counting practice, have students reverse the process by rolling the die and placing the eggs back in the baskets for the next pair to use!

Snack Center
Bunny Food
Following directions

Encourage your preschoolers to eat like rabbits as they make their own easy snacks at this center! Create simple pictorial directions like the ones shown; then set out a bowl of baby carrots or carrot sticks, paper plates, a squeeze bottle of ranch dressing, and a class supply of small condiment cups. A child at this center counts out five carrots, then squeezes some dressing into an itty-bitty basket (a condiment cup). Then he's ready to dip and eat this bunny treat!

Count 5.   Squeeze.   Dip.

Girl Bunny Head Pattern
Use with "Bunny Headbands" on page 190.

Boy Bunny Head Pattern

Use with "Bunny Headbands" on page 190 and "'Ears' to You" on page 192.

Basket Pattern
Use with "Basket Patterns" on page 192.

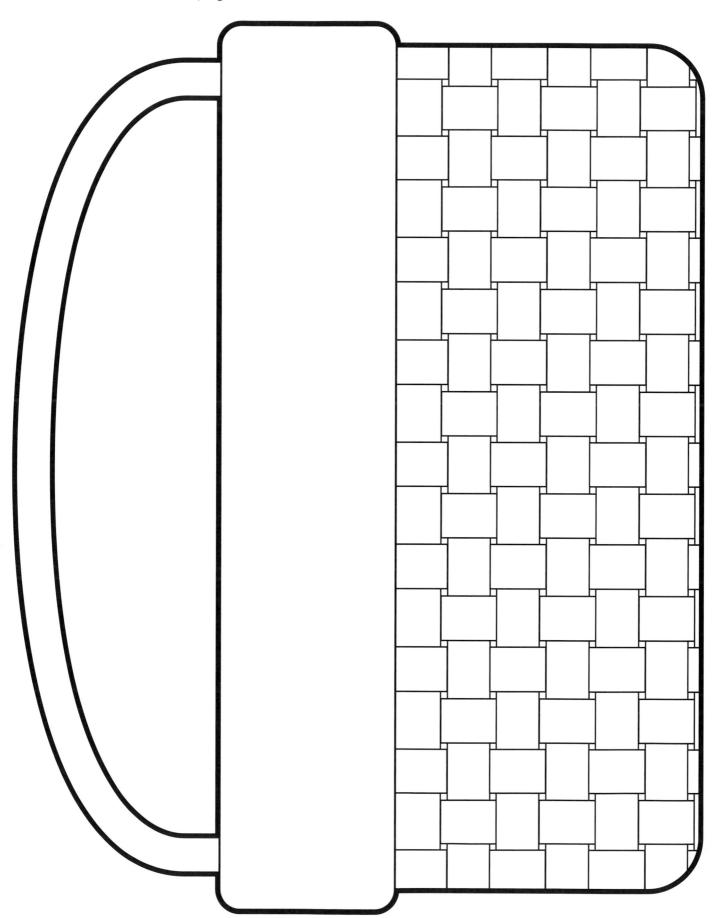

Fantastic Flower Centers

Learning is in full bloom when youngsters use this bouquet of center activities!

ideas by Gerri Primak

Dramatic Play Center
Flowers for Sale
Engaging in play

Calling all little florists! Transform your dramatic-play area into a fun-filled flower shop. Stock the center with a variety of real or artificial flowers, plastic vases, foam blocks, bows, ribbons, play dollar bills, and a toy cash register. Also provide blank cards for youngsters to use to add notes to their flower arrangements. Invite students who visit this center to set up a flower shop. Encourage them to play the roles of the florist, the cashier, and the customer. How fun!

Math Center
Every Seed Counts!
Counting, ordering numbers

Counting skills are sure to flourish when little ones "plant" seeds at this center! In advance, purchase five inexpensive plastic flowerpots (or use plastic cups). Label each flowerpot with a different numeral from 1 to 5. Place the flowerpots and a container with 15 large brown pom-poms (seeds) at a center. When a child visits the center, she identifies the number on a flowerpot. Then she counts out the corresponding number of seeds and places them in the pot. She continues in this manner for the remaining flowerpots. After all the seeds have been planted, the youngster then places the flowerpots in order from 1 to 5. Now that's a center to count on!

Art Center
Fanciful Flower Garden
Using fine-motor skills

It certainly looks like spring when youngsters make these bright and colorful flower gardens! Prepare a few homemade stamp pads by pouring different colors of paint into foam trays lined with damp paper towels. Cut green chenille stems in half to make a large supply. Provide each student with a strip of paper and a variety of flower-shaped sponges (you can make these by cutting flower shapes from sponges and hot-gluing them onto film canister handles). Invite her to use the supplies to create a colorful row of flowers. After the paint is dry, help each youngster tape a chenille stem to the back of each flower. Use the strips as a colorful bulletin board border or make a flower garden display. What a great way to brighten a rainy spring day!

Literacy Center
Letters in Bloom
Matching letters

A-tisket, a-tasket, a letter-flower basket. Youngsters are sure to enjoy matching a basketful of letter flowers to flower-pots at this sweet center. To prepare, make three colorful copies of the flower patterns on page 200. Cut out the patterns; then label each flower with a different letter and glue it to a green craft stick. Store the flowers in a basket. Program six plastic flowerpots (or plastic cups) each with a different letter to match a letter on a flower. Add a small amount of play dough inside each pot. Place the programmed pots and the flower basket at a center. A visiting youngster removes one flower from the basket and names its letter. Then he finds the matching pot and places the flower stem into the play dough. He continues in this manner until all the flowers have been matched to their flowerpots.

Blocks Center
A Flower Tower
Using spatial reasoning

Building giant flowers is sure to delight your little sprouts! Transform your large blocks into flowers and stems by using green construction paper strips and flower cutouts. In advance, enlarge or reduce the flower patterns on page 200 so that they are about the same size as your blocks. Copy the patterns onto various colors of construction paper; then cut them out. Tape the flowers and strips to a supply of blocks as shown. Place the flower and stem blocks at a center and invite little ones to build different sizes of flowers. Encourage them to compare sizes by using words such as *taller, smaller, shorter,* and *bigger.* What a unique way to make an oversize flower garden!

198

Game Center
Spinning for Petals
Recognizing numerals, counting

This counting game is a sure cure for spring fever! Make a tagboard copy of the spinner pattern on page 200; then cut it out. Poke a hole through the center and fasten a paper clip to it with a brad to complete the spinner. Also make a copy of the flowerpot pattern on page 201 for each student. Cut a supply of two-inch petal shapes from wallpaper samples or construction paper and store them in a container. Place the petal container, the copies, and the spinner at a center. When a pair visits the center, each student takes a flowerpot pattern. In turn, each player spins the spinner and identifies the number. Then he removes the corresponding number of petals from the container and places them around his flower. Play continues until each youngster's flower has petals all around the flower's center. Youngsters may then return the petals to the container and play again or glue the petals around their flowers' centers.

Writing Center
Say It With Soil
Using fine-motor skills, understanding left-to-right progression

Little ones dig getting their hands dirty while they practice writing at this center! To prepare, add a layer of potting soil to the bottom of two shallow boxes. Place them at a center along with various "writing tools" such as artificial flowers, plastic shovels, and craft stick flowers. Display a list of students' names, alphabet letters, or color words at the center. When a student visits the center, encourage her to choose a writing tool and write one of the posted words in the soil. Next, direct her to read the word and then smooth out the soil to erase her writing. Have her continue to write other words in this manner. Youngsters' writing skills are sure to grow!

Fine-Motor Center
Buds Are Blooming
Using fine-motor skills

Spring is in the air! These colorful blooming buds are a great way to welcome spring. At a center, cover a table with newspaper. Use four different colors of food coloring to tint four separate bowls of water. Place the tinted water, four eyedroppers, and a supply of coffee filters at the center. Invite a visiting youngster to take a coffee filter and flatten it out. Then have him use an eyedropper to squeeze drops of colored water onto his coffee filter, allowing the colors to blend together. After the water dries, help each youngster pinch the middle of his coffee filter and wrap a green chenille stem around the pinched area to create a flower with a stem. Then spread out the flower and watch it bloom!

199

Flower Patterns
Use with "Letters in Bloom" and
"A Flower Tower" on page 198.

Spinner Pattern
Use with "Spinning for Petals" on page 199.

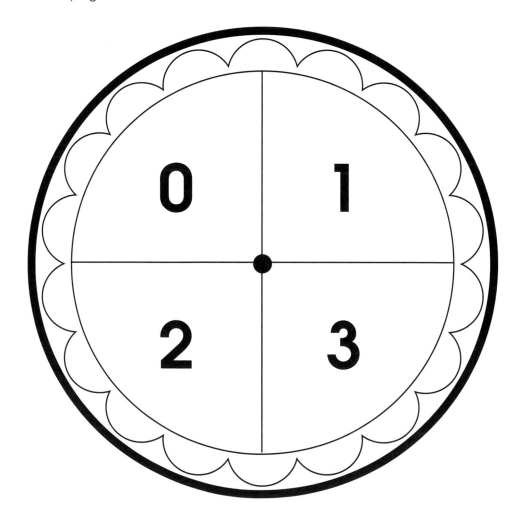

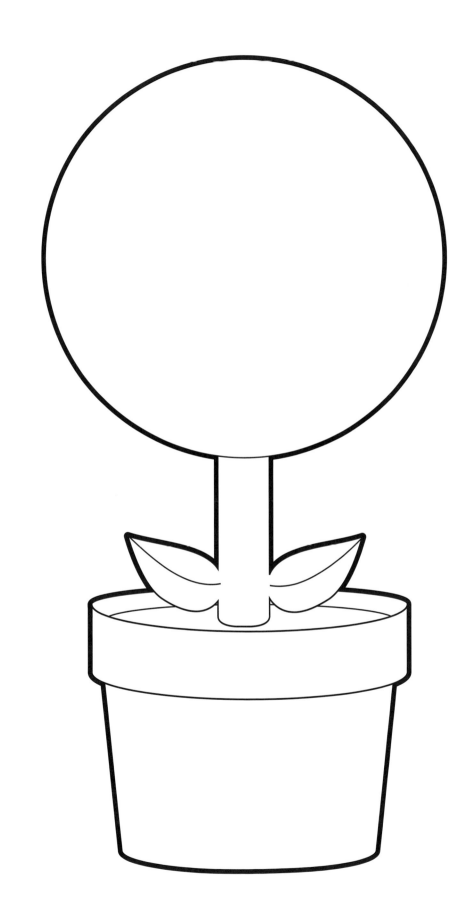

A Picnic? Perfect!

Pack a basket with these fun and easy ideas for lending
your classroom centers a picnic theme!

ideas by Ada Goren, Winston-Salem, NC

Discovery Center
What's in the Basket?

Have your preschoolers employ their sense of touch at this
center. Into a large handled basket, put several items that might
be used on a picnic, such as a paper plate, a plastic spoon, a
plastic cup, a napkin, and some plastic picnic foods from your
housekeeping center (such as an apple, a chicken leg, and a
banana). Lay a heavy towel over the top of the basket so the
items aren't visible. Have a child reach under the towel, feel an
item, and try to guess what it is before pulling it out to check
his guess. Have him continue in this manner until the basket is
empty.

Games Center
Picnic Memory

Plates are great for a game of Picnic Memory! Gather a
supply of paper plates; then make two copies of the picnic
patterns on page 206. (Discard one pair of ant patterns.)
Color the picture pairs identically; then cut them apart and
glue each picture to a separate paper plate. Lay the plates on
the floor in rows, picture side down. Have children play the
game like a traditional game of Memory. Or vary the game by
labeling paper plates with matching pairs of letters, numbers,
or shapes.

Reading Area
Teddy Bear Picnic
Spread a blanket in your reading area and add a few large handled baskets filled with appealing books. Also provide a few teddy bears that look hungry for a good story! Then invite a child at this center to select a book and a teddy. Have her sit on the blanket to read aloud to her stuffed friend.

Block Center
Tables for Teddies
What else might teddy bears need on a picnic? How about some tables and benches? Put some teddy bears in your block area for inspiration; then set your young builders to work making picnic tables and seats sized for the bears. Also provide a few large baskets so your builders can tote their blocks to the work site of their choice!

Math Center
Whoa! What a Watermelon!
Introduce your preschoolers to the idea of circumference with this picnic-perfect measurement idea! Purchase a small watermelon. Then cut a length of string or yarn to fit exactly around its middle. Next, cut a string that's too short and another that's too long. Display the watermelon in an empty water table in your math center, along with the three strings. Ask each child to estimate which string will exactly fit around the watermelon. Then have her test her choice by wrapping it around the watermelon. After the results have been discovered, cut and serve the melon for a cool summertime snack. Hey, measuring is easy!

Art Center
A Red and White Delight

Ask your petite picnickers to create these paper versions of a traditional red and white checkered picnic cloth—with a traditional picnic visitor! In advance, purchase plastic ants. Duplicate the checkerboard pattern on the back of the centerfold onto white construction paper to make a class supply. Then cut out eight 1½" x 1½" squares of red construction paper per child. At your art center, have a child glue a red square over each dotted square on her white paper. Finish the project by having her use a bit of tacky glue to attach a plastic ant to the cloth wherever she desires. It's picnic time!

Literacy Center
Letters? Check!

Here's a letter-perfect way to use a traditional red and white checkered tablecloth pattern! To prepare, make one copy of the checkerboard pattern on the back of the centerfold. Mask the dots on the pattern; then make several copies. On each sheet, program every other square with a letter to which students have been introduced. Color the remaining squares red. Laminate the letter boards for durability.

At your literacy center, set up the picnic cloths and a basket of magnetic letters. Have a child pull out a magnetic letter and match it to the letter on a square of the cloth. If he doesn't have the letter on his board, he puts the magnetic letter back in the basket. Have him continue until he has filled his board. "I found *M!*"

Play Dough Picnic

Roll your picnic theme into your play dough area by inviting
youngsters to create plates full of faux food! Provide various
shades of play dough, cookie cutters in basic shapes, and a paper
plate for each child. Demonstrate how to create picnic foods from
the basic shapes, such as by placing two white squares on either
side of a pink circle to represent a bologna sandwich, putting chips
on a tan circle cookie, or forming a yellow crescent for a banana.
Have each child create a few foods and display them on her plate.
Encourage little ones to show off their creations when center time
is over.

Snack Center

Picnic Mix

Put your youngsters' counting skills to work as they create
a simple snack to enjoy picnic-style! Set up bowls of Teddy
Grahams crackers, fish-shaped crackers, and cereal. Give
each child at this center a plastic bag; then have him follow
visual directions, such as those shown, to count out the
correct number of each type of snack food. Spread a blanket
nearby, and invite your preschoolers to sit down together to
enjoy their picnic mix!

Sensory Center

Watch Out for Ants!

Pack your basket, but watch out for those pesky ants! That's
the key to this sensory center idea. To prepare, make a few
copies of the picnic patterns on page 206 on tagboard. Color
the pictures if desired; then cut them apart. Hide them in a
sensory table partially filled with red and white crinkled paper
shreds. Give each child at this center a basket. Have her hunt
for foods to pack in her picnic basket. She can keep going until
she uncovers an ant. Then she has to empty her basket back
into the sensory table and start again!

Picnic Patterns

Use with "Picnic Memory" on page 202 and "Watch Out for Ants!" on page 205.

LITERACY UNITS

That's My Name!

To a preschooler, the most meaningful word in the world is his name. As he learns the letters of his own name, he begins to notice letters and their sounds in other names and words. Opportunities to recognize names are great literacy builders. This unit contains numerous nifty opportunities to help your preschoolers recognize and learn from their names.

Who's Here?

While they're bright eyed and bushy tailed, have your youngsters find their names as a way of taking the morning's attendance. For each child, program one side of an index card with her name and glue her photo on the other side. Laminate the cards for durability. Each morning, arrange the cards randomly in a pocket chart with students' names facing out. As each child arrives, ask her to find her name card and turn it over to show her smiling face. You can tell at a glance who's at school, and the children will get daily practice finding their names. There's no better way to start the day!

Kristin Niles—PreK ESE
Blackburn Elementary School
Palmetto, FL

My Name Marks the Spot

Call your little ones to circle time anytime with this musical invitation! In advance, prepare a name strip for each child. Invite each youngster to decorate his strip with stickers or stamps. Before circle time, arrange the name strips in your large group area. Then sing the first verse of the song below. Have each child find his name and have a seat! When circle time is over, sing the second verse and collect the name strips as students file past you and return to their seats. z

(sung to the tune of "London Bridge")

Find your name and sit right down,
Sit right down, sit right down.
Find your name and sit right down.
Let's have circle time!

Bring your name back up to me,
Up to me, up to me.
Bring your name back up to me.
See you next time!

Wanda R. Hostas—Three- and Four-Year-Olds
God's World Christian Child Care and Preschool
Prescott Valley, AZ

Scurrying Off to Centers

Send students scurrying off to centers with this useful name-recognition transition! Write each child's name on an individual index card. Before center time, scatter the cards randomly on the floor in your group area. Pick up one card at a time and ask if anyone recognizes the name on it as her own. After a child reads her name, invite her to choose a center or proceed to the one already selected. If a child doesn't recognize her name, invite classmates to help read the card or simply say her name; then allow her to choose a center.

Karyn Abele—PreK
Elmwood School
Syracuse, NY

Special Name, Special Helper

When a preschooler discovers that he has been selected to be a special helper, he'll have one more reason to consider his name special! First, create a name card for each child in your class. Stack the cards and bind them together with one or two metal rings. When you need a helper, randomly flip to a child's name card, show it to the group, and say, "This child may pick a book for me to read" or "This child may choose the next song we sing." Whenever you reach for the helper cards, your whole class will be eager to read the name you pick! In fact, it will help them learn to identify classmates' names too!

Jennifer Schear—Preschool
Clover Patch Preschool
Cedar Falls, IA

Where Is My Name?

Here's a name-recognition game you won't want to pass up! Have your little ones sit in a circle; then make each child his own name-and-picture card (or use the ones from "Who's Here?" on page 208). Play some music or simply sing a favorite song as students pass the name cards around the circle. When the music stops, have youngsters hold the cards with the names facing out. Choose a child and have him try to find his own name card. When he selects his name, have the child holding the card flip it over to reveal the picture. If it is the player's name card, he trades the card he's holding for his own card and returns to his spot. If not, he may guess again until he finds his own name.

Destiny Simms—Two- and Three-Year-Olds
Kiddie Academy Learning Centers
Laurel, MD

Magical Rubbings

Your students will really get a feel for their names with this activity, which engages their sense of touch! To prepare, write each child's name on a piece of tagboard. Trace over the letters with thick craft glue or gel glue; then allow the glue to dry thoroughly. Invite each youngster to locate his name strip among the others, run his fingers over the letters to feel their shapes, and name any letters he recognizes. Then have him make a name rubbing. Tape the name strip to a tabletop; then tape a sheet of paper over the strip. Have the child rub the side of a peeled crayon over the entire sheet of paper. Don't miss the look of delight when he sees his name emerge on the paper! It's magic!

Later, encourage children to choose classmates' names for rubbings too. Some children may start by making rubbings of names that have the same beginning letter as theirs.

Donna Pollhammer—Three-Year-Olds
YMCA Chipmunk Preschool
Westminster, MD

Mobile, Marvelous, and Mine!

These easy-to-make placemats will help your preschoolers with both name recognition and name writing. They're especially useful if you can't permanently label the tables in your room with students' names. To make a placemat, use a colorful sheet of paper with a fun seasonal border around the edge or add interest with stamps or die-cuts. Write a child's name near the center top. Then glue the placemats to tagboard, if desired, before laminating them for durability.

Each day, randomly put the placemats on your tables. Challenge each child to find his name and have a seat. Then pass out dry-erase markers and encourage each youngster to trace over his name and copy his name on the open space on his mat. The marker will wipe right off, and the placemat will be ready for more name recognition and writing practice on another day!

Jennifer Schear—Preschool
Clover Patch Preschool
Cedar Falls, IA

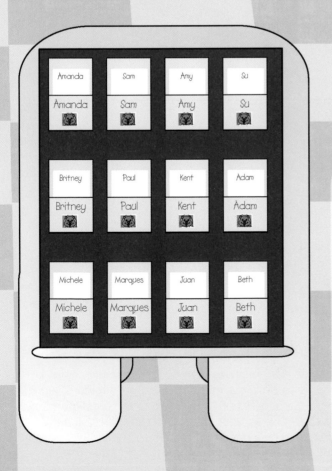

Pick Your Pocket

Make a name pocket for each child, and watch as your little ones not only recognize their names but learn to write their names on their projects too! To prepare, gather a class supply of library pockets. On the front of each one, write a child's first name. Then add a photo of the child. Next, write the child's first name at the top of a 3" x 5" index card (as shown) and slip the card into the pocket. Display all the pockets together in a convenient location in your classroom. When a child needs to write her name on a paper, have her find her name pocket and remove her name card. Instruct her to take her card to her seat, copy her name onto her work, and then return the card to its pocket. After a child has mastered writing her first name, program the card in her pocket to include her last name too!

Brenda Horn—PreK
Livingston Elementary
Livingston, IL

211

Rhyme With

Autumn is the perfect time to teach little ones about rhyming. Just watch as they scamper and scurry through these ideas, which will help prepare them for a lifetime of literacy!

ideas by Angie Kutzer—Garrett Elementary, Mebane, NC

Nutty About Rhyming
Matching rhyming pictures

Youngsters move about looking for rhyming words with this nutty activity. To prepare for the game, make a copy of the rhyming pictures on page 215. Color and cut out each picture; then glue each one to a construction paper nut. Cut out three pairs of gray construction paper ears and staple them to sentence strip headbands.

To play, designate three students to be squirrels, and have them wear the headbands. Then give each of the other children a different nut and instruct him to hold it so that the picture side shows. Have students spread out around the room. Instruct the squirrels to look at each nut and group the youngsters holding nuts with rhyming pictures. After each group has been made, have the children say the rhymes aloud, and instruct the squirrels to rearrange the nuts if needed. Then pick new squirrels, redistribute the nuts, and play another round. Gray squirrels, gray squirrels, find the nuts that rhyme!

Possible Rhymes

Ring (Swing)
Four (Door)
Ball (Wall)
Bag (Flag)
Wrench (Bench)
Key (Tree)
Hand (Sand)
Sock (Clock)
Star (Car)
Train (Chain)
Hat (Mat)
Bear (Chair)

On the Lookout for Rhymes
Identifying rhyming objects

Send your little raccoons on a rhyming rumpus with this scavenger hunt idea. In advance, purchase a plain black eye mask for each child. (Check the Halloween section of your local discount store.) For each child, collect an item that rhymes with an object located in or around your school. (See the list at the left for ideas.) Tell students that they are going to pretend to be raccoons, but instead of searching for food, they're going to look for rhyming objects. Have each child put on her mask, and give her an item from your collection. Review the name of each child's object. Then take your raccoons on a trek, purposely passing your predetermined rhyming objects. Pause from time to time to stare at an object, whisper its name, and scratch your head. As each child identifies her matching rhyme, snap a photo of her holding her item while standing next to the rhyming object. After the rhyme hunt is finished, return to the classroom and review the rhyming pairs of objects. When the photos are printed, create a class book of rhymes starring your rascally raccoons!

—jtiptonbennett

Forest Friends

A Mouse Walk
Identifying words in a rhyming family
Send your little mice scampering down this rhyming path to find a cheesy treat! Draw eight pawprints on tagboard and then cut them out. From magazines or clip art, cut out a collection of pictures that rhyme with one another and also cut out a few pictures that do not rhyme. (Use the rhyming pictures from page 215 if desired.) For example, cut out pictures of a cat, a bat, a mat, a hat, a bear, a key, and a train. Glue each picture onto a separate pawprint. Arrange the pawprints on the floor and tape them in place. Have students help you name the pictures on the pawprints. Instruct each little mouse, in turn, to walk along the path stepping only on pawprints that rhyme with one another as he says the rhyming words aloud. Reward each student's effort with a few cheese-flavored snack crackers. After each child has had a turn, swap several cards to create a different path. Squeak! Squeak!

The Berry Patch Crew
Sorting rhyming pictures
Students pick berries and get rhyme-matching practice at this berry patch! Use green poster board to create two berry bushes. Cut slits in the bushes to create pockets. Attach the bushes to a wall within students' reach. Cut out 16 berry clusters from purple construction paper to fit the slits in the bushes. Glue a different picture from page 215 on each cluster. Select two sets of rhyming berries, mix them up, and then randomly position them on the bushes. Label each of two baskets with a corresponding rhyming picture to match your picture sets. Place the baskets on the floor in front of the bushes. Have each child pick a cluster of berries, look at its picture, and decide in which rhyme basket it belongs. After youngsters master sorting those two sets of rhyming pictures, switch the berries to give them more rhyme-sorting practice!

"Whooo" Can Make a Rhyme?
Generating a rhyming word

This quick and easy game helps you informally assess who can generate rhymes. Make a copy of the owl pattern on this page. Color and cut out the pattern. Tape the cutout to a large craft stick or paint stick. Then teach youngsters the chant below. To play, have youngsters pass the owl around the circle while reciting the verse. When you designate a word with which to rhyme, have the child holding the owl respond with a rhyming word at the end of the verse. If a child has difficulty, give clues to help in his success. After each correct response, invite everyone to cheer by making owl sounds. Then start another round of play. Whoo! Whoo!

Round and round the owl flies,
Looking for a child who is wise
And making rhymes for all to hear.
If you can do it, we will cheer.
Can you make a rhyme for me?
Let's rhyme with [pig]. One, two, three!

Owl Pattern
Use with "'Whooo' Can Make a Rhyme?" on this page.

Rhyming Picture Cards

Use with "Nutty About Rhyming" on page 212 and "A Mouse Walk" and "The Berry Patch Crew" on page 213.

A Letter Recognition
BLIZZARD

Get ready for a flurry of fresh letter recognition activities in this clever unit. Your little ones are going to have "snow" much fun matching, recognizing, and identifying letters!

ideas by Jana Sanderson, Rainbow School, Stockton, CA

Snowflake Bingo

No two snowflakes are alike, even in this snowflake bingo game. To prepare, cut white construction paper into 1½" x 12" strips. Staple three strips together in a snowflake design. Write three different letters on each snowflake as shown. Cut out the snowflake letter cards on the centerfold. To begin, give each child a snowflake and a handful of mini marshmallows. Then select a card, say its letter, and show it to students. Instruct each youngster to place a mini marshmallow marker on the letter if he has it on his snowflake. Monitor the game and offer assistance when necessary. Continue play until each child has covered all the letters on his snowflake. Then, to reward good work, invite each youngster to eat his marshmallows.

Recognize to Accessorize

Letter recognition is cool when youngsters help this snowman get decked out for winter. Make a copy of page 221 for each child and make one copy of the game spinner and hat and scarf patterns on page 222. Using the hat and scarf patterns, trace and cut out a construction paper hat and scarf for each child. Provide each student in a small group with a hat, a scarf, two craft sticks (arms), and four cereal pieces (buttons). Glue the spinner pattern to tagboard, hole-punch the center, and attach a paper clip with a brad to complete the spinner. Have each youngster, in turn, spin the spinner, match the letter on the spinner with one of the letters on her paper, and then place the corresponding accessories on her snowman. If she has already added the accessories, it becomes the next child's turn. Instruct students to continue play until each child has completely accessorized her snowman. After a round or two, have each youngster glue the accessories to her snowman. Perfectly accessorized!

ICY INITIALS

Icy Initials

The first letter of a child's name is often the first letter of the alphabet that he recognizes, so your preschoolers will be thrilled to identify and paint their first initials. With a white crayon, program a sheet of dark blue construction paper for each child with the first letter of his name. Then pour white paint in a pan to make a thin layer. Instruct each child to search through the labeled papers to find one with his initial on it; then have him identify the letter. Next, instruct him to use a spool dipped in paint to make prints along the lines of his letter to resemble snowflakes. Attach the projects to a bulletin board and title the display "Icy Initials!"

Cooperative Ice Crystals

Letter matching is in the forecast for this snowflake-cutting activity. Write the word *SNOW* on several sheets of paper; then cut apart each letter. Next, fold each of a class supply of white coffee filters in half three times. Program each filter with the letters *S, N, O,* and *W* and outline each letter as shown. Divide children into groups of four. Provide each child with one of the letter cards and a folded coffee filter. Instruct her to identify the letter on her card and then locate its match on her filter. Then have her cut along the lines around the matching letter on the filter. Direct each child to pass her letter card to the child to her right. Have that child repeat the process with the new letter. Direct children to continue to pass cards and cut around the letters until all of the letters have been cut out. Then have each child unfold her filter to reveal a beautiful snowflake. Let it snow; let it snow; let it snow!

Stack a Snowflake

This craft stick project stacks up to be a great letter identification game. Make enough copies of page 223 so that each child will have one copy of the snowflake shadow pattern. Write a different letter at the top of each copy; then, for each copy, program a set of four craft sticks with the same letter.

To play, mix five sets of sticks and place them facedown on a table. Provide each of five children with a prepared snowflake shadow pattern and a bottle of glue. Have each child, in turn, choose a stick and look to see whether its letter matches the one on his paper. If it does match, instruct him to say the letter's name and then lay the stick along one of the shadows. If the letters do not match, direct him to return the stick to its facedown position. With each round, have the child glue his matching sticks together, as shown, using the shadows as a guide. (Do not glue the first stick to the paper.) The game continues until youngsters have completed their snowflakes. When the glue is dry, invite students to paint their snowflakes and then sprinkle glitter on the wet paint. Add a loop of ribbon, and this pretty snowflake is ready for hanging!

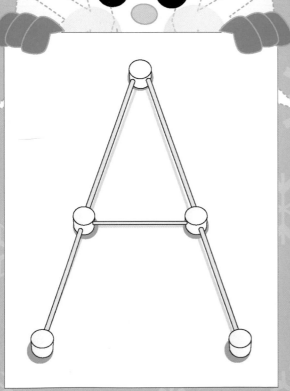

Snowball to Snowball

Little ones connect mini marshmallow snowballs with dry spaghetti pieces for this fun letter activity. Program sheets of construction paper with large letters. (Choose letters that do not include curved lines.) Place sticky dots at each line end and at the intersecting points of each letter as shown. Laminate the letter cards for durability. Invite each child to select a card, name the letter, and then trace it with her finger. Next, have her put a mini marshmallow (snowball) on each dot and then use dry spaghetti to connect the snowballs. After she forms her letter, encourage her to disassemble it, choose a new card, and then repeat the process with another letter. When children are finished, have them throw away their spaghetti pieces and marshmallows. Then offer youngsters fresh marshmallows (snowballs)!

Snatch a Snowflake

These snowflakes are guaranteed not to melt once youngsters catch them, and they will ensure wintry fun! Program each of a set of three-inch doilies with a letter. Hole-punch each doily and hang it from a long piece of yarn. To play, tie the yarn between two trees, or have two volunteers hold the yarn ends. Sing the song below, substituting a child's name and a letter in the fourth line. Have the child run up to the snowflakes, search for his letter, and then pull it off the yarn. Play continues until everyone has had a turn identifying a letter and snatching a snowflake.

(sung to the tune of "Twinkle, Twinkle, Little Star")

Snowflake, snowflake, snowflake white,
Falling from the sky so bright.
Each one different as can be.
[Child's name], find letter [letter] for me.
Snowflake, snowflake, snowflake white,
Falling from the sky so bright.

Letter Snow Globes

Shake up some letter recognition fun with these child-made snow globes. Collect a supply of clean, empty water bottles. Remove the label from each one. Place a funnel in a bottle and invite a child to drop in a few pinches of white glitter or snowflake confetti. Then have her add several letter beads. Next, hold the funnel as she pours water into her bottle, filling it to the top. While students watch from a safe distance, apply a bead of hot glue to the inside of the bottle cap; then screw it on tightly. Instruct each child to shake her snow globe and identify the letters as they drift in the bottle.

Sledding In to Letter Recognition

Your preschoolers will "brrr-st" with excitement as they slide into this letter recognition game. Follow the directions below to make four sleds. Then mask the letters on the spinner on page 222 and copy it. Label the spinner with the letters *S, L, E,* and *D.* Glue it to a piece of tagboard, hole-punch the center, and attach a paper clip with a brad as shown.

Invite a group of four children to play. Give each youngster a sled and four counters or plastic animal markers. Have each child, in turn, spin the spinner, name the letter it lands on, and place a marker on the corresponding letter on her sled. If a child spins a letter she has already covered, play continues with the next child. The game continues until each child has covered the letters on her sled. Then invite each child to slide her sled down a hill (propped cookie sheet) to see whether her markers can stay on for the ride!

Directions for one sled:

1. Lay three tongue depressors side by side on waxed paper.
2. Glue two craft sticks on the tongue depressor seams.
3. Prop a craft stick on its side along the outer edge of each of the glued craft sticks to create blades. Glue them in place.
4. When the glue is dry, turn each sled over and glue a length of yarn to one end as shown.
5. Cut and glue a 2¼-inch piece of craft stick to the sled to cover the yarn ends.
6. Label the sled as shown.

"Soup-er" Letter Recognition

Wrap up this letter recognition unit by warming up some alphabet soup and inviting each youngster to add a sprinkling of shredded-cheese snow. Then encourage each preschooler to try to identify the letters in each spoonful. I see *T!* Down goes *O!*

Cool Dressing

Listen for directions.

Spinner Pattern

Use with "Recognize to Accessorize" on page 216 and "Sledding In to Letter Recognition" on page 220.

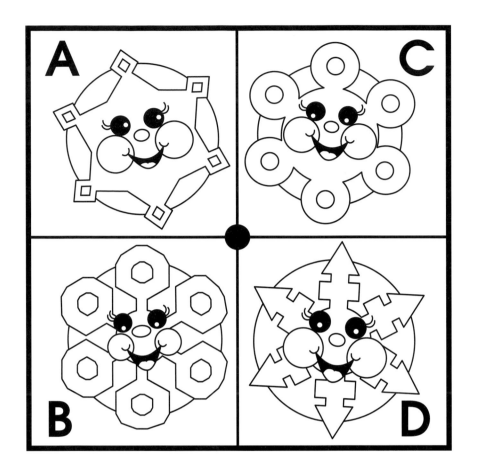

Hat and Scarf Patterns

Use with "Recognize to Accessorize" on page 216.

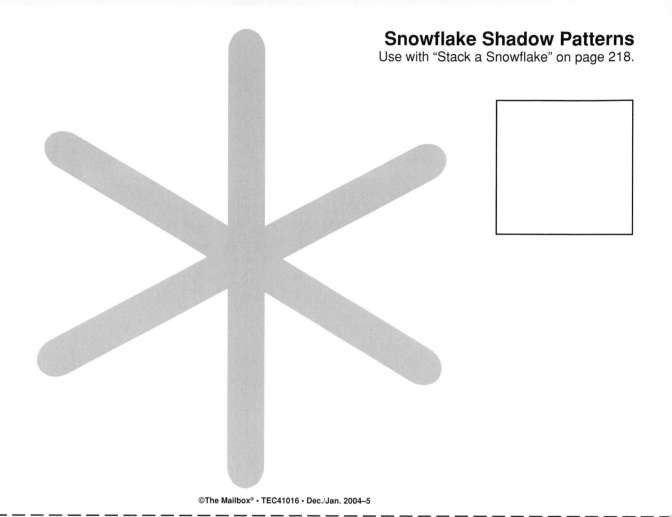

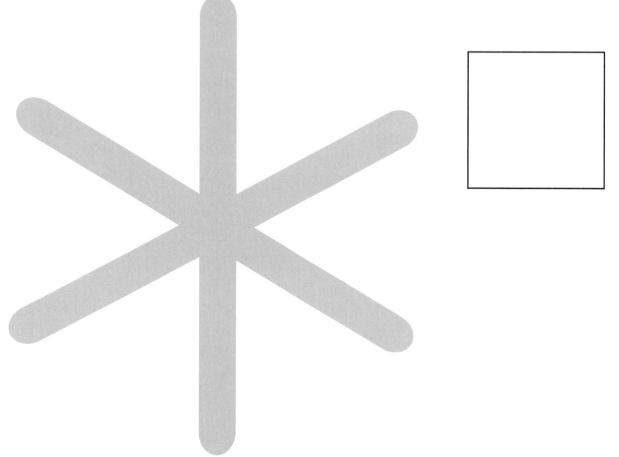

Chugging Into Print Awareness

All aboard for these activities, which help preschoolers understand conventions of print!

by Ada Goren, Winston-Salem, NC

Choo-Choo-Choose a Cover!
Book covers tell about the story inside.

Get this look at books on track by starting at the beginning—a book's cover! Gather students and display three or four books in front of them. Explain that a book's cover and title usually tell the reader something about the story that's inside. Read each book title aloud. Give a short synopsis of one of the stories; then ask whether anyone can identify the book's cover. After a child has correctly identified the cover, talk about how the cover and the story go together. Then move on and give synopses of the other books and have students match those covers too.

Bookmakers
A book is created by an author, an illustrator, and a publisher.

Your preschoolers know that a book's title is on its cover. But what about those names? Hold up a big book and read aloud the author's and illustrator's names, as well as the publisher's name from the title page. Ask whether anyone knows who these people are and why their names are on the book. Explain to students that an author writes a story, an illustrator adds the art, and a publisher is responsible for putting the book together. Then teach youngsters this chant to reinforce these bookmakers' jobs. Invite three children at a time to play the roles of author, illustrator, and publisher. Have them stand in front of the group and point to the appropriate parts of a big book as indicated.

(chanted to Brown Bear, Brown Bear, What Do You See?)

Author, author, what do you do?
I write the words in a book for you.   Point to text.

Illustrator, illustrator, what do you do?
I make the pictures in a book for you.   Point to illustration.

Publisher, publisher, what do you do?
I put the book together for you!   Close book and point to cover.

Cover to Cover
Hold and handle books properly.

Here's an activity engineered to help preschoolers practice handling books correctly and with care! For each child, affix a small sticky note to the front cover of a book. Draw on the sticky note an arrow that points upward. Give each child a book and then ask her to hold the book so that she can see the arrow pointing up. Sing the song at right as youngsters follow along!

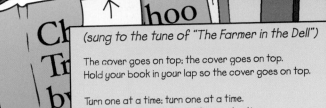

(sung to the tune of "The Farmer in the Dell")

The cover goes on top; the cover goes on top.
Hold your book in your lap so the cover goes on top.

Turn one at a time; turn one at a time.
Turn the pages in your book one at a time.

Turn front to back; turn front to back.
Turn the pages in your book from front to back.

Treat your book with care; treat your book with care.
Whenever you read a book, treat that book with care!

Green Means "Go," Red Means "Stop"
Print flows top to bottom and left to right.

Train your little ones to recognize the starting points for reading with some colorful cues! On several green sticky dots, write the word *go*. On several red dots, write the word *stop*. Place each dot on a small sticky note. Choose a page in a big book and display it in front of your group. Point to the top of the page and the bottom of the page. Ask a child to tell you which place you should start reading. Have him place a "go" note at the top of the page. Then ask where to stop reading this page. Have another volunteer put a "stop" note at the bottom of the page. Next, do the same thing with each line of print on the page. Have youngsters mark the left side of each line with green sticky dots and the right side with red ones. Finally, read the page aloud to your group, running your hand under the print to demonstrate the correct starting and stopping points and to emphasize the return sweep at the end of each line.

Story Trains
A story has a beginning, a middle, and an end.

It's full steam ahead when your preschoolers explore the basic parts of a story! Make one copy of the train patterns on pages 226 and 227; then color them. After sharing a story with your students, explain that each story is like a train on a track. Display the engine pattern for the group and write in the title of the book. Then display the train car marked "Beginning." Ask student volunteers to recall what happened at the beginning of the book; then write their dictation on the car. Continue in the same manner with the other boxcar and the caboose. Then review all the parts and remind students that every story has a beginning, a middle, and an end. If desired, repeat the activity on another day with a different story and another set of train car patterns.

Engine and Train Car Patterns

Use with "Story Trains" on page 225.

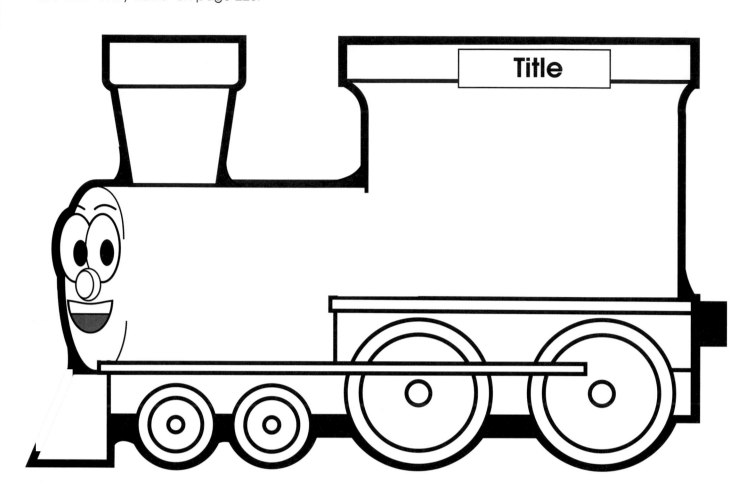

Title

Beginning

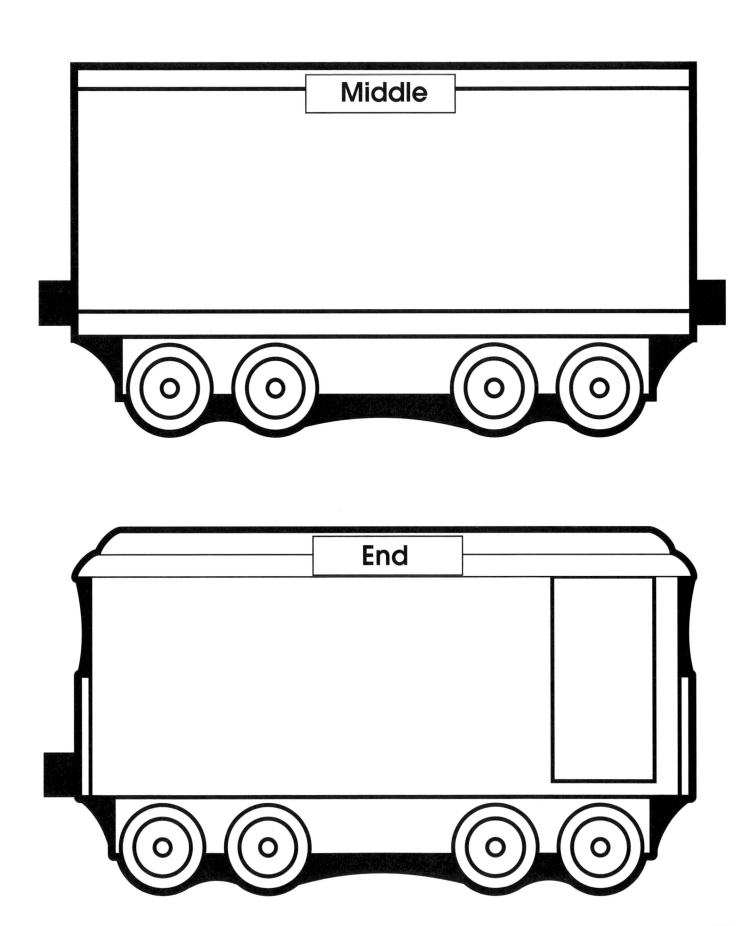

Middle

End

Wiggle With Beginning Sounds!

Youngsters dig these ideas, which focus on beginning consonant sounds!

ideas by Roxanne LaBell Dearman, Western NC Early Intervention Program for Children Who Are Deaf and Hard of Hearing, Charlotte, NC

Wiggle Worms
Recognizing beginning consonant sounds

Youngsters wiggle their way through sound-matching skills with this energetic song. Have students stand, and teach them the song below. After each verse is sung, hold up two objects or picture cards and say each item's name (make sure you share at least one item or picture that begins with the song's featured letter sound). When youngsters hear an item that begins with the sound sung in the song, have your little worms wiggle down to the ground. Repeat the song several times, substituting the sounds in line 3 to match sounds with which your class is familiar. Wiggle, wiggle!

(sung to the tune of "The Farmer in the Dell")
The earthworm hears a sound.
The earthworm hears a sound.
The earthworm hears a [/p/, /p/, /p/]
Then wiggles in the ground!

Earthworms on the Hunt
Identifying beginning sounds

Little ones dig this hunt in mud when their fingers (worms) search for pictures with the same beginning sounds! To prepare, attach three or four stickers that begin with the same letter—such as ball, bird, and bell stickers—to the inside of a resealable plastic bag. Seal the bag and place it inside a larger resealable plastic bag. Pour half a cup of brown paint into the outer bag to represent mud. Seal the bag and then use clear packing tape to secure the bag's opening. Make several more mud bags to reinforce the sounds that you would like students to practice. Have each child choose a bag, lay it on a table, and then use her little worms to search for pictures in the mud. Encourage each child to determine which sound is heard at the beginning of each picture's name. Have youngsters repeat the activity with a different mud bag. We dig it!

Worm Match
Matching beginning sounds

Help Mr. Worm find Mrs. Worm in this sound-matching game! To prepare, nearly fill two containers with sand. Gather 20 large craft sticks. For each pair of sticks, label one end of each stick with a sticker or picture that begins with the same beginning sound. Cover the stickers or pictures with clear tape to protect the images. On the opposite end of each stick in the pair draw either a girl face or a boy face so that the pair creates a couple. Place all of the Mr. Worms in one sand container picture side down and all of the Mrs. Worms in the other container picture side down. Invite two children to take turns selecting a worm from each tub of sand. Have the pair say the names of the pictures shown on each worm and determine whether the beginning sounds match. If a match is made, the child keeps the worms. If a match isn't made, the worms are returned to the sand. Have youngsters continue play until all of the worms have been paired. Mr. Worm, Mrs. Worm—they're a match!

Night Crawler Search
Matching beginning sounds

Your little ones will need to use their eyes and ears to catch these night crawlers. In advance, make a copy of the worm cards and labels on page 231. Color and cut out the worm cards; then laminate them for durability. Place the worms in an empty water table filled with green Easter grass. Glue each label to a different plastic jar with a lid. Then encourage youngsters to use flashlights and plastic tweezers to find the night crawlers in the grass. When a night crawler is found, have the child say its picture's name and decide which jar is labeled with the matching beginning sound. Instruct him to put his night crawler in the appropriate jar. Creepy-crawly fun!

229

Walk the Worm
Identifying beginning sounds, pronouncing sounds

Wee learners get lots of practice making consonant sounds as they walk along this winding worm! In advance, attach strips of masking tape to the floor to make a long twisting worm. Place several objects at one end of the worm. Invite a small group of children to join you at the worm. Select one child to be the worm walker. Have her choose an object, name it, and then say its beginning sound. Next, instruct her to walk on the worm while repeatedly saying her featured beginning sound. Encourage the rest of the group to say the sound along with her. Continue play until each child has walked the worm. That's /t/, /t/, /t/, terrific!

/t/, /t/, /t/

Juicy Worms
Matching beginning sounds

What's worse than finding a worm in your apple? Finding half a worm in your apple! Students search for the other half of the worm during this activity. Make a copy of the worm patterns on the back of the centerfold. Color and cut out the worms; then laminate them for durability. Next, cut each worm in half as shown. Place one half of each worm in an empty, clean apple juice can and place the corresponding halves faceup on a table. Gather a small group of children at the table. Invite a child to choose a worm half from the can. Have the group say the name of the picture on the worm. Then encourage students to find the worm half whose picture begins with the same sound. When the match is found, have the child position the halves to form a whole worm. Continue play until all the worms are put together. Place the worm halves at a center for more practice. What wormy learning fun!

Ss Letters and Sounds

These ideas help set your little ones afloat in the vast waters of letters and sounds! Encourage them to sail through this skill-building series of ideas!

ideas by Angie Kutzer, Garrett Elementary, Mebane, NC

My Name Is Nifty!
Recognizing beginning sounds in words

Youngsters' names are important to them, and this idea uses names as an entry point into literacy practice. Write the song shown on chart paper, leaving blanks where indicated. Laminate the chart and then post it in front of your group. Choose one student's name to feature. Use a dry-erase marker to write the beginning letter of her name in the blanks in the first verse. (Students will sing the letter's sound in this verse rather than sing the letter's name.) Have the child name a word that begins with the same sound and letter as her name and then write it and her name in the second verse as shown. Teach youngsters the song; then, after singing, simply use a dry paper towel to erase the chart to ready it for a different child's name. You're guaranteed to have a sea of hands volunteering to be featured in the song!

(sung to the tune of "The Farmer in the Dell")

My name begins with [K].
My name begins with [K].
[K, K, K, K, K, K]
My name begins with [K].

My name starts like [kite].
My name starts like [kite].
[Kaleigh, kite; Kaleigh, kite]
My name starts like [kite].

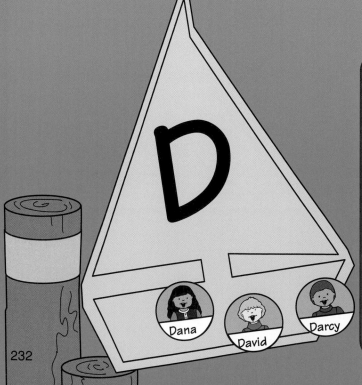

First Mates
Matching beginning letters in names

If you have a photo of each of your students and some construction paper, you're well on your way to creating a seaworthy letter-matching center. To prepare, make enough construction paper copies of the sailboat pattern on page 235 so that you will have one for each letter represented at the beginning of students' first names. (If three children's names begin with *s,* for example, you will only have one *s* boat.) Label each boat with a different letter. Cut a photo of each child into a circle and label it with the child's name.

To play, have each child choose a photo, say the pictured child's name, and then look at the name's first letter to decide in which boat her friend belongs. Instruct her to position the picture on the boat. All crew members accounted for!

A Nautical Environment

Recognizing beginning letters in familiar words

Lots of environmental print is collected for this literacy display. Prepare the display by covering a bulletin board with blue bulletin board paper. Use white chalk to draw waves on the paper. Then make three to four copies of the sailboat pattern on page 235. Program each sailboat with a different letter you want students to practice; then attach each boat to the board. Have each student bring in environmental print showing words that begin with the designated letters. Encourage each youngster to share his environmental print; then staple each piece below the corresponding sailboat. We're sailing through literacy!

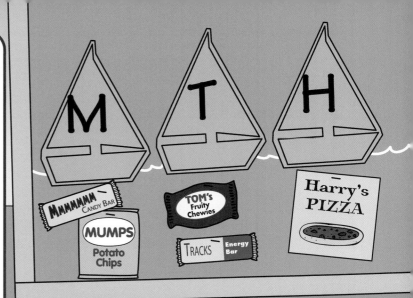

Wonderful Water Crafts

Tracing, the /s/ sound

These mobiles help students really make connections between letters and their sounds. Make a construction paper copy of the sailboat pattern on page 235 for each child. Cut out each boat so that the sail and the hull are separate as shown. Use a highlighter to write a capital *s* on the sail and a lowercase *s* on the hull. Next, cut out two waves from blue construction paper for each child. Give each child the waves and sailboat cutouts along with a marker, access to clip art or pictures from old magazines, and glue. (Make sure to have mostly letter *s* pictures plus a few other pictures in your supply.)

To make a mobile, have the child trace the letters on the sail and the hull. Then instruct him to find two pictures from the supply that begin with the letter *s*. Have him glue each picture to a different wave. Next, use a hole puncher to make holes in the cutouts as shown. Finally, use paper clips to connect the pieces and add a yarn length for hanging. Allow each child to share his sailboat and then hang the completed projects for an eye-catching display.

Set Sail!

Matching objects to beginning letters

This unit wouldn't be complete without some actual sailing on real water, so head for the water table! In advance, collect an assortment of small, lightweight items that begin with a letter with which students are familiar and a few objects that do not begin with the letter. Cut out a triangle from construction paper to resemble a sail. Program the sail with the chosen letter. Prepare the sail by gluing it to a jumbo craft stick and inserting the stick into a lump of clay positioned in the middle of a clean foam tray. Place the objects in a basket near the water table and put the boat in the water. Have each child visit the water table and sort the objects by placing those that begin with the letter on the boat. Let's sail!

Monogrammed Sails

Letter-sound association, forming letters

This quick and easy idea simply needs lengths of rope (Wikki Stix creatables) to get these monogrammed sailboats in shape! In advance, make a class set of the sailboat pattern on page 235. Program each pattern with one of two letters. Then give each child a pattern and several lengths of Wikki Stix Creatables. Say a letter sound and have each child determine whether the letter on his sail matches the letter sound. Instruct youngsters with the correct letter to use their manipulatives to form the letter. After several rounds, have each youngster trade sailboats with a classmate and then repeat the activity. No doubt, youngsters will be sailing along with letter-sound association!

Letter Lotto

Matching the letters m and t and their sounds

Students set sail with this small-group lotto game that focuses on the letters *m* and *t*! Make one copy of the gameboards and three copies of the letter cards on page 236. Cut out the board and cards; then laminate them for durability. Place the letter cards in a bag. Invite a group of three children to play. Give each student a gameboard. Have each child, in turn, remove a card from the bag. Instruct him to look at the letter and decide whether there is a picture on his board that begins with that letter's sound. If so, he puts the card on that picture. If not, the card goes back into the bag. Play continues in this manner until each child fills his board. Letter lotto!

Sailboat Pattern

Use with "First Mates" on page 232, "A Nautical Environment" and "Wonderful Water Crafts," on page 233, and "Monogrammed Sails" on page 234.

Lotto Boards and Letter Cards
Use with "Letter Lotto" on page 234.

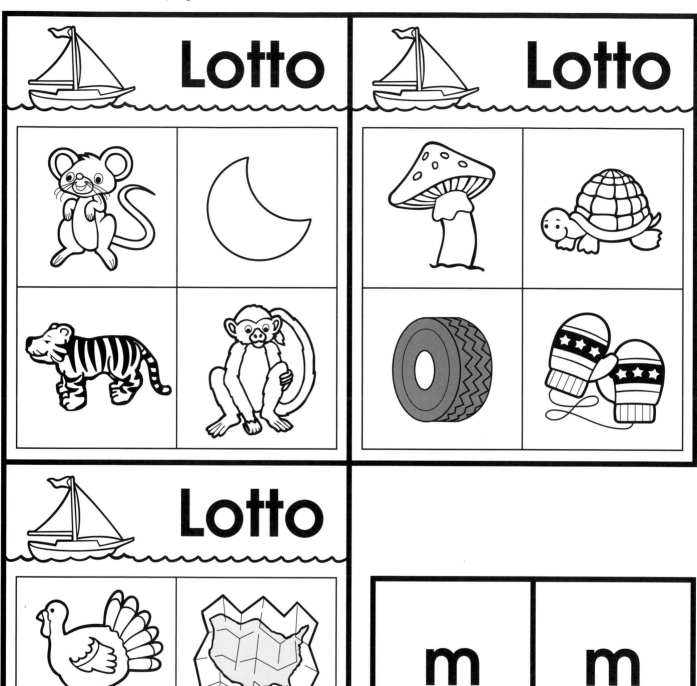

Lotto

Lotto

Lotto

m	m
t	t

MATH UNITS

A PALETTE OF COLORFUL LEARNING

Mix these ideas into your teaching and help paint a pretty picture about colors for your little ones.

ideas by Angie Kutzer, Garrett Elementary, Mebane, NC

COLORFUL LEIS
identifying matching colors

There's a lot of lei switching going on during this color-matching game! Purchase a solid-colored plastic lei for each child so that half the class will have one color and the other half of the class will have another color. Instruct each child to wear her lei as you play some lively music. Stop the music at random and have each youngster switch leis with someone whose lei is the same color. Periodically during play, review the colors of the leis. As more colors are introduced, add new sets of leis to the game. Hey, we're both wearing yellow!

A BLOOMING BOUQUET OF COLOR
identifying colors

These bouquets will make lovely refrigerator works of art and will also help little ones learn their colors! To prepare, make a copy of the vase pattern on page 240 for each child. Gather several different colors of artificial flowers, and provide a shallow dish of corresponding paint for each bloom.

Have each youngster color his vase pattern. Help each child cut out the vase pattern and glue it to the bottom of a 12" x 18" sheet of construction paper. Have him use a green crayon to draw stems and leaves coming out of the vase. Next, instruct him to choose a flower and dip it in the matching paint color. Have him make prints on his paper, as shown, in three or more different colors. Encourage him to use three or four different blooms for a vivid display. After each child finishes, have him tell you which colors he used in his painting. Beautiful!

238

BUBBLE GUM, BUBBLE GUM
naming colors, identifying colors

This adaptation of a traditional jump rope chant gets your youngsters calling out color names! To prepare, put a supply of large pom-poms into a clear fishbowl. Chant the rhyme shown; then call out a student's name at the end. Have him name a color of gumball he'd like to have, and then invite him to take a pom-pom from the bowl. Continue in this manner until everyone has had a turn.

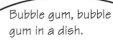

Bubble gum, bubble gum in a dish.

For which color of gumball do you wish?

OVER THE RAINBOW
naming colors

Youngsters learn all the colors to reach this pot of gold! Gather a sheet of construction paper in each of the following basic colors: red, orange, yellow, green, blue, purple, black, and brown. Tape them to the floor in order, creating a rainbowlike path. At the end of the path, place a plastic cauldron (found in discount stores during Halloween) filled with gold-wrapped chocolate coin candy. When a child is ready to recite all of the colors, have her start at the beginning of the path and name each color as she steps on it. If she makes it to the end of the path, naming all of the colors correctly, reward her with a piece of gold!

A COLOR-MIXING PALETTE
mixing colors

Get ready for lots of oohs and aahs when you show your youngsters this color display! To prepare, make three transparency copies of page 241. Use permanent markers to color each copy as shown. Place the blue copy on your overhead projector. Point to the color word and read it aloud. Next, place the red copy over the blue and read the corresponding color words. Finally, add the yellow copy and finish reading. Follow up this activity by letting budding artists paint and do some color mixing of their own!

First Copy
(Color blue.)

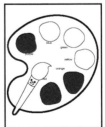

Second Copy
(Color red.)

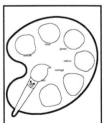

Third Copy
(Color yellow.)

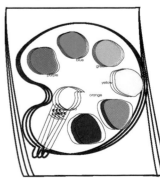

239

I'm learning my colors.
Yes, it's true.

This bouquet has more colors
Than one or two.

Let me name each one
For you!

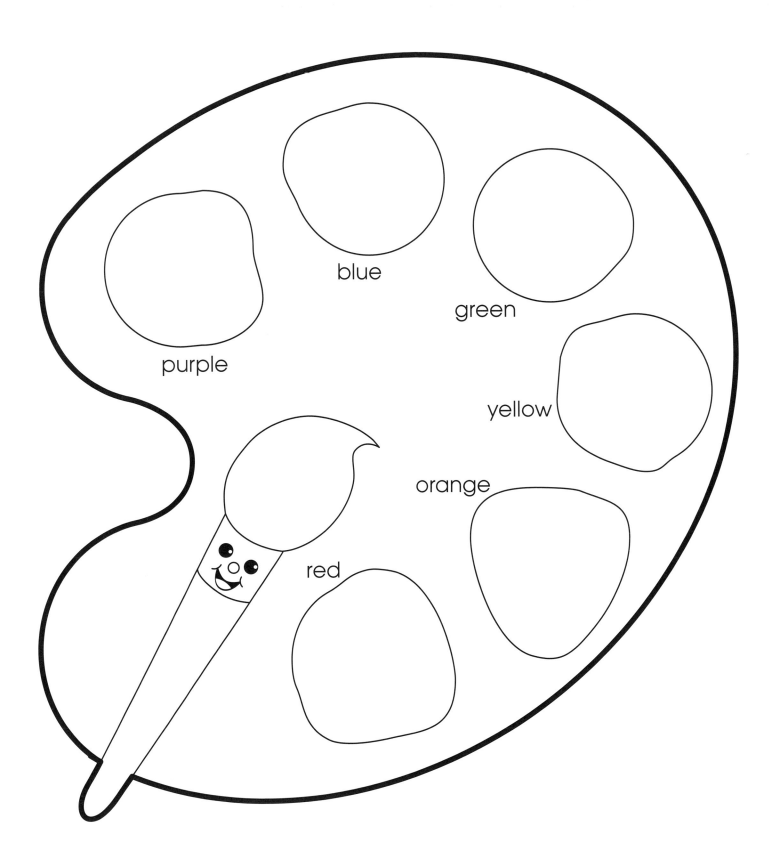

purple

blue

green

yellow

orange

red

Circles, Triangles, and Squares—
With Spiders EVERYWHERE!

Here's a wonderful web of ideas for teaching your youngsters about the basic shapes—all with the help of some not-so-scary spiders!

ideas by Ada Goren, Winston-Salem, NC

There's a Spider on the Shape
Identifying shapes

Start your shape study on a musical note! After reviewing the three basic shapes—circle, square, and triangle—give each child in a small group a paper version of each shape. Also give him a large black pom-pom or a plastic spider ring. Teach youngsters the song below and have them bounce or crawl their spider on each shape as you sing about it.

(sung to the tune of "If You're Happy and You Know It")

There's a spider on the [square], on the [square].
There's a spider on the [square], on the [square].
Look at that spider go!
It is moving to and fro.
There's a spider on the [square], on the [square].

Which Web?
Sorting shapes

Put a new spin on shape sorting with this wonderful web center! Duplicate the three webs on pages 246 and 247. Then die-cut a supply of circles, triangles, and squares from construction paper. Have a child at this center sort the paper shapes onto the webs of the corresponding shape.

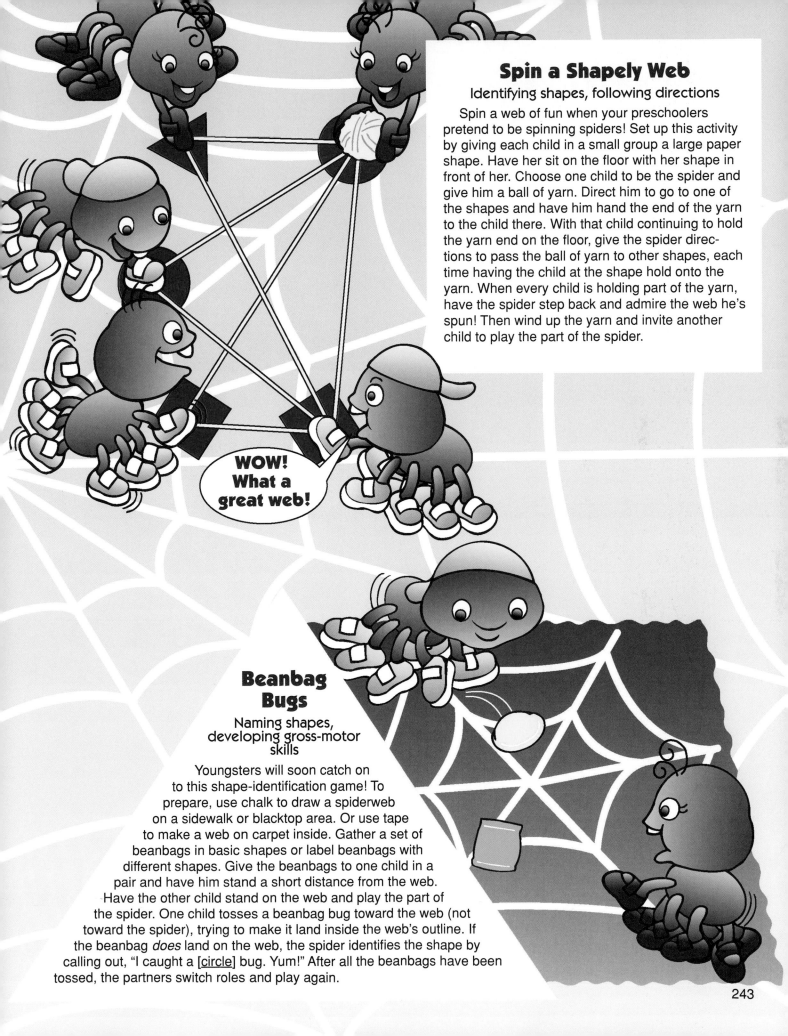

Spin a Shapely Web
Identifying shapes, following directions

Spin a web of fun when your preschoolers pretend to be spinning spiders! Set up this activity by giving each child in a small group a large paper shape. Have her sit on the floor with her shape in front of her. Choose one child to be the spider and give him a ball of yarn. Direct him to go to one of the shapes and have him hand the end of the yarn to the child there. With that child continuing to hold the yarn end on the floor, give the spider directions to pass the ball of yarn to other shapes, each time having the child at the shape hold onto the yarn. When every child is holding part of the yarn, have the spider step back and admire the web he's spun! Then wind up the yarn and invite another child to play the part of the spider.

WOW! What a great web!

Beanbag Bugs
Naming shapes, developing gross-motor skills

Youngsters will soon catch on to this shape-identification game! To prepare, use chalk to draw a spiderweb on a sidewalk or blacktop area. Or use tape to make a web on carpet inside. Gather a set of beanbags in basic shapes or label beanbags with different shapes. Give the beanbags to one child in a pair and have him stand a short distance from the web. Have the other child stand on the web and play the part of the spider. One child tosses a beanbag bug toward the web (not toward the spider), trying to make it land inside the web's outline. If the beanbag *does* land on the web, the spider identifies the shape by calling out, "I caught a [circle] bug. Yum!" After all the beanbags have been tossed, the partners switch roles and play again.

The Spider Goes Round and Round

Naming shapes

Shape up your circle time with this "spider-ific" activity! Seat your little ones in a circle. Give each child a paper shape to place in front of her. (Use the paper shapes from "There's a Spider on the Shape" on page 242.) Give one child a pom-pom or a plastic spider ring. Play some music and have the child holding the spider walk around the circle, touching the spider to each shape as she passes. Stop the music, have the child stop the spider on a shape, and then instruct everyone to chant, "The spider crawls round and round. Tell us which shape she's found." Ask the child holding the spider to identify the shape the spider is on. Then have her give the spider to that child and sit down in her place. Restart the music for another round of play.

Spider Hider

Naming shapes, using critical-thinking skills

There's a sneaky spider hiding out in this activity! To prepare, cut four large shapes from construction paper—a circle, a square, a triangle, and a rectangle. Duplicate the spider from page 247, color it, and cut it out. Then gather a small group at a table. While your preschoolers cover their eyes, hide the spider cutout beneath one of the shapes. Then have students open their eyes. Give a clue about the hiding place, such as, "This shape has no corners," or "This shape has four sides that are all the same." Have a student volunteer point to and name the shape he thinks is the hiding place. Then invite him to look under the shape and see if the spider is there. If he is incorrect, give another clue about the hiding place. After the spider is found, hide it again for another child to find.

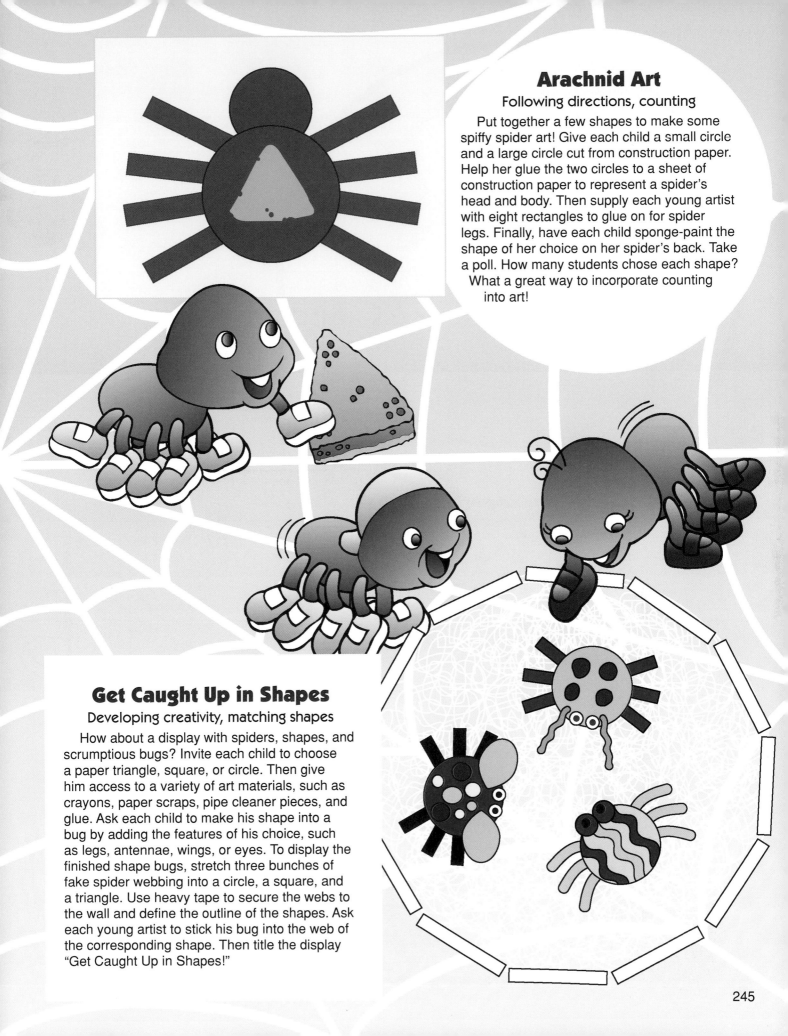

Arachnid Art
Following directions, counting

Put together a few shapes to make some spiffy spider art! Give each child a small circle and a large circle cut from construction paper. Help her glue the two circles to a sheet of construction paper to represent a spider's head and body. Then supply each young artist with eight rectangles to glue on for spider legs. Finally, have each child sponge-paint the shape of her choice on her spider's back. Take a poll. How many students chose each shape? What a great way to incorporate counting into art!

Get Caught Up in Shapes
Developing creativity, matching shapes

How about a display with spiders, shapes, and scrumptious bugs? Invite each child to choose a paper triangle, square, or circle. Then give him access to a variety of art materials, such as crayons, paper scraps, pipe cleaner pieces, and glue. Ask each child to make his shape into a bug by adding the features of his choice, such as legs, antennae, wings, or eyes. To display the finished shape bugs, stretch three bunches of fake spider webbing into a circle, a square, and a triangle. Use heavy tape to secure the webs to the wall and define the outline of the shapes. Ask each young artist to stick his bug into the web of the corresponding shape. Then title the display "Get Caught Up in Shapes!"

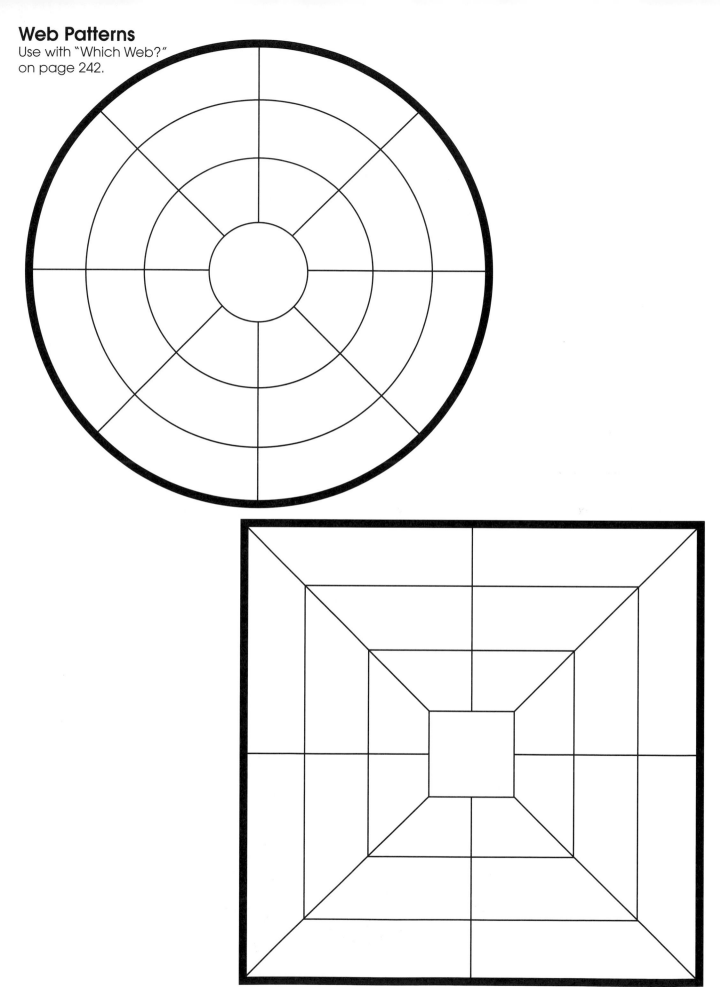

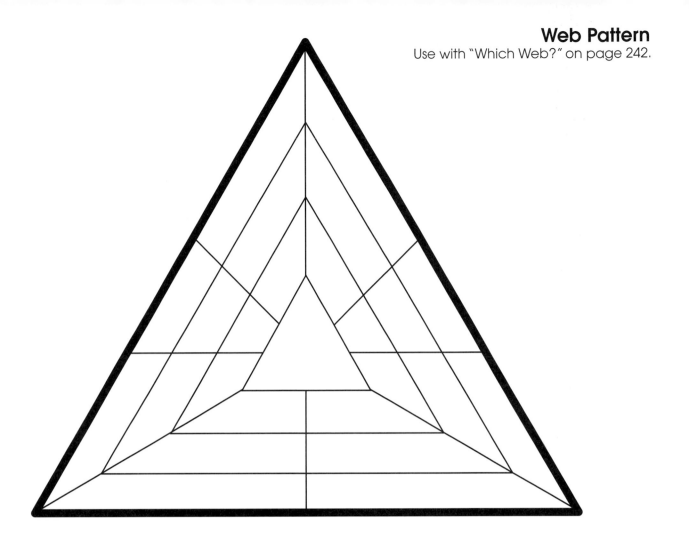

Spider Pattern
Use with "Spider Hider" on page 244.

One-to-One Correspondence— Something to Bark About!

No bones about it, youngsters will dig this collection of ideas centered around one-to-one correspondence and man's best friends—puppy dogs!

ideas by Roxanne LaBell Dearman, WNC Early Intervention Program for Children Who Are Deaf or Hard of Hearing, Charlotte, NC

Buried Bones

Dig up some one-to-one correspondence practice at your sand table with this easy idea. To prepare, bury a desired number of bone-shaped dog treats in your sand table. Place the same number of plastic dog dishes or bowls nearby. Add a small shovel or scoop to the table for digging. Tell students that puppies have buried bones in the sand table. Invite each child, in turn, to the center and have him dig through the sand to find the bones. As each bone is found, encourage the child to place it in a dog bowl. Have him continue until there is one bone in each dish. Then instruct him to bury the bones in the sand for the next center visitor.

Doggie Dash

Youngsters dash to distribute dog supplies to some furry canine friends with this exercise. Have five children stand in a line. Position five stuffed dogs at the opposite end of your room. Give each child a basket with five identical dog-related items in it, such as clean or new balls, chew toys, leashes, collars, or dog dishes. In turn, have each child walk to the dogs and place one item from her basket in front of each dog. When her basket is empty, have her go to the end of the line and sit down. Continue the dash until each child has distributed her dog supplies. Then discuss with youngsters the items each dog has—one ball, one chew toy, one leash, one collar, and one dish. Lead them to realize that each dog has the same items and the same number of each item. This doggie dash is done!

Bowwow Collars

Every pup needs a collar, and this activity has youngsters taking care of that! To prepare, make two tagboard copies of the tags on page 251. Cut six tagboard strips to serve as collars. Position six stuffed dogs in front of students. Have students help you think of six dog names. Write each name on a different tag. Staple the ends of each strip to make a collar. Next, place the hook side of a Velcro fastener on the back of each dog tag; then put its corresponding loop side on a dog collar. Invite a child to choose a dog's tag and attach it to a collar. Have her put the collar around the neck of a dog of her choice. For older preschoolers, vary the number of dogs and collars. Ask students to complete the activity and then use terms such as *more, less,* and *same* to describe the outcome.

Cozy Canines

Transform your dramatic-play area into a cozy slumber area for pooches. Stock the center with a desired number of stuffed dogs and enough of the following items so that each puppy can have one of each: a cardboard box (dog bed), a small blanket, and a chew toy. Encourage your little pet owners to place one dog into each bed, cover each one with a blanket, and then give each pooch a chew toy. When the pooches wake up, have their masters gather the blankets, toys, and dogs into a large basket for the next visitors at the center. Night-night, doggies!

Play Dough, Pups, and Pals

Transform your play dough center to ready each puppy for a walk—complete with a leash and a collar! To prepare, make several copies of the child and dog patterns on page 251. Color, cut out, and laminate the patterns for durability. Have each child fashion a dog collar from play dough for each dog and then roll another piece of play dough into a rope to make a leash for each one. Instruct him to connect each leash from a dog's collar to a child's hand. Have him continue until each pup is paired with a pal and ready for a walk!

Hound Hunt

Play this small-group game to reinforce color names and color matching while encouraging one-to-one correspondence. To prepare, make enough copies of the dog and child patterns on page 251 to equal the number of colors that you would like to review. For each pair, color the dog's collar and the child's shirt the same color. Cut out the patterns and then laminate them for durability. To play, position the child cards faceup in a row and place the dog cards facedown on a table. Explain to youngsters that each child owns one dog whose collar color matches the child's shirt. In turn, have each student select a dog card, name the collar color, and then find its matching owner. Have him place the dog next to its owner. Continue until each hound has been located and reunited with its master. For an added challenge, vary the number of dog patterns or child patterns. Have youngsters use terms such as *more, less,* and *same* when describing the outcome.

Puppy Pieces

After playing with puppies, your preschoolers will have dog-size appetites! Have them make this dog-inspired treat to tame their hunger and practice one-to-one correspondence. Personalize a disposable bowl (dog dish) for each child. Purchase four varieties of cereal (kibble) and pour each kibble type into a separate plastic bowl. Invite a group of four children to join you at a table. Instruct each child to find her dog dish; then line up the dishes on the table. In turn, give each child a serving spoon and a different bowl of kibble. Have her scoop a spoonful of kibble into each dog dish. When each type of kibble has been distributed, invite your pups to dig in!

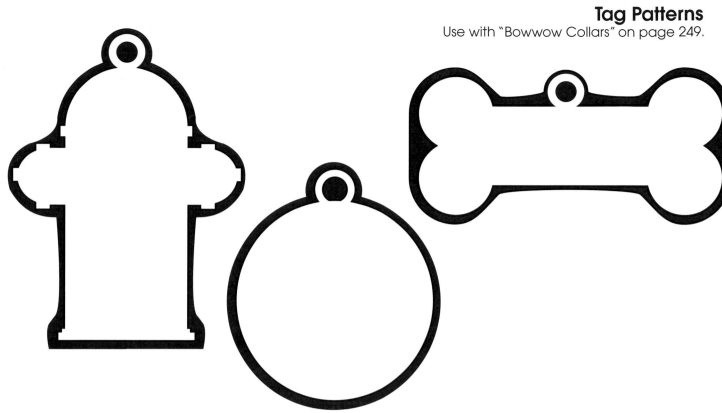

Child and Dog Patterns
Use with "Play Dough, Pups, and Pals" on page 249 and "Hound Hunt" on page 250.

Leaping Lizards Count

Camouflage counting skills with these fun ideas that help preschoolers focus on counting lizards!

ideas by Jana Sanderson, Rainbow School, Stockton, CA

Leaping Lizards Count
Counting to ten
Preschoolers jump for joy as they count along with this clever rhyme about lizards!

One, two, my belly's blue.
Three, four, I catch bugs galore.
Five, six, I run on sticks.
Seven, eight, my tail is straight.

Nine, ten, my count now ends.
1, 2, 3, 4, 5, 6, 7, 8, 9,10—
Leaping lizards!

Pat belly with hands.
Pretend to catch bugs.
Run in place.
Place hands behind back with fingers touching.

Count on fingers.
Jump.

Tacky Toes
Representing and counting sets
Whether counting sticky fingers or tacky toes, students are sure to stick around for more counting practice with this activity. To prepare, make construction paper copies of the gecko pattern on page 255. For each copy, place a different number of sticky dots on each of the gecko's front feet (use a different color for each foot to distinguish the two number sets). Show youngsters one gecko at a time. Have each child hold up the corresponding number of fingers on each hand to match the set of dots on each of the gecko's feet. As a group, count each set of fingers held up and determine the total number. Then count the dots on the gecko's toes to check students' work. Four little toes in all!

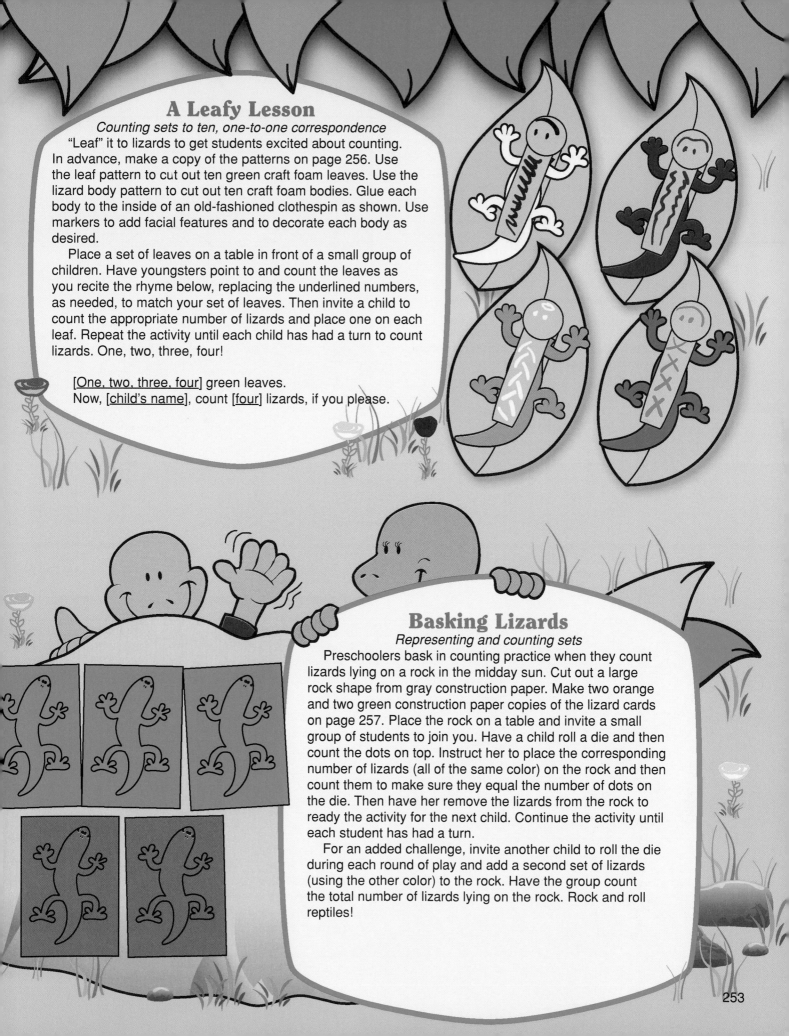

A Leafy Lesson

Counting sets to ten, one-to-one correspondence

"Leaf" it to lizards to get students excited about counting. In advance, make a copy of the patterns on page 256. Use the leaf pattern to cut out ten green craft foam leaves. Use the lizard body pattern to cut out ten craft foam bodies. Glue each body to the inside of an old-fashioned clothespin as shown. Use markers to add facial features and to decorate each body as desired.

Place a set of leaves on a table in front of a small group of children. Have youngsters point to and count the leaves as you recite the rhyme below, replacing the underlined numbers, as needed, to match your set of leaves. Then invite a child to count the appropriate number of lizards and place one on each leaf. Repeat the activity until each child has had a turn to count lizards. One, two, three, four!

[One, two, three, four] green leaves.
Now, [child's name], count [four] lizards, if you please.

Basking Lizards

Representing and counting sets

Preschoolers bask in counting practice when they count lizards lying on a rock in the midday sun. Cut out a large rock shape from gray construction paper. Make two orange and two green construction paper copies of the lizard cards on page 257. Place the rock on a table and invite a small group of students to join you. Have a child roll a die and then count the dots on top. Instruct her to place the corresponding number of lizards (all of the same color) on the rock and then count them to make sure they equal the number of dots on the die. Then have her remove the lizards from the rock to ready the activity for the next child. Continue the activity until each student has had a turn.

For an added challenge, invite another child to roll the die during each round of play and add a second set of lizards (using the other color) to the rock. Have the group count the total number of lizards lying on the rock. Rock and roll reptiles!

Crunchy Counting

Counting sets, using problem-solving skills

Your preschoolers will eat up this counting activity, which has hungry lizards dining on flies for lunch. To prepare, make one construction paper copy of the gecko pattern on page 255 and the fly cards on page 257. Laminate the patterns and cards and then cut them out. Place the gecko and two sets of flies on a table in front of a small group. Then recite the poem below, replacing the underlined words with the appropriate numbers to match the fly sets. Instruct youngsters to count the total number of flies the lizard ate for lunch. That's one way to munch on math!

The very hungry lizard ate [three] flies for lunch.
Then he ate [one] more—crunch, crunch, crunch.
In all, how many did he munch?

Ten Little Lizards Lineup

Counting, sequencing numerals

This mathematical melody is sure to be a classroom favorite. Make copies of the lizard cards on page 257 so that you have ten cards. Color the lizards and cut out the cards; then use a permanent marker to label each one with a different number from 1 to 10. Glue a square of felt to the back of each lizard to ready it for flannelboard use. Place the lizards, one by one, in proper sequence on the flannelboard as you sing the song below.

For an added challenge, remove one lizard from the lineup. Have youngsters guess which lizard is missing. Count the lizards in order to check students' guesses. Then repeat the song and place the missing lizard back in its proper order in line. Ten little lizards all lined up!

(sung to the tune of "Ten Little Indians")

One little, two little, three little lizards,
Four little, five little, six little lizards,
Seven little, eight little, nine little lizards,
Ten lizards in a line.

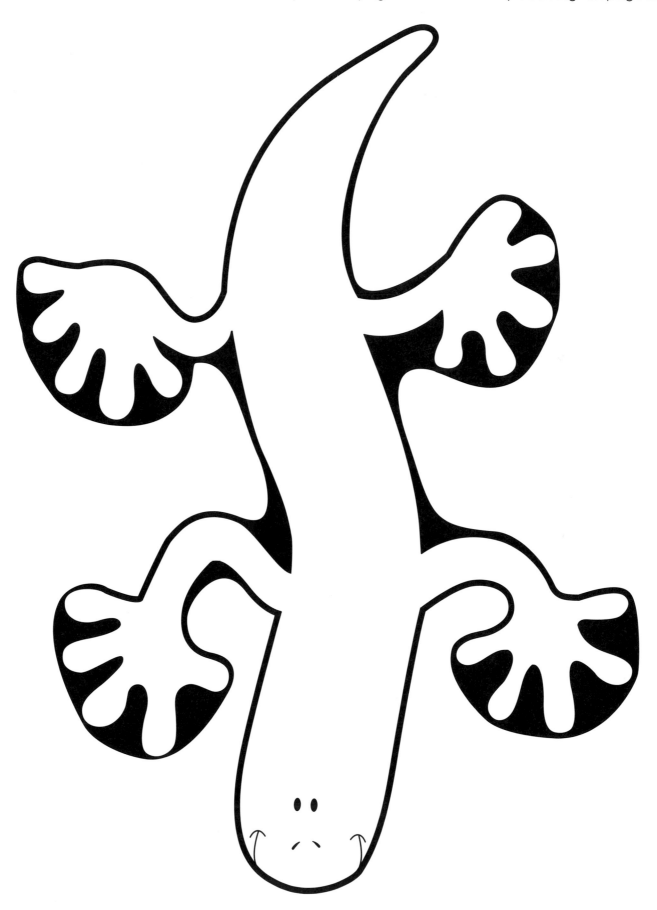

Leaf and Lizard Body Patterns
Use with "A Leafy Lesson" on page 253.

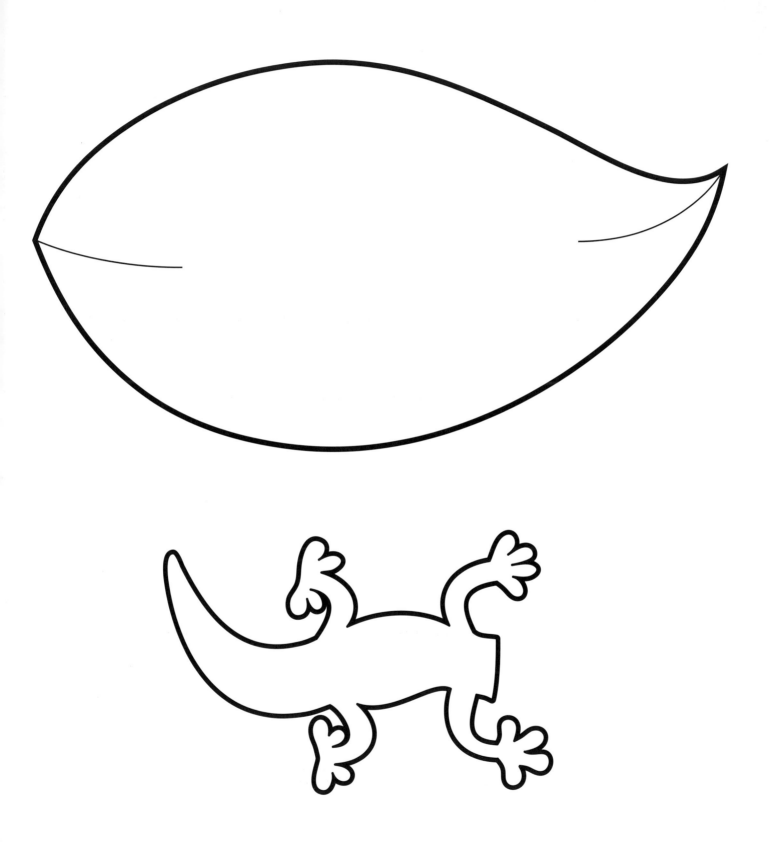

Lizard Cards

Use with "Basking Lizards" on page 253 and "Ten Little Lizards Lineup" on page 254.

Fly Cards

Use with "Crunchy Counting" on page 254.

A Numbers Race

Not too fast and not too slow—present the ideas in this unit at just the right pace to help youngsters increase number identification from 1 to 6. It's a winner!

ideas by Suzanne Moore, Irving, TX

Race Warm-Up
Identifying numbers, forming numbers

Students are ready for a race warm-up when they take these cute turtle puppets on a walk—a number formation walk, that is! Stock a center with rings cut from cardboard tubes, copies of the turtle puppet pattern on page 261, crayons, scissors, and glue. Make large number cards by programming each of six sheets of card stock with a different number from 1 to 6. Program each card with arrows showing the correct formation of the number. Cut lengths of Con-Tact covering slightly larger than each number card. Press a piece of covering over each card to adhere it to a table.

To make a puppet, have each child color and cut out a turtle puppet pattern and glue it to a cardboard ring. Instruct him to choose a number card, name the number on it, and then slip his puppet on his fingers. Have him take his turtle on a walk, using his fingers to trace over the number. Encourage him to choose another card and repeat the activity. Now that's a nice warm-up!

Feed the Turtles
Identifying numbers, counting

These turtles are hungry for a prerace snack! To prepare, paint the backs of six paper bowls green to resemble turtle shells. Glue a green craft foam head, a tail, and legs to each shell. Write a different number from 1 to 6 on the back of each shell. Remove at least 261 leaves from silk greenery and put them in a basket. Place the turtles and the basket at a center. A child chooses a turtle and identifies the number on its shell. Next, she counts the appropriate number of leaves and then feeds the turtle by slipping the leaves beneath its shell. Yum, yum!

Turtle Training

Identifying numbers, ordering numbers

As part of their training, youngsters help little turtles come out of hiding and line up in order. To prepare, make six copies of the turtle pattern on page 261. Color and cut out the turtles, write a different number from 1 to 6 on each shell, and then laminate the turtles for durability. Have students cover their eyes while you hide the turtles around the room. Then invite six volunteers to search for the turtles. While they're looking, have the rest of the class say the first chant below. When all the turtles have been caught, have each child holding a turtle identify the number on it. Next, instruct the turtle catchers to line up so that the turtles are in order from one to six. Then have the class say the second chant, pointing at the turtles in order while saying the final line. Repeat the activity until each child has had a chance to participate in the hunt. These turtles are lined up and ready to race!

Six turtles are hiding. Where can they be?
Each little turtle says, "You can't catch me!"

Six turtles were hiding. We found all six.
Each little turtle says, "Fiddlesticks!"
One, two, three, four, five, six!

Race Day Numbers

Identifying numbers

Every racer needs a number! Use this simple idea to have youngsters practice number identification. In advance, on bulletin board paper, draw a turtle with a large shell similar to the turtle on page 261. Divide the shell into six sections; then label each section with a different number from 1 to 6. Place the turtle on the floor. Have each child, in turn, toss a small beanbag on the turtle target and then identify the number on which the beanbag lands.

Prerace Rest

Identifying numbers, matching numbers to sets

These little turtles need to rest up before the big race, and a sunny log is just the place! Cut six log shapes from brown grocery bags. Draw knothole swirls on each log corresponding to a different number from 1 to 6; then laminate the logs. Place the logs and turtles numbered from 1 to 6, such as those made in "Turtle Training" on this page, at a center. Have each child who visits the center choose a turtle, identify its number, count the knotholes, and then place the turtle on the log with the corresponding number of holes. Ahh, well-rested turtles!

259

Spiffy Spots

Forming numbers, creating sets, counting

Slow and steady, that's the pace when little ones read these cute turtle-shaped number booklets. In advance, duplicate the booklet title on page 261 for each child. Cut enough six-inch paper plates in half so that each child will have seven halves. Stack the plate halves and staple them together as shown. Cut out a head, a tail, and two legs from green construction paper for each child.

To begin, have each student cut out the booklet title and glue it to the front of his booklet. Next, help each child write a different number from 1 to 6 on each page. Then have him identify the number on each page and use a green ink pad to make a corresponding number of thumbprint spots on the page. Help each child glue or staple the head, tail, and legs to the back of the last page of the booklet. Invite each youngster to read his book, counting the spots on each page. We're picking up the pace!

Race On Home!

Recognizing numbers

On your mark. Get set. Go! Here's a fun number chant that has little ones racing to reinforce number recognition. Cut out a log shape from brown paper or use one from "Prerace Rest" on page 259. Place the log on the floor and attach a frog sticker to it. Make six copies of the turtle pattern on page 261 and label each one with a different number from 1 to 6, or use the numbered patterns from "Turtle Training" on page 259. Randomly position the turtles on the log. Have a child, in turn, remove the appropriate turtle after the class says the poem below. Continue repeating the poem, substituting a different number from one to six in the last line until there are no turtles left. Repeat the activity until each child has had a chance to race a turtle home!

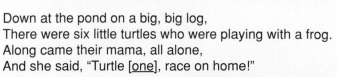

Down at the pond on a big, big log,
There were six little turtles who were playing with a frog.
Along came their mama, all alone,
And she said, "Turtle [one], race on home!"

Turtle Puppet Pattern
Use with "Race Warm-Up" on page 258.

Booklet Title
Use with "Spiffy Spots" on page 260.

How Many Spots Are on the Turtle's Shell?

by _____

©The Mailbox® • TEC41019 • June/July 2005

Turtle Pattern
Use with "Turtle Training" and "Prerace Rest" on page 259
and "Race On Home!" on page 260.

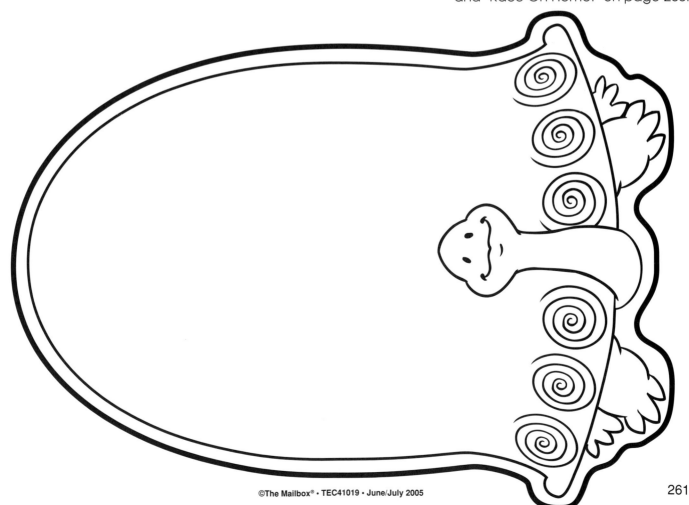

Stripes, Spots, ... Patterns!

Natural patterns are all around us, even in the fur coats that animals wear! Stripes and spots are common on animal coverings and make marvelous motifs for preschool patterning practice.

ideas by Lucia Kemp Henry, Fallon, NV

Animal Patterns

Describing patterns, locating patterns

Introduce your youngsters to the pleasing patterns of a zebra's zippy stripes and a leopard's spiffy spots with a flannelboard activity. To prepare, make a copy of the zebra and leopard pattern cards on page 266. Color and cut out the cards; then prepare them for flannelboard use. Begin by showing students pictures from magazines or books of a zebra and a leopard. Encourage them to describe each animal's fur. Write youngsters' responses on a chart. Next, display a leopard and a zebra pattern card on the flannelboard. Prompt students to name the animal that matches each pattern. Then discuss the repeated stripes and spots seen on the cards. Explain to youngsters that we can see patterns all around us, even in nature. Have students search for patterns in the classroom and then outside; then talk about the components of each pattern. Found a pattern!

Stripes and Spots
Duplicating and extending patterns

Invite little ones to use animal fur cards in this linear patterning activity. Make two copies of the cards on page 266 and prepare them for flannelboard use. Line up leopard and zebra pattern cards on the flannelboard to create a six-card *AB* pattern. Reinforce the pattern in the minds of your youngsters by having them chant the pattern names in sequence: "Stripe, spot, stripe, spot, stripe, spot!" Then ask a volunteer to duplicate the pattern on the flannelboard by lining cards up below the first set. Prompt youngsters to repeat the chant as the child arranges the cards.

For an added challenge, use the cards to display a pattern and have a volunteer extend the sequence. Have the class chant the pattern to check for accuracy. As students build patterning skills, vary the difficulty of the task by introducing different patterns. Soon your students' patterning skills will hit the spot!

Diagram A

Diagram B

Pattern Center
Duplicating and extending patterns

Pattern savvy students will enjoy sharpening their skills in this independent patterning center. To prepare, cut out multiple copies of the pattern cards on page 266; then cut each card in half. Arrange and glue several pattern cards to construction paper to make patterning boards as shown. Follow diagram A to make boards for duplicating patterns and follow diagram B to make boards for extending patterns. Place the patterning boards at a center along with a supply of pattern cards. Then invite pairs of students to visit the center for a patterning session with stripes and spots. What a fun way for students to earn their patterning stripes!

Leopard and Zebra Headbands
Creating a pattern

Here's a fun way for your little ones to wear the spots and stripes they've studied. To prepare, cover two tables with newspaper. Cut enough 3" x 24" strips of white and yellow bulletin board paper or construction paper so that each student can choose to make a zebra headband or a leopard headband. To prepare a zebra painting station, place brushes and a pan containing a thin layer of black paint on one table. To prepare a leopard painting station, place several two-inch round sponge stampers and a pan containing a thin layer of black paint on the other table. (To make a sponge stamper, pinch and pull out or cut out the center from a sponge for a leopard spot result. Hot-glue a film canister to the back of the sponge to make a handle.) Have each child choose to paint zebra stripes or leopard spots and give her the corresponding headband. Instruct each child to put on a paint smock. Write each child's name on the back of the headband; then direct her to the appropriate table to paint a pattern on her headband. When the paint is dry, fit each child's headband to her head and staple the ends together. Finally, help the child glue black paper zebra ears or yellow paper leopard ears to her headband as shown. Use the headbands to add fun and interest to the next two ideas!

Pattern Lineup
Extending a pattern

After youngsters have made their leopard or zebra headbands (above), invite students to put them on for a different kind of patterning practice! Line several students up in front of the class to create a leopard, zebra, leopard, zebra pattern (*AB* pattern). Reinforce the pattern by having children chant the animal names or make the animals' sounds in sequence as you point to each child in the line. Then, in turn, have each of the remaining students help extend the pattern by joining classmates who are already in line.

Later, vary the difficulty by introducing different, more complex patterns such as *AABB, ABBA,* or *AAB.* Your little learners will want to do this patterning activity again and again!

Stripes and Spots Rubbings

Creating a pattern, using fine-motor skills

It's fun to make rubbings, and the patterns produced are perfect for a patterning project. To prepare, use a hole puncher to make a supply of craft foam dots. Glue the dots to an index card as shown. Tape the card to the table in a center stocked with yellow paper and black paperless crayons. Next, cut narrow strips of foam and glue them to an index card in a striped pattern. Tape the card to the table in a center stocked with white paper and black paperless crayons. Have each child make several rubbings on one sheet of paper in each center. Then help him cut out his rubbings and glue them to a strip of construction paper to create a pattern. To extend the idea, have each child make additional rubbings, cut them out, and then take them home along with his pattern strip to practice extending a pattern with his family.

Percussion Patterns

Recognizing patterns of sound, duplicating a pattern

Spotlight different learning styles with this child-centered sound patterning activity. First, gather a supply of rhythm instruments such as wood blocks and rhythm sticks. Next, ask students to put on their animal headbands from "Leopard and Zebra Headbands" on page 264. Then have students form a zebra group and a leopard group. Give all the children in one group the same kind of instrument. For example, zebras might clap wood blocks while leopards might tap rhythm sticks. Then use both instruments to model an *AB* sound pattern at a slow pace. Have youngsters duplicate the pattern several times. After youngsters get the hang of playing the instruments in a pattern, introduce new patterns and encourage them to duplicate them. Tap, clap, tap, clap!

265

Zebra and Leopard Pattern Cards
Use with "Animal Patterns" on page 262 and "Stripes and Spots" and "Pattern Center" on page 263.

THEMATIC UNITS

Preschool Roundup

Welcome your little buckaroos to school with this rootin'-tootin' roundup of ranch-themed activities. They'll be ready to saddle up for some preschool learning fun!

ideas contributed by Lucia Kemp Henry, Fallon , NV

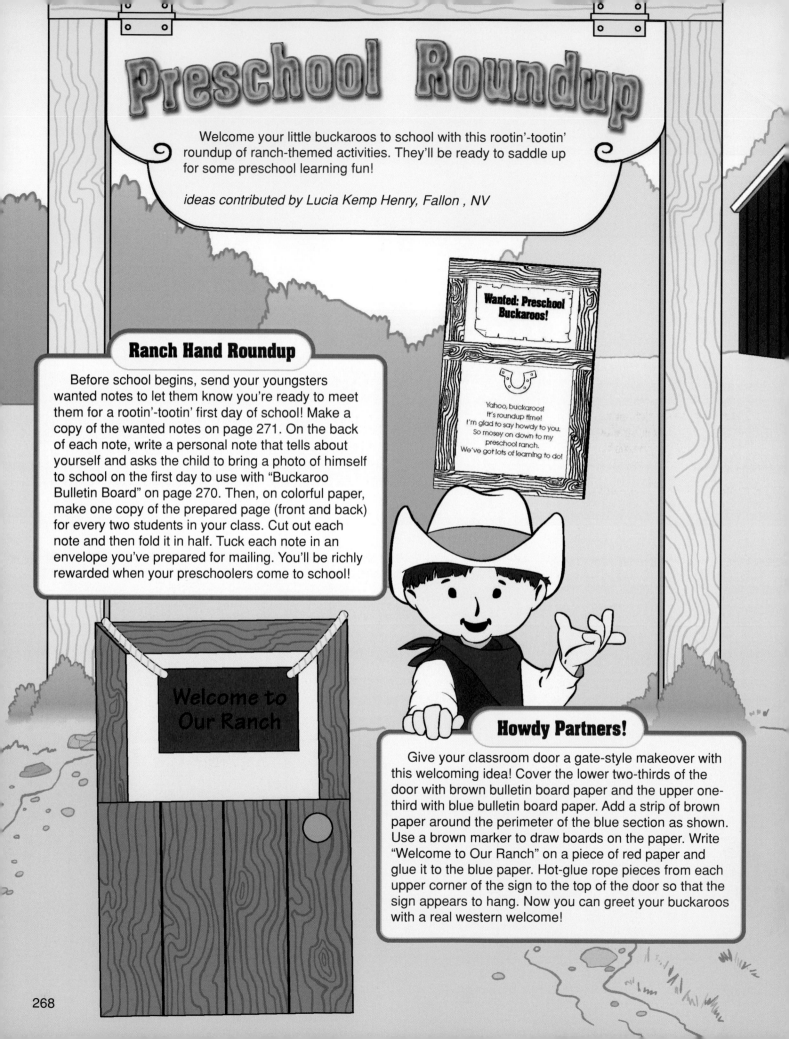

Wanted: Preschool Buckaroos!

Yahoo, buckaroos!
It's roundup time!
I'm glad to say howdy to you.
So mosey on down to my preschool ranch.
We've got lots of learning to do!

Ranch Hand Roundup

Before school begins, send your youngsters wanted notes to let them know you're ready to meet them for a rootin'-tootin' first day of school! Make a copy of the wanted notes on page 271. On the back of each note, write a personal note that tells about yourself and asks the child to bring a photo of himself to school on the first day to use with "Buckaroo Bulletin Board" on page 270. Then, on colorful paper, make one copy of the prepared page (front and back) for every two students in your class. Cut out each note and then fold it in half. Tuck each note in an envelope you've prepared for mailing. You'll be richly rewarded when your preschoolers come to school!

Welcome to Our Ranch

Howdy Partners!

Give your classroom door a gate-style makeover with this welcoming idea! Cover the lower two-thirds of the door with brown bulletin board paper and the upper one-third with blue bulletin board paper. Add a strip of brown paper around the perimeter of the blue section as shown. Use a brown marker to draw boards on the paper. Write "Welcome to Our Ranch" on a piece of red paper and glue it to the blue paper. Hot-glue rope pieces from each upper corner of the sign to the top of the door so that the sign appears to hang. Now you can greet your buckaroos with a real western welcome!

Ranch Hat Headbands

Here's a crafty cowboy hat that serves as a back-to-school nametag too! To prepare, make a copy of the hat pattern on page 272 for each child. Prepare a two-inch wide headband strip for each child. To make his Texas-style topper, invite each child to color the hat with crayons and cut it out. Have him glue a 1" x 4" strip of decorative paper to the hat for a band. Use a marker to write the child's name on the band. Next, lay the hat on the headband strip. Staple the middle five inches of the brim to the strip, leaving the brim's ends free as shown. Fit the band to the child's head and staple the ends together.

A Western Welcome

Invite each child to wear his hat as you sing this song to introduce him to the group.

(sung to the tune of "Mary Had a Little Lamb")

Howdy, [child's name]! How are you?
How are you? How are you?
Howdy, [child's name]! How are you?
We welcome you to school. Yahoo!

Buckaroo Bulletin Board

Lasso a photo of each child to display on this getting-to-know-you bulletin board. Photocopy the lasso pattern on page 273 for each child. Have him color his lasso as desired. Help him cut out his lasso around the outer edge. Then glue the pattern to a 9" x 12" piece of construction paper in the child's favorite color. Glue a copy of the child's photograph to the center of the lasso. Use a marker to write the child's name below his photo. Next, provide the child with paint and a star-shaped sponge stamper. Have the child print a star shape in each corner of the construction paper as shown. Help the child sprinkle glitter on each star while the paint is wet. Finally, display the personalized lasso frames on a bulletin board titled "Star Buckaroos!"

Star Buckaroos!

Annie

Josh

Penny

Terrance

Sally

Henry

Cafeteria

Around the Ranch

Use this rootin'-tootin' sign idea to give your first-of-the-year classroom or school tour western appeal. To make one sign, copy the lasso pattern on page 273 onto yellow paper. Cut out the pattern along the outer edge and glue it to a patterned sheet of scrapbook paper. Use a western font on your computer to generate the text for your sign; then print it, cut it out, and glue it to the center of the lasso as shown. (Alternately, use a wide marker to write the sign's text.) Display these signs around your classroom and the school. Remember to make signs for the office, music room, computer lab, art room, and cafeteria. Then take youngsters on the trail that leads to these important places.

I'll learn my 123's

Five Buckaroos

Invite groups of five little cowpokes to act out this fingerplay. Then encourage your buckaroos to share what they want to do and learn at school.

Five buckaroos galloped off to school.	*Wiggle five fingers.*
The first one said, "Yahoo! School is cool!"	*Point to thumb.*
The second one said, "There's learning to be done."	*Point to index finger.*
The third one said, "There's also time for fun."	*Point to middle finger.*
The fourth one said, "I'll learn my ABCs."	*Point to ring finger.*
The fifth one said, "I'll learn my 123s."	*Point to pinky.*
"Yippee!" said the five as they learned all day.	*Wiggle five fingers.*
Then the five buckaroos galloped off to play.	*Move hand behind back.*

Wanted: Preschool Buckaroos!

Yahoo, buckaroos!
It's roundup time!
I'm glad to say howdy to you.
So mosey on down to my
preschool ranch.
We've got lots of learning to do!

©The Education Center, Inc. • *The Mailbox*® • TEC41014 • Aug./Sept. 2004

Wanted: Preschool Buckaroos!

Yahoo, buckaroos!
It's roundup time!
I'm glad to say howdy to you.
So mosey on down to my
preschool ranch.
We've got lots of learning to do!

©The Education Center, Inc. • *The Mailbox*® • TEC41014 • Aug./Sept. 2004

Hat Pattern

Use with "Ranch Hat Headbands" on page 269.

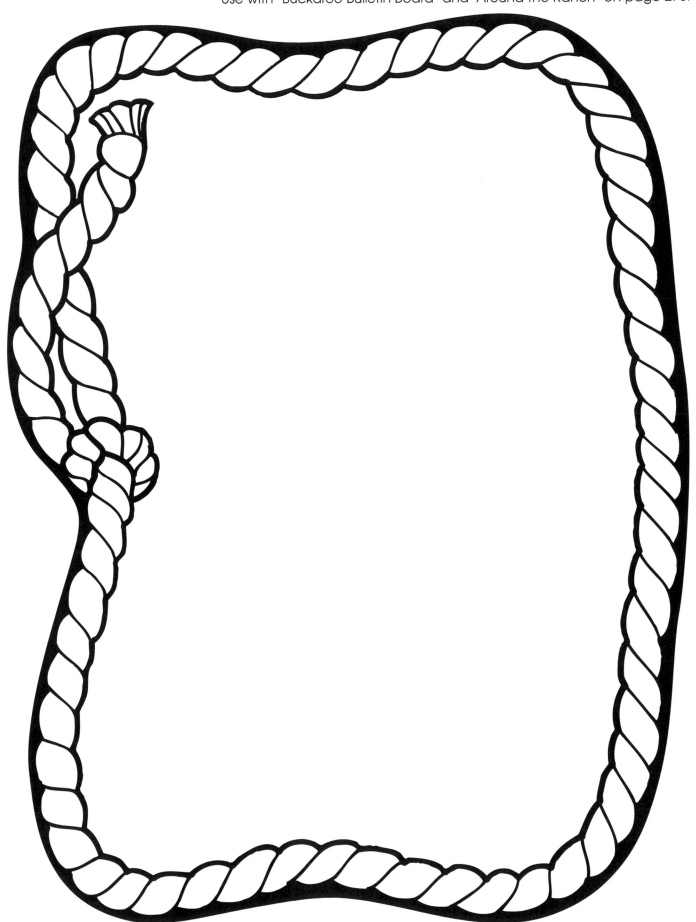

All About Our Bodies

Youngsters are always eager to learn about things that belong to them—and their bodies are no different! Use the activities in this unit to review body parts and introduce a few concepts that may be new to your students.

ideas contributed by Lenny D. Grozier

Body Brainstorming

Two eyes, two ears, one nose—the list goes on and on when little ones brainstorm the things they know about the human body. As students brainstorm, record their responses on a large body outline drawn on bulletin board paper. Use this resource to begin your exploration and investigation of the human body. Throughout this unit, revisit the chart and add to it as needed. You will be amazed at what your youngsters learn, and so will they!

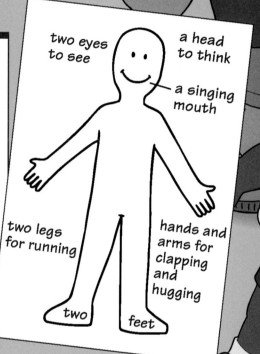

two eyes to see

a head to think

a singing mouth

two legs for running

hands and arms for clapping and hugging

two feet

I could smile.

I can swing high.

I will learn to read.

Betsy

See How We've Grown!

Bodies change and grow a lot from birth to preschool! To help preschoolers see how they've grown, take a photo of each child during the first few weeks of school and have the film developed. Ask parents to send in a copy of one of their child's baby photos. (Label the backs of photos with initials or first names.) Display the pictures and lead a discussion about what things students could do as babies, what things they can do now, and what things they hope to do when they grow bigger. Label students' pictures with their responses. Then give each child a sheet of construction paper and have her draw a picture of herself when she's older. Label her portrait with her future aspirations. Post the two pictures of each child along with the self-portrait on a bulletin board titled "See How We've Grown!"

Put a spin on a traditional game of Duck, Duck, Goose! by playing Eyes, Eyes, Nose! Have students sit in a circle in a large open area facing out. Choose a child to be It. Have her choose a body part for her sit word and another body part for her go word. As she goes around the circle, have her point to and say the chosen body part until she's ready for a chase. Continue the game until each child gets a turn. This game will keep little ones on their toes since each new It will be able to select her own body part key words. Eyes, Eyes, Nose!

Nose!

Pin the Part on the Person

Get your little ones laughing and moving with this classic party game! Begin by making two copies of the body pattern on page 277. Color each copy as desired and laminate it for durability. Then cut one body pattern into the following parts: head, trunk, arms, and legs. Mount the uncut body outline on a magnetic surface at the students' level. Add a strip of magnetic tape to the back of each body part and place the parts in a bag. Have a child choose a body part out of the bag and identify it. Blindfold him and guide him to the body outline; have the child place the part where he thinks it belongs. Then take the blindfold off the child and ask him whether he positioned the part correctly. If he says no, give him an opportunity to place the body part where it belongs. Continue until all body parts have been positioned. Get ready for some silliness and lots of learning along the way!

The Happy Health Song

Here's a great song to get the body moving and to teach your little ones some basic body-care concepts. Have fun staying fit!

(sung to the tune of "The Wheels on the Bus")

To stay healthy we go to sleep,
Go to sleep, go to sleep.
To stay healthy we go to sleep
To keep our bodies strong!

Pretend to sleep.

To stay healthy we eat good foods,
Eat good foods, eat good foods.
To stay healthy we eat good foods
To keep our bodies strong!

Pretend to eat.

To stay healthy we exercise,
Exercise, exercise.
To stay healthy we exercise
To keep our bodies strong!

Do jumping jacks.

To stay healthy we wash our hands
Wash our hands, wash our hands.
To stay healthy we wash our hands
To keep our bodies strong!

Pretend to wash hands.

Body Riddles

Get your little ones thinking critically with these body part riddles! Read the riddles below. As a child figures out the riddle, have him point to that body part. After children have chosen the body part, have them tell you the words in the riddle that gave them the clues to their answers. That's the way to use your noodle!

I use these parts to see
Objects big and small in size.
I have two that can open and close.
They are my eyes!

I use these parts to listen to sounds
Both far and near.
Some sounds are loud, and some are soft.
I hear them with my ears!

I use this part to smell many things
From cookies to a rose.
Breath in deep and take a guess.
This body part is my nose!

With these ten I can feel
Many, many things.
Some things feel hard, and some feel soft.
Have you guessed yet? I'm talking about my fingers!

I've used this part to taste new foods
Since I was very young.
I have just one inside my mouth.
This body part is my tongue!

Fall for Fall Veggies!

Carrots, corn, and potatoes—yum, yum! Autumn vegetables are packed with good nutrition and good learning, so harvest a bumper crop of these activities and prepare a learning feast for your little ones!

ideas by Roxanne LaBell Dearman—Preschool
Western NC Early Intervention Program for Children Who Are Deaf or Hard of Hearing,
Charlotte, NC

Sounds Delicious!

Listening to oral clues, identifying vegetables
Take the guesswork out of fall veggies when you play this game with your group! In advance, slip a carrot, potato, sweet potato, fresh ear of corn, and squash into an opaque bag. During circle time, tell students you have a bagful of vegetables that grow all summer and ripen in the fall. In turn, give clues about each vegetable. For example, when describing a carrot, you could say, "It's orange, long, and thin. The part we eat grows underground. We think rabbits like them a lot!" Or when describing a squash say, "It's yellow on the outside and white on the inside. It grows on a vine and rhymes with the word *wash!*" Next, encourage volunteers to name the mystery vegetable. When the correct name is given, dramatically pull it from the bag and begin giving clues about a different veggie. When your bag is empty, proudly pronounce your preschoolers as produce pros!

Harvest Ditty

Song participation, introducing vegetable growth habits
Cultivate youngsters' interest in vegetables with this energetic tune. It's perfect for a hoedown!

(sung to the tune of "Skip to My Lou")

Corn on the cornstalks grows above ground.
Corn on the cornstalks grows above ground.
Corn on the cornstalks grows above ground.
Let's go harvest our garden!

Potatoes in the dirt grow underground.
Potatoes in the dirt grow underground.
Potatoes in the dirt grow underground.
Let's go harvest our garden!

Continue with other verses:
Squash on long vines grows above ground.
Carrots are roots; they grow underground.

Tater Toss
Counting, developing gross-motor skills

One potato, two potato, three potato four! This counting game gets the wiggles out and more! To prepare, make ten little potatoes. To make a potato, stuff a newspaper ball into a clean knee-high stocking. Twist the free end of the stocking and then pull it over the ball. Repeat the last step; then knot the open end of the stocking and cut off any excess. If desired, add potato eyes with a permanent marker. Place the potatoes along with an empty basket on the floor in a center area. Invite a child in this center to pick up each tater and toss it into the basket. When all the taters have been tossed, have him count how many landed in the basket and how many landed outside the basket. Then have him pretend to plant each potato in a neat row for the next child. Small potatoes, big fun!

Carrot Patch Match
Matching same letters

Your little harvesters will be eager to try this 26-carrot activity! Prepare a carrot patch workmat by gluing a 9" x 24" piece of brown construction paper to the bottom half of an 18" x 24" piece of light blue construction paper. Next, make five white construction paper copies of the carrot patterns on page 281. Color each carrot. Program each top and bottom with an alphabet letter. Laminate the patterns for durability. Cut out the carrots and then cut the top off of each one. Store the carrot tops and bottoms in separate envelopes near the carrot patch mat. To complete this activity, a child selects ten carrot tops and places them on the blue part of the mat. Then he chooses the matching carrot bottoms and places them on the brown part of the mat as shown. When he finishes, he may clear the mat and repeat the activity with another set of carrot tops and bottoms.

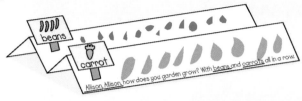

Preschool Produce
Completing a sentence
How do your preschoolers' gardens grow? With fall veggies and literacy skills all in a row! In advance, program a sheet of paper with the question and answer shown, leaving out the underlined words. Then make a class supply on tan construction paper. For each child, accordion fold a prepared sheet to create four sections. Then unfold the paper, and invite her to think about which two fall vegetables she would plant in her garden. Read the sentence starter aloud; then write as she dictates to complete it. Next, encourage her to illustrate each garden row to match her dictation. Then help her label each row with a small sticky note sign as shown. Refold students' papers and display the completed gardens on tabletops for little ones to read and enjoy. Hey—that's my friend's name! She grew beans and carrots!

Corn Cobs
Following directions, developing fine-motor skills
Sometimes it's fun to be a little corny! These colorful ears of corn are a creative addition to any fall vegetable study. In advance, collect a short cardboard tube for each child. Provide each child with a tube, a sheet of yellow construction paper, yellow tissue paper, an old paintbrush, green tissue paper, and water-thinned glue. Have each child tear yellow paper into small pieces to resemble corn kernels. Next, instruct him to brush glue on the tube and cover it with paper kernels to resemble an ear of corn. Wrap a half sheet of green tissue paper around the cob to represent husks. When the projects are dry, crumple yellow tissue paper and stuff it in one end of the tube to represent the top end of the corn ear. Display the ears of corn on construction paper stalks to create a classroom cornfield.

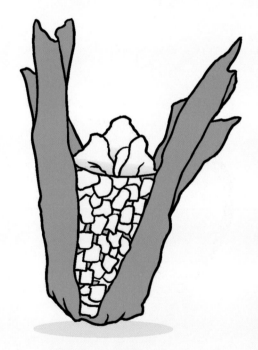

Some Grow Underground...
Identifying vegetables, sorting
...and some grow above the ground! This tasty sorting activity provides a healthy ending for your fall vegetable study. Purchase several cans of Veg•All mixed vegetables and warm the contents along with some precooked squash. Give each child a paper plate and a small spoonful of vegetables. Guide each child to identify her vegetables, discuss where they grow (above ground or below ground), and then have her sort like vegetables on her plate. When the veggies have been sorted and checked, invite each youngster to munch on a healthy harvest snack. Dig in!

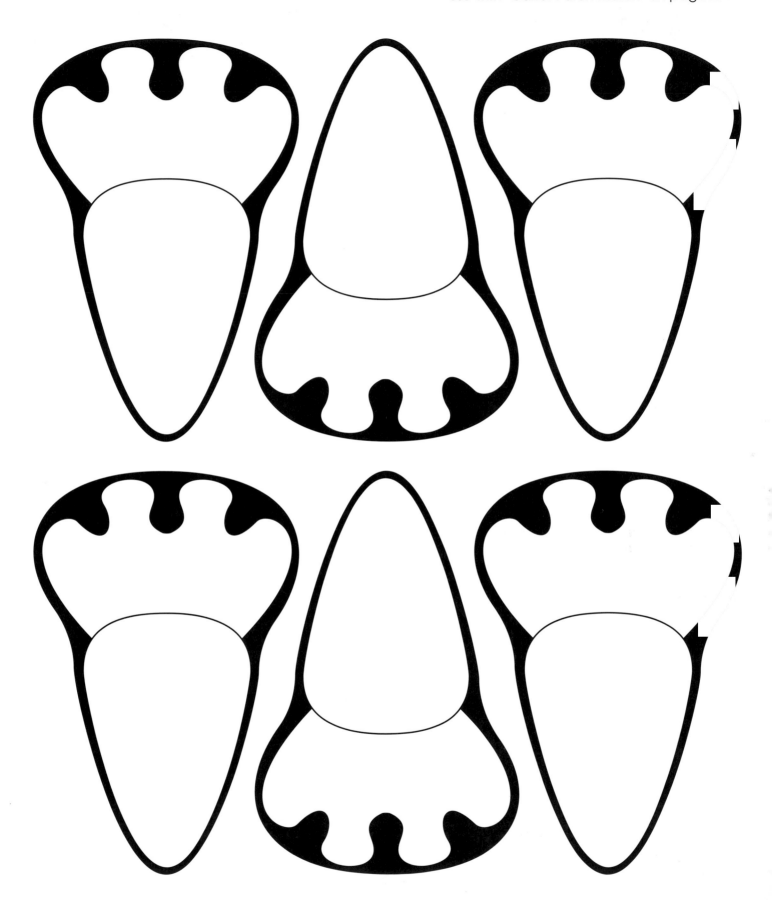

Fire Safety—a Hot Topic

Calling all junior firefighters! These clever ideas help your little ones become knowledgeable about firefighters and fire safety.

ideas by Jana Sanderson—PreK, Rainbow School, Stockton, CA

One Firefighter Went Out to Spray

After teaching youngsters this catchy rhyme, invite students to pretend to be firefighters. Choose a child to be the first firefighter. Have him hold a long jump rope (hose) as the first verse is recited. When another firefighter is called to join him, instruct the two to walk around the room pretending to spray a fire while saying the rhyme. The last firefighter to join the line calls the next firefighter until all the children are walking around the room. After all children are holding the hose, have them recite the last verse.

[One] firefighter(s) went out to spray
Water on a red-orange flame one day.
The fire got big and hot that day.
So [he] called a friend to help [him] spray.

All the firefighters went out to spray
Water on a red-orange flame one day.
The big, hot fire was soon put out
By the brave firefighters, without a doubt!

Flashy Fire Hats

Children will be fired up to make these colorful hats to wear as you study fire safety. To prepare, cut thin strips of red, yellow, and orange tissue paper and metallic gift wrap. Make enough copies of the firefighter badges on page 286 so that each child will have one. Cut an 18" x 24" length of Con-Tact covering for each child. Pull back one half of the paper backing to expose a 12" x 18" sticky area. Tape the corners of the covering to a table to prevent it from moving. Have each child color and cut out a badge and add it facedown to his project as shown. Then instruct each youngster to cut the prepared strips into little pieces, allowing them to fall on the sticky surface. When each child has finished cutting the strips, pull off the remaining paper backing and fold the covering over the project. Cut each child's Con-Tact covering as shown to make a firefighter's hat. Encourage youngsters to sport their hats while completing the remaining activities in this unit.

Rule Out Fire

"Stop, drop, and roll" is an important fire safety rule for little ones to know and practice. After practicing this method for extinguishing flames, reinforce the activity with an art project to remind youngsters what to do if their clothes catch on fire. In advance, write or type "STOP," "DROP," and "ROLL" on a sheet of paper several times. Make enough copies so that each child will have one set of words. Trace a shirt pattern on the fold of a sheet of white construction paper for each child. Have each student cut out his shirt. Next, direct him to dip a long length of dental floss in red paint and lay it inside the fold of his shirt cutout, leaving a free end trailing out. Then press the folded paper as the child pulls the floss out. Repeat the process with orange and yellow paint until the shirt is covered in colorful flames. Unfold the cutout and allow the paint to dry. Have each child cut apart his set of words. Finally, assist him as he glues the commands on his painted shirt. Post the shirts on a wall and refer to them daily.

Truckloads of Tasks

Youngsters will drive away with a better understanding of our fire fighting friends after making this nifty class book. Make a white construction paper copy of the fire truck page on page 285 for each child. Read *I Want to Be a Firefighter* published by Firefly Books Ltd. Give each child a copy of page 285, and have her draw a firefighter in the window of the truck. Then have her use watercolors to paint the truck and ladder. Next, invite her to add glitter glue to the lights on the truck. When the paint and glue are dry, have each student dictate to complete the sentence at the bottom of the page. Bind the pages between red construction paper covers, and title the book "Firefighters!" Share the book with the class and then put it in your reading area. This book is sure to be a hot reading selection!

Hot Tips

Stop! Don't get burned. A tip a day keeps the firefighter away! Make a copy of pages 287 and 288. Color and laminate the stop sign on page 287. Post the stop sign on a wall within students' reach. Color (if desired) and cut out the safety cards on page 288. Number the backs of the cards as shown, and then laminate them. Tape each card on the sign as shown. Each day, have a different child remove a card from the wall. Read and discuss the tip on the card. Encourage youngsters to guess what is hidden beneath the cards. Post the safety cards around the display and review them each day. Continue selecting cards, reading the safety tips, and guessing what is hidden until the stop sign is revealed. Stop! Don't touch!

A Calculated Climb

Enthusiasm for math climbs to a new level as young firefighters count the rungs of their ladders all the way to the top. To prepare, make a game spinner as shown. Use chalk to draw several ladders with ten rungs each on pavement outdoors. Make a house for each ladder from a box, including a cardboard tube chimney. Stuff a small piece of red tissue paper in the tube to represent fire. Place a spray bottle filled with water next to the house.

To play, have each child, in turn, spin the spinner. If the spinner lands on a number, the child pretends to climb the ladder that number of rungs. If the spinner lands on the flame, she moves down her ladder one rung to symbolized that the fire is too hot. When a child reaches the top rung, invite her to use the water bottle to spray the tissue paper flames!

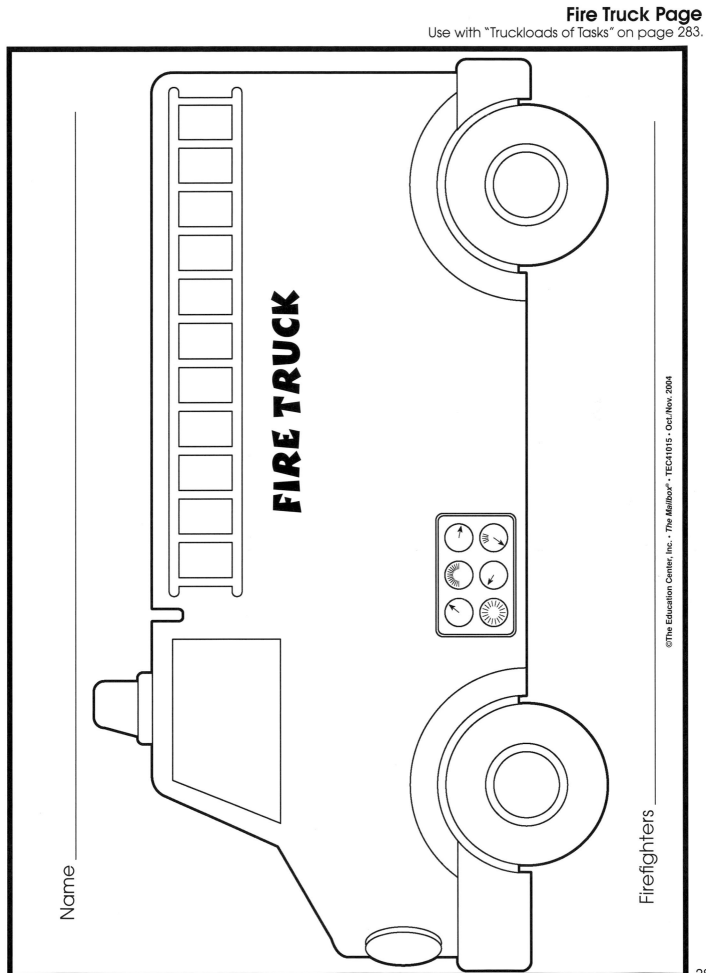

FIRE TRUCK

Name

Firefighters

Firefighter Badge
Use with "Flashy Fire Hats" on page 282.

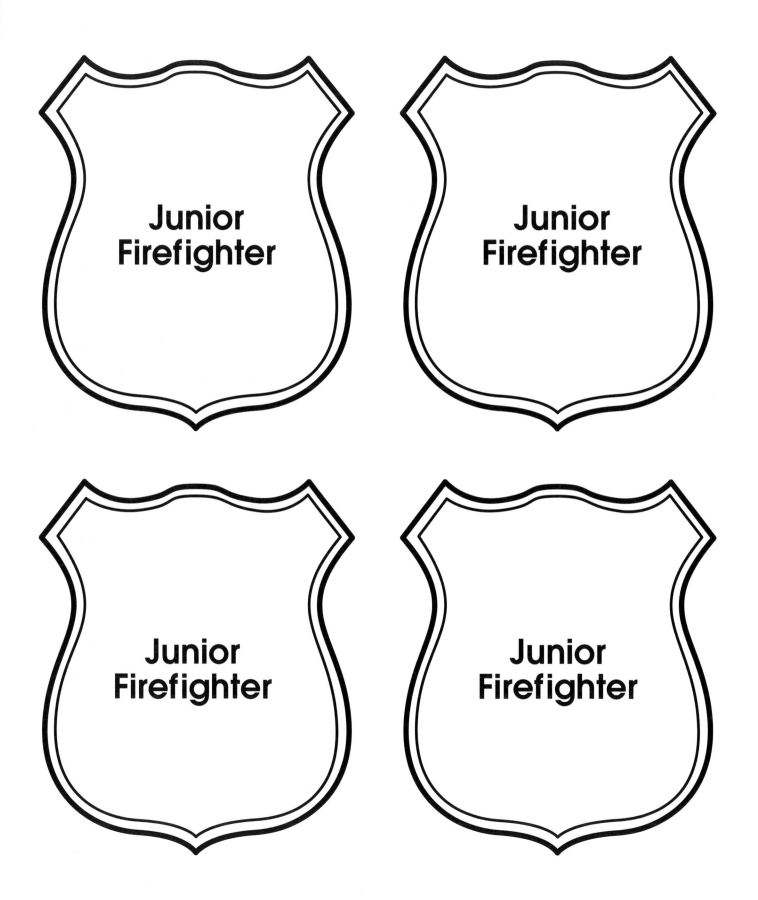

Junior
Firefighter

Junior
Firefighter

Junior
Firefighter

Junior
Firefighter

Fire Safety Cards
Use with "Hot Tips" on page 284.

Don't touch fire.

Don't touch matches.

Don't touch a hot grill.

Don't touch a hot slide.

Don't touch a hot stove.

Don't touch a hot iron.

Don't touch hot bath water.

Don't touch a hot heater.

Don't touch a hot curling iron.

'Tis the Season for Learning

Deck the halls with lots of learning…fa, la, la, la, la! Use the excitement of the season to help your little ones get hooked on learning using this ornament-related thematic unit.

ideas by Angie Kutzer, Garrett Elementary, Mebane, NC

Festive Letters

● *Observing the shapes of letters* ●

Make learning letters more festive with this decorative idea. Program a sheet of construction paper for each child with her first initial. Provide her with a bingo dauber to dot over the penciled lines. Then show each child how to draw a hook on several dots to create ornaments. Invite each child to share her letter with the class. For added interest, provide youngsters with holiday stickers to decorate the areas around their letters. Bind the pages between construction paper covers and title the book "Festive Letters."

A Perfect Pick

● *Using vocabulary, visual discrimination* ●

Reinforce the use of descriptive vocabulary with this circle-time guessing game. Place an assortment of eight to 12 ornaments in front of youngsters. Secretly choose one to describe. For example, you might say, "I see an ornament that is flat. It's shiny. It has curvy lines." With each new clue, pause a moment to allow youngsters to look over the collection. After giving your description, encourage students to point to the appropriate ornament. Then start again with a new ornament description. After youngsters understand the game, invite a volunteer to describe an ornament of his choice. Continue play until each child has had a turn.

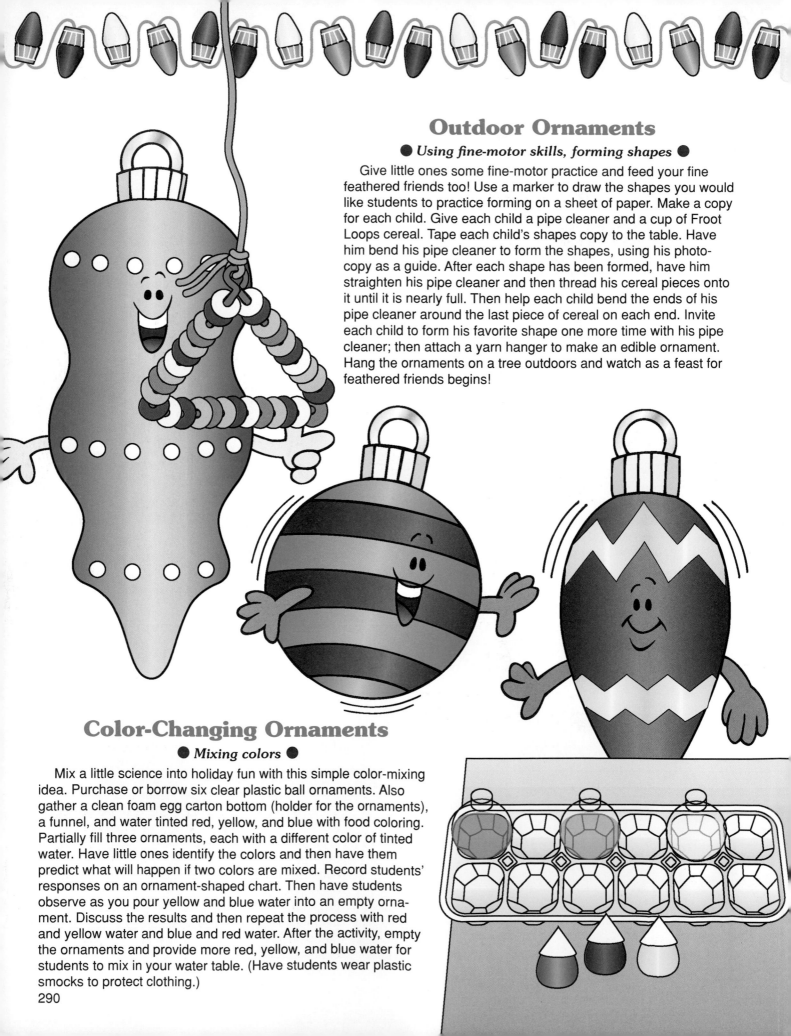

Outdoor Ornaments

● *Using fine-motor skills, forming shapes* ●

Give little ones some fine-motor practice and feed your fine feathered friends too! Use a marker to draw the shapes you would like students to practice forming on a sheet of paper. Make a copy for each child. Give each child a pipe cleaner and a cup of Froot Loops cereal. Tape each child's shapes copy to the table. Have him bend his pipe cleaner to form the shapes, using his photocopy as a guide. After each shape has been formed, have him straighten his pipe cleaner and then thread his cereal pieces onto it until it is nearly full. Then help each child bend the ends of his pipe cleaner around the last piece of cereal on each end. Invite each child to form his favorite shape one more time with his pipe cleaner; then attach a yarn hanger to make an edible ornament. Hang the ornaments on a tree outdoors and watch as a feast for feathered friends begins!

Color-Changing Ornaments

● *Mixing colors* ●

Mix a little science into holiday fun with this simple color-mixing idea. Purchase or borrow six clear plastic ball ornaments. Also gather a clean foam egg carton bottom (holder for the ornaments), a funnel, and water tinted red, yellow, and blue with food coloring. Partially fill three ornaments, each with a different color of tinted water. Have little ones identify the colors and then have them predict what will happen if two colors are mixed. Record students' responses on an ornament-shaped chart. Then have students observe as you pour yellow and blue water into an empty ornament. Discuss the results and then repeat the process with red and yellow water and blue and red water. After the activity, empty the ornaments and provide more red, yellow, and blue water for students to mix in your water table. (Have students wear plastic smocks to protect clothing.)

I'm a Little Ornament

● *Singing a song* ●

Sing this quick song with your little ones to get those wintry wiggles out and get youngsters ready for learning!

(sung to the tune of "I'm a Little Teapot")

I'm a shiny ornament, big and round.
I'm hanging on the tree while watching the ground.
When the children come in with a bound,
I dance and wiggle to their joyful sound!

Hold arms out in front, making a big circle.
Put hand above eyes as if searching below.
Jump.
Sway back and forth.

Children paint tree

Jump 12 times.

Countdown to Christmas

● *Reviewing skills* ●

This "undecorating" idea leads to lots of fun skills review. To prepare, cut out a large tree shape from green bulletin board paper and mount it near your calendar. Make several colorful construction paper copies of the ornament patterns on page 293 so that you will have one pattern for each school day in December. Program each cutout with a different activity, such as "Sing the alphabet," "Jump 12 times," or "Name your favorite color." Cut out the patterns and attach them to the tree. Each day during calendar time, have a different student remove an ornament from the tree. Read the activity aloud and encourage youngsters to complete the given task. Just a few more days to go!

Trim the Tree
● *Sorting letters and numbers* ●

Youngsters will love decorating as they discriminate between letters and numbers. In advance, purchase a large supply of nonbreakable ornaments. Tie a yarn hanger to each one. Then set up two small artificial trees at a center. Top each tree with a tagboard star labeled with either a letter or a number. Use a marker or programmed sticky dots to label the ornaments, each with a different letter or number. Store the ornaments in a gift bag. Invite each child to take a turn at the center and sort the ornaments. Then have him use the ornaments to trim the appropriate tree. After each child has had a turn, encourage youngsters to sort the ornaments by different attributes, such as shiny or painted, metal or plastic, or heavy or light and then decorate the trees again. The possibilities for this sorting activity are nearly endless!

A Class Snack
● *Following directions* ●

Eat an ornament? Sure! Culminate this unit by using refrigerated sugar cookie dough to bake one large cookie in a pizza pan. After the cookie has cooled, invite little ones to help turn it into a gigantic ornament. Provide tubes of colored frosting and small candies and guide youngsters to use them to create patterns on the cookie. Add a length of red licorice for a hook. Be sure to take a photo of your little bakers with the finished product before everyone digs in!

Be a Smart Cookie— Use Your Senses!

Sounds abound and the smells are swell when you bake a batch of Christmas cookies! Use these ideas centered around baking cookies to help youngsters understand their five senses.

ideas by Ada Goren, Winston-Salem, NC

The Case of the Missing Cookie
Sense of sight, visual memory

Now you see it; now you don't! That's just what happens in this activity, which puts your little ones' visual memories to the test. To prepare, duplicate the cookie patterns on page 297 onto tagboard. Color each one as desired and cut it out. Then add a piece of magnetic tape to the back of each one. Sit with a small group and display a number of cookies on a metal cookie sheet. Ask youngsters to look carefully at all the cookies. Explain that you are going to take one cookie away and that they'll have to figure out which one is missing. After students have a chance to study the cookies, ask everyone to close his eyes. Remove one cookie; then have the children open their eyes. Who can guess which cookie is gone?

Cookie Shapes
Sense of touch

Stars, trees, candy canes...holiday cookies come in lots of shapes! Gather a variety of distinctively shaped plastic holiday cookie cutters for a festive feely box activity! First, trace each shape onto a sheet of construction paper. Display the paper next to your feely box at a center. Put the cookie cutters inside the feely box. Have a child reach inside, choose a cookie cutter, and use his sense of touch to carefully examine the shape of the cutter. Have him look at the sheet of traced shapes and determine which shape he is holding. Then have him pull out the cookie cutter to check his guess. Have him reach in and identify another cookie cutter until he's found them all!

Tappity-Tap
Sense of hearing, auditory memory

What's the essential equipment for baking cookies? Bowls and spoons, of course! Give each child in a small group a metal bowl and a wooden spoon and invite her to pretend to mix up a batch of cookie dough. Then ask youngsters to use their bowls and spoons to exercise their sense of hearing! Ask them to listen carefully as you tap your own spoon on your bowl a number of times. Then ask them to imitate your taps. If necessary, help younger preschoolers by counting aloud as you tap. Older preschoolers may be up to the challenge of copying a pattern, such as tap, tap-tap, tap, tap-tap.

Name That Scent!
Sense of smell, critical thinking

One of the most delightful things about baking cookies is the delicious smell. Ask your preschoolers to put their noses to work as they explore some common cookie scents! To prepare, put some or all of the following in individual margarine tubs: peanut butter, chocolate syrup, ground cinnamon, coconut extract, and vanilla extract. Poke holes in the plastic lids so that youngsters can smell the substances inside but can't see them. Sit with one small group at a time. Pass around one tub at a time and after each child has sniffed the scents, recite the following rhymes for each one. Can your little ones guess each scent by using the clues and their noses?

Peanut butter:
This smell starts a growl in my belly.
It tastes so very good with some jelly!

Chocolate:
A favorite flavor, my, oh my!
Find it in cakes, candy bars, shakes, and pie.

Vanilla:
This flavor makes lots of things taste just right.
It's the flavor of ice cream that's just plain white.

Cinnamon:
Mix it with sugar; give it a sprinkle or shake.
Yummy with toast, apple pie, or oatmeal you make.

Coconut:
This stuff comes in little flakes of white.
Yummy in cake, pie, or cookies to bite!

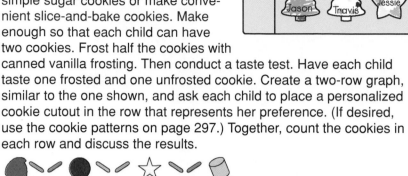

Do You Favor Frosting?
Sense of taste, graphing

All this talk of cookies is bound to have your preschoolers wishing they could eat a few! So mix up a batch of simple sugar cookies or make convenient slice-and-bake cookies. Make enough so that each child can have two cookies. Frost half the cookies with canned vanilla frosting. Then conduct a taste test. Have each child taste one frosted and one unfrosted cookie. Create a two-row graph, similar to the one shown, and ask each child to place a personalized cookie cutout in the row that represents her preference. (If desired, use the cookie patterns on page 297.) Together, count the cookies in each row and discuss the results.

Do You Favor Frosting?				
Yes	Beth	Mikayla	Sharon	Jon
No	Jason	Travis	Jessie	

Song of the Senses
Senses review, rhythm and rhyme

After inviting children to participate in baking a batch of cookies, teach them this song to review how they've used their five senses.

(sung to the tune of "If You're Happy and You Know It")

If you're going to bake some cookies, use your ears.
If you're going to bake some cookies, use your ears.
Hear the mixer mix the dough.
Is it going fast or slow?
If you're going to bake some cookies, use your ears.

If you're going to bake some cookies, use your hands.
If you're going to bake some cookies, use your hands.
Roll the dough out smooth and flat.
With your hands, give it a pat.
If you're going to bake some cookies, use your hands.

If you're going to bake some cookies, use your nose.
If you're going to bake some cookies, use your nose.
Smelling cookies bake is fun!
Your nose will tell you when they're done!
If you're going to bake some cookies, use your nose.

If you're going to bake some cookies, use your eyes.
If you're going to bake some cookies, use your eyes.
Choose the frosting that's just right;
Make them such a pretty sight!
If you're going to bake some cookies, use your eyes.

If you're going to bake some cookies, use your mouth.
If you're going to bake some cookies, use your mouth.
Eat the cookies when they're through.
Do they taste yummy to you?
If you're going to bake some cookies, use your mouth.

Love Is in the Air!

Youngsters will fall in love with the valentine-related ideas in this thematic unit. Let the love of learning begin!

by Roxanne LaBell Dearman, Western NC Early Intervention Program for Children Who Are Deaf or Hard of Hearing, Charlotte, NC

Valentines for All
Recognizing names, developing literacy

Get everyone involved in this heartfelt ditty by using each child's name in the song! To prepare, print each child's name on a large construction paper heart. On the back of each cutout, print a three-syllable message such as "I like you," "You are nice," or "We are friends." Hold up a heart and have youngsters identify whose name is on it. Then instruct students to sing the song below, substituting the selected child's name and message in the verses.

(sung to the tune of "Mary Had a Little Lamb")

[Kayla] has a valentine, valentine, valentine.
[Kayla] has a valentine,
And this is what it says:

(Turn the heart over and read the message before singing the second verse.)

The valentine says, "[You are nice]," "[You are nice]," "[You are nice]."
The valentine says, "[You are nice]."
Happy Valentine's Day!

Special Delivery
Counting to 10, recognizing numerals

This first-class activity will have preschoolers practicing counting skills while delivering valentines. To prepare, label the back of each of several valentine cards with an action such as "walk," "hop," "tiptoe," etc. Cut out ten construction paper hearts and number them 1 to 10. Then adhere the hearts to the floor with clear Con-Tact covering to make a trail. Position a mailbox at one end of the trail. Invite a small group of children to join you at the trail's other end. Have each child, in turn, select a valentine. Then read the action on the back of his card to the group. Have him count each heart as he hops or steps on his way to the mailbox. After he reaches the box, have him say, "Happy Valentine's Day," as he slips the card inside. Repeat the activity until each child has had a turn to deliver a valentine. That's first-rate fun!

To practice numeral recognition, label index cards with one number on each side so that when added together the sum equals ten. For example, use numbers two and eight on the same card. During play, have a child draw a card, say the number on one side, take that number of steps, say the number on the other side, and then take the remaining number of steps to deliver the card.

Love Puzzles
Completing a sentence

Little ones put together a loving message, piece by piece, with these heartfelt puzzles. Make a tagboard copy of the valentine on page 301 for each child. Have each youngster think of someone to whom he would like to send a valentine. Then write each child's dictation to complete the sentence on his paper. Have him draw a picture to depict his words. Use a pencil to lightly draw lines on the valentine that, when cut, will make a three- or four-piece puzzle. Have each youngster cut out the valentine and then cut along the puzzle lines. Encourage each student to put his puzzle together before placing the pieces into an envelope to deliver to someone special.

I love *you because you* *read books to me.*

Sweet Shapes
Identifying and matching shapes

Put those beautiful, empty candy boxes to good use by making this matching game. Cut several shapes from brown craft foam to resemble chocolates (rectangle, heart, circle, oval, and square). Trace the shapes on the bottom of a candy box. Place the candy shapes in a bag. Invite one pair of students to play at a time. Have each child, in turn, reach into the bag, pick up a candy, feel its shape, and use the outlines in the bottom of the box as a guide to help guess its shape. Then instruct her to remove the candy from the bag and position it on its shape in the bottom of the box. Play continues until all of the candy pieces have been placed. Sweet learning!

Alphabet Love Letters
Understanding letter-sound correspondence

Transform your literacy center into a little post office and have youngsters prepare these special valentines for delivery! Make a copy of the animal labels and stamp patterns on the back of the centerfold. Next, prepare eight envelopes by coloring and cutting out the animal labels and then gluing one label to each envelope as shown. Seal the envelopes and laminate them for durability. Color, cut out, and laminate the stamp patterns. Attach the hook side of a piece of Velcro fastener to each envelope where the stamp should go, and attach the loop side of each corresponding piece to the back of each stamp.

To play, have each child attach the corresponding stamp to the appropriate envelope by matching the animal's beginning sound to the correct letter stamp. You have mail!

Sunny Valentines
Using fine-motor skills, name writing

Youngsters warm up to this art activity in no time! Give each child a paper plate and have him paint it yellow. After the paint has dried, cut each child's plate into a sun shape. Invite each little sweetheart to use heart stamps and ink pads to make prints on her sun. On the back of each project write "Valentine, you are my sunshine!" Have each child sign her name under the sentiment. Display the suns from your ceiling for several days before sending them home with students. Hooray!

Love Potion
Mixing colors

Mix a little science into your valentine unit with a color-mixing drink! In advance, use food coloring to tint one container of water red and another container of water blue. Pour the colored water into ice cube trays and freeze. Give each child a clear cup half-filled with a lemon-lime soda. Help him add red ice cubes and blue ice cubes to his cup. Then instruct him to stir his potion with a straw and observe any changes. Talk about what students observe as the ice cubes begin to melt and then invite them to sip on their purple love potion.

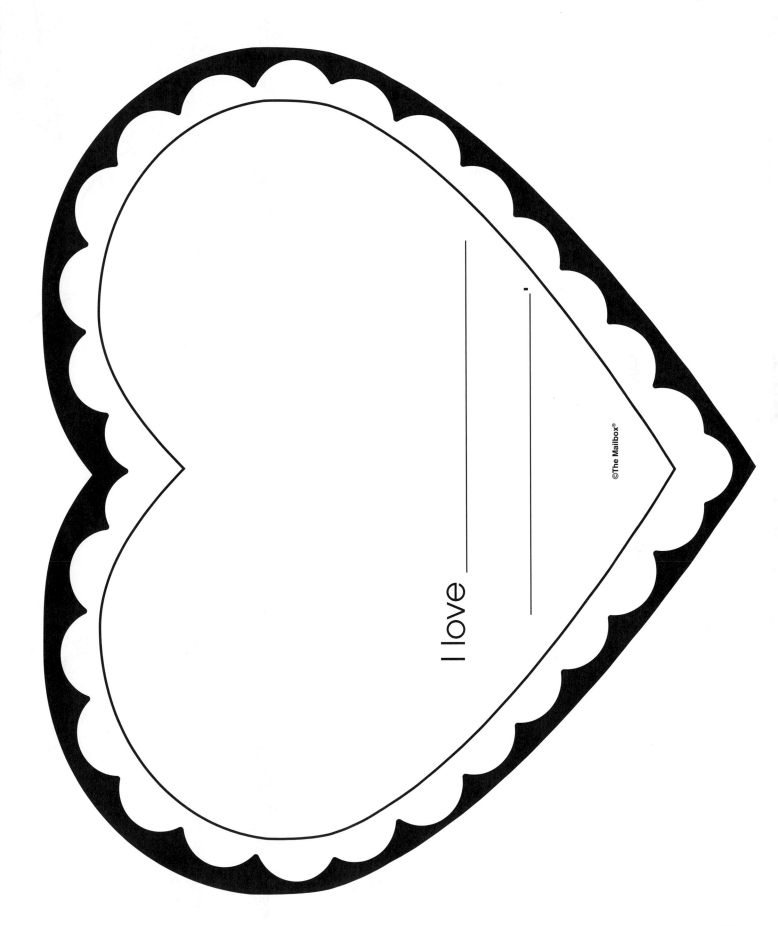

I love _____

©The Mailbox®

Up, Up, and Away With Kite Fun!

Youngsters are sure to soar into spring with these high-flying ideas focused on kites!

ideas by Suzanne Moore, Irving, TX

blowing bubbles

swinging

riding a bike

playing ball

Lucky Song

Encourage creative thinking and build oral language skills with *Lucky Song,* a simple and charming tale by Vera B. Williams. Before reading the story, ask youngsters what they enjoy doing on a windy day; jot down responses on a kite-shaped chart. Then introduce students to Evie by displaying the cover of the book, and ask youngsters what they think she might enjoy doing on a windy day. Share the book with your class and then discuss Evie's lucky day. What kinds of things make it lucky? Then ask youngsters to talk about their own lucky days. Volunteers will be eager to sing their own lucky day songs for the group.

Kite Flight

Big or little; simple or ornate—kites come in all shapes, sizes, and designs. The only thing that makes a kite a kite is that it soars through the air at the end of a line. A light wind, along with the string and a few artful tugs, keeps a kite in the air. Kick off your kite studies by inviting a kite-flying guest to give a demonstration for students. Then have your highfliers make and fly some simple kites with "Round Up" on page 303.

302

Round Up

Who says kites have to be diamond shaped? Paper plates and yarn are the only supplies needed for students to make a circular kite. In advance, prepare the plates by punching four holes in each one as shown. Cut five 14" lengths of yarn per plate. Invite each child to decorate her plate with stickers. Help each child tie one end of each yarn length to a different hole; then tie the free ends of the strings together to form one knot. Assist her in tying the fifth string to the knot. Encourage students to run holding the kite string. It flies!

Attach the Tail to the Kite

Here's a fun twist to Pin the Tail on the Donkey that will have your students jumping for joy. In advance, cut a large kite from poster board. Invite youngsters to decorate the kite by using colorful markers to write their names on it. Tape the kite to the wall, just high enough to be out of students' reach. Next, cut a 24" length of crepe paper and attach a loop of tape to one end of the strip. Invite children to take turns trying to attach the tail to the kite. They'll have a jumping good time doing it!

Steven Amy Daniel Cathy Pete Maria Debbie

Flying High

Your little kite lovers will get a spatial relations workout that focuses on the concepts of over and under when they manipulate their kite puppets and sing this high-flying song. In advance, make a class set of the kite pattern on page 306. Invite each student to color her pattern as desired; then assist her in gluing a ten-inch yarn tail to the bottom of the kite. Last, have her tape a jumbo craft stick to the back of her kite. Encourage your little ones to manipulate their stick puppets and sing the song below.

(sung to the tune of "The Bear Went Over the Mountain")

My kite flies over the table.
My kite flies over the table.
My kite flies over the table.
My kite can fly so high.

My kite flies under the table.
My kite flies under the table.
My kite flies under the table.
My kite can swoop so low.

The Sky's the Limit

With a movement activity like this, the sky's the limit! Begin by inviting students to create a kite headband. Make a class set of the kite pattern on page 306. Have students color their kites. Next, give each child a 16" strip of crepe paper. Have him cut and then glue scrap paper bows to the crepe paper, creating a kite tail. To complete the kite headband, staple a sentence strip to fit each child's head. Then staple the kite onto the back of the band. Now your little kite lovers are ready to move! Play instrumental music and invite students to don their headbands and pretend to be kites leaping, soaring, dancing, and dipping around the classroom.

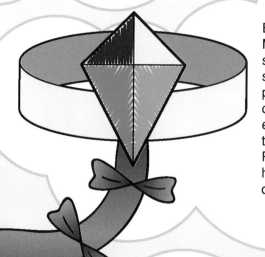

Shape Up!

The traditional shape of a kite is a diamond. Show children two large attribute block triangles. Recite to your children the poem below while putting the triangles together to form a diamond. Then give each child his own pair of triangles so he can make a diamond too!

Here is a triangle—one, two, three.
Triangles have three sides, as you see.
Put two together just like so.
Now it's a diamond. This I know!

Kite Names

Name recognition is the name of this game. To prepare, make a class set of the kite pattern on page 306. Invite each child to color his kite as desired. Collect the kites and write each child's name twice on his completed project, as shown, using a black permanent marker. Cut out the kites and laminate them for durability. Cut the laminated kites in half, mix them up, and place them in a basket. Challenge your youngsters to put the kites together by matching the names on the pieces.

What Would You See if You Were a Kite?

Where would you go? Would you fly over the school? Over the zoo? Over the mountains? During this discussion, students' imaginations will soar to new heights! In advance, cut a supply of kite shapes from 12" x 18" construction paper. Sing the song below and then invite children to discuss the places they'd like to fly and the things they would see if they were kites. Follow the discussion by inviting children to illustrate on their kites what they would see. Write each student's dictation below her picture. When the illustrations are complete, have each child glue a crepe paper tail to her kite. Mount the completed projects on a bulletin board titled "Kites in Flight."

(sung to the tune of "Man on the Flying Trapeze")

If you were a kite, tell me, where would you go?
Would you fly way up high and then dip down so low?
Would you float in the clouds and then soar through the sky?
Oh please, tell me, where would you fly?

If you were a kite, tell me, what would you see?
When you fly in the air over houses and trees?
Would you wave to your friends, your mother, and me?
Oh please, tell me, what would you see?

Kite Bite

After all this kite activity, your little ones will be hungry for a snack—a kite-shaped snack, that is! In advance, cut a class set of whole wheat tortillas into kite shapes using clean kitchen scissors. Invite children to help mash two three-ounce packages of softened cream cheese with a splash of milk and one tablespoon of cinnamon sugar. To prepare this yummy snack, encourage each child to spread the cream cheese mixture on a tortilla. Then add pretzel sticks as shown. Children will enjoy flying these delicious kites straight into their mouths!

Kite Pattern

Use with "Flying High" and "The Sky's the Limit" on page
304 and "Kite Names" on page 305.

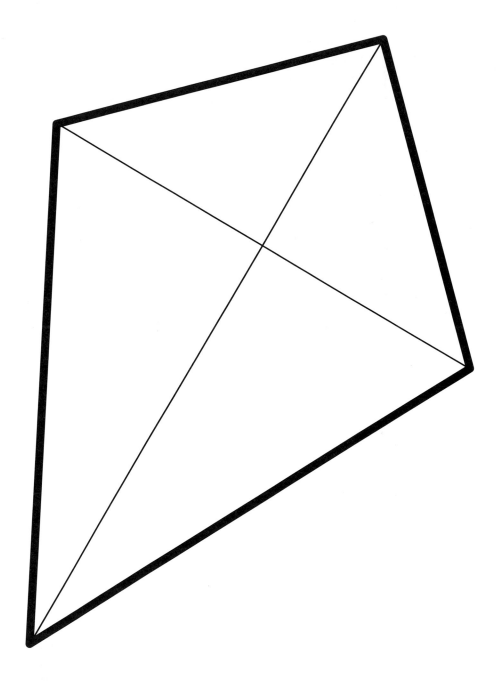

The Preschool Circus

The circus is coming! Use these ideas and invite your little circus lovers to step right up for the greatest show in preschool!

ideas by Lucia Kemp Henry, Fallon, NV

The Stars of the Circus

Using vocabulary, singing a song

Introduce youngsters to a colorful tentful of circus stars by reading *Circus* by Lois Ehlert. After reading and discussing the story, lay a large Hula-Hoop toy in the center of your circle-time area. Invite each child, in turn, to step into the ring, name a circus animal or performer from the book, and then move like her selected big top star. After each child has had a chance to perform, remove the hoop. Have students imagine that they are all inside a circus ring as they sing the song below and perform the suggested actions. Lead students in singing four more verses of the song, replacing the underlined words with "Little dogs are dancing," "Acrobats are twirling," "Elephants are marching," and "Jugglers are performing."

(sung to the tune of "Short'nin' Bread")

Everybody's going to the circus, circus.   *Wave.*
Come on, everybody, it's circus time!
Who's at the circus? What do we see?   *Put hand above eyes as if looking at something.*

[Clowns are making faces] for you and me!   *Point to a friend and then to yourself.*

Block Center Circus

Using imaginative play

Transform your block center into a special circus! To make a tent, copy the tent pattern on page 309; then color it and cut it out. Glue the pattern to one side of a cereal box and cut out an opening on both sides of the box to make a stand-up circus tent. Glue colorful streamers to the top of the tent. Set several tents in your block center along with small plastic hoops or bangle bracelets and small plastic or plush animals. Add a supply of colorful plastic cups to use as animal performance platforms. Invite each child to visit the center and use the props to create her own circus show. Hurry! The circus is about to begin!

307

Circus Stunts
Using gross-motor skills

Circus acrobats perform some amazing stunts! Set up a child-friendly performance space with a length of masking tape on the floor (tightrope), Hula-Hoop toys, and small activity cones. Provide each child in a group of four students with a long cardboard gift wrap tube with crepe paper streamers taped to the ends. Then invite each child, in turn, to hold the tube for balance as he pretends to be an acrobat walking across the tightrope, hopping in and out of the hoops, and jumping over the cones.

Paper Plate Clown Mask
Using fine-motor skills, using shapes

Who are the most popular performers in the circus? Clowns, of course! Invite youngsters to make clown masks from paper plates so each child can have a chance to be a clown! Instruct the student to glue precut paper or craft foam shapes and other materials, such as yarn or pom-poms, to a large paper plate to make a clown face. Cut eyeholes and then tape a jumbo craft stick to the back of the mask to create a handle. Have each child hold up her mask as she acts out the motions in the chant below. Hee, hee! These clowns are funny!

Funny clown, funny clown, start the show!
March round the ring and bow down low.
Walk like a duck and stamp your feet.
Put on your hat; you look so neat!
Walk on a tightrope way up high;
Then climb down and wave goodbye!

Wave to the crowd.
March in place.
Waddle like a duck and then stamp feet.
Pretend to put on a hat.

Pretend to balance and walk on a tightrope.

Tiger Tricks
Matching uppercase and lowercase letters

Here's a small-group literacy game that will put letter matching in the center ring! Copy, color, and cut out the tiger and platform patterns on page 310. Program each tiger and platform pair with a matching set of uppercase and lowercase letters. To make a game mat, draw a large circle (circus ring) on a piece of bulletin board paper. Glue the platform pieces to the circle. To play, each child, in turn, places a tiger on top of its matching platform. Terrific tricks!

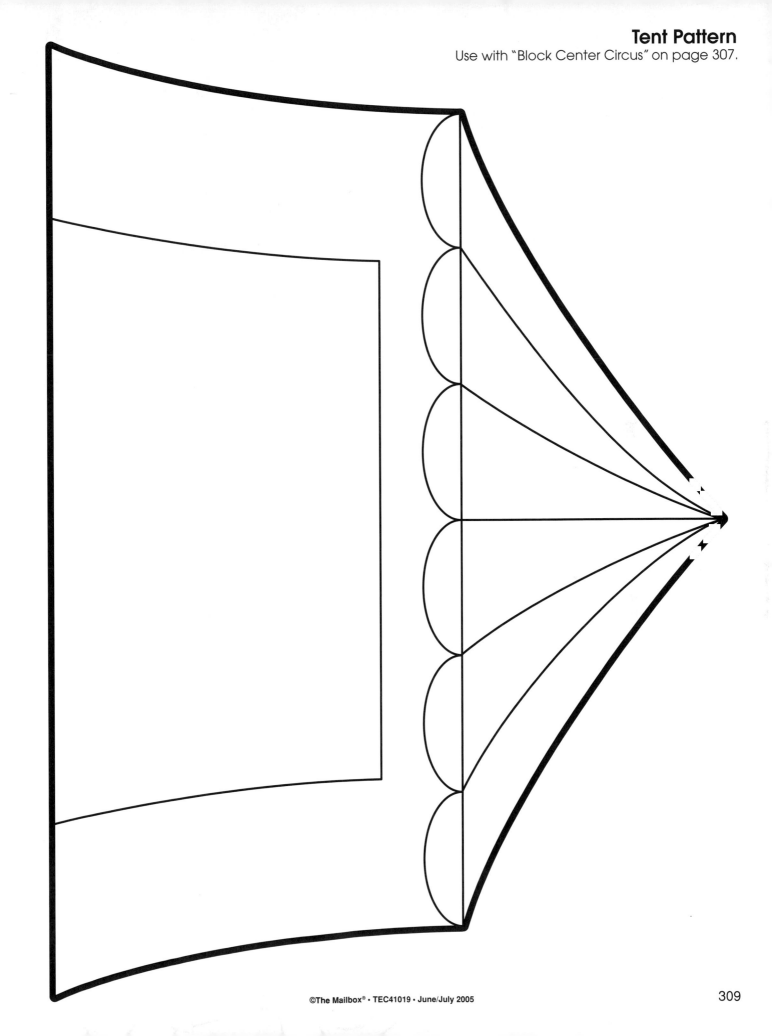

Sweet Strawberries

Handpicked and ready to provide little ones with lots of learning, these ideas are all focused on strawberries!

ideas by Roxanne LaBell Dearman, Western NC Early Intervention Program for Children Who Are Deaf and Hard of Hearing, Charlotte, NC

Autographed Berries
Tracing letters

These berries smell as good as they look and are as unique as your students! To prepare, cut out a white construction paper strawberry shape for each child. (Or mask the words on the strawberry pattern on page 313 and make white construction paper copies.) Use a pencil to lightly label each cutout with a different child's name. Then mix one packet of unsweetened strawberry Kool-Aid drink mix with one half cup of warm water to make scented paint. (You may need to make more than one batch of paint depending on the number of students in your class. One batch will paint about ten strawberries.) Place the cutouts on a table. Have each child find his strawberry and then use a black crayon to trace over his name and draw small strawberry seeds. Next, instruct him to paint his berry. Use the berries as cubbie or table labels or for a sweet-smelling bulletin board display!

Mmm, Strawberry Pie!
Counting

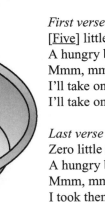

Serve up this catchy song that has little ones counting! In advance, gather five large red pom-poms (berries) and a small pie pan. Place the berries on the floor to create a berry patch. Have youngsters count the berries and then sing the first verse. At the end, remove a berry and place it in the pie pan. Have youngsters recount the berries in the patch and sing the song again. Continue singing until there are no berries left in the patch; then sing the last verse. Pie, anyone?

(sung to the tune of "Short'nin' Bread")

First verse
[Five] little strawberries in a berry patch.
A hungry bear came by—
Mmm, mmm, mmm.
I'll take one home and make a pie;
I'll take one home and make a pie!

Last verse
Zero little strawberries in a berry patch.
A hungry bear came by—
Mmm, mmm, mmm.
I took them home and made a pie;
I took them home and made a pie!

311

Berries Sound Good
Matching beginning sounds

Take a small group of youngsters on a trip to the strawberry patch without leaving your classroom! To prepare, make one red construction paper copy of the strawberry cards on page 314. Then cut out the cards. Choose two letters you would like students to practice. Divide the cards into two sets of four and program each card in a set with a different picture that begins with one of the chosen letters. Next, label each of two berry baskets with one of the letters and a picture that begins with that letter. Arrange the cards on a table to create a strawberry patch. Invite a group of four children to play. Have each student, in turn, pick a strawberry, say its picture's name, and then place it in the corresponding container. Continue play until all the berries have been picked and placed!

Handmade Strawberry Desserts
Using dramatic play

Turn your play dough center into a bakery that specializes in strawberry desserts! Mix one packet of unsweetened strawberry Kool-Aid drink mix into your favorite play dough recipe to make scented dough. Place the play dough at a center along with a variety of baking pans, such as mini-muffin tins, pie pans, and small cake pans. Add plastic utensils and a child-size rolling pin. Encourage your little bakers to use the dough to make all kinds of strawberry desserts!

Strawberry Treats
Writing

Lots of yummy things are made from strawberries. This writing activity has little ones eager to share their favorites! Have youngsters brainstorm a list of goodies made with strawberries. Record students' responses on a strawberry-shaped chart cut from red bulletin board paper. Then give each child a copy of page 313. Have him write his name and then dictate his favorite strawberry treat as you write his response to complete the sentence. Have him illustrate his treat and color the remainder of the strawberry. Stack the completed pages between construction paper covers and title the book "Strawberries! Strawberries! Oh So Sweet!" Then read the book while students snack on fresh strawberries!

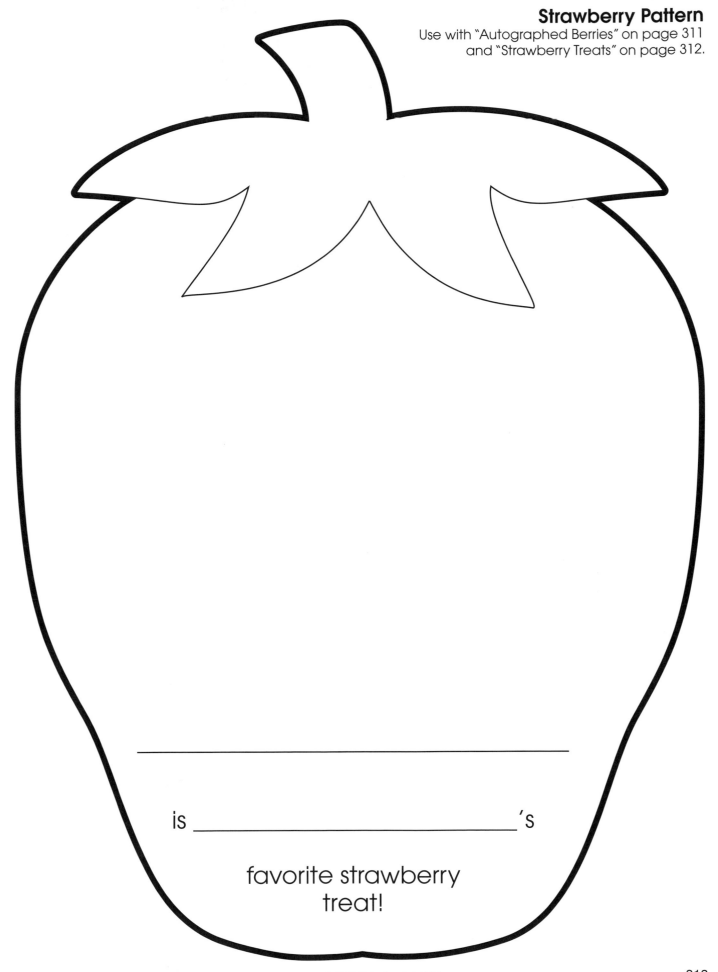

Strawberry Pattern
Use with "Autographed Berries" on page 311
and "Strawberry Treats" on page 312.

is _____'s

favorite strawberry
treat!

Strawberry Cards

Use with "Berries Sound Good" on page 312.

Index